10/02

Llewellyn's

635.7 10/02

Herbal Almanac

2003

Edi

I

C

Co

Yo

a

Lle

onli

to

requ

click o

Online F

ISBN 0-7387-0073-8
Llewellyn Worldwide
P.O. Box 64383, Dept. 0-7387-0073-8
St. Paul, MN 55164

ontents

Growing and Gathering Herbs

Culinary Herbs

Herbs for Health

Herbs for Beauty

Herb Crafts

Herb History, Myth, and Magic

Introduction to Llewellyn's Herbal Almanac

What is old is new again, wrote the poet. In the case of the 2003 edition of Llewellyn's *Herbal Almanac*, the sentiment is entirely appropriate. In this, the fourth edition of a now-old book, we are taking some new approaches in looking at the wide range of current research on, and expanding use of, herbs as medicine, as culinary spice, as beautifying cosmetic, and as magical item. This year in particular we tap into some of the world's most ancient knowledge—the magic and healing power of ayurvedic and traditional Chinese medicine, for instance, as well as the lore regarding the use of herbs in Mexico and Africa. And we bring to these pages some of the most innovative and original thinkers and writers on herbs.

This focus on the old ways—on times when men and women around the world knew and understood the power of herbs—is important today, as it seems the balance of the world has been thrown off kilter. Terrorists, water shortages, hatred, internecine battles, militant religious fervor, all seem to be holding sway over the good things in life—such as beauty, good food, health, love, and friendship. While we don't want to assign blame or cast any other aspersions, this state of affairs perhaps is not surprising considering so many of us—each one of us—is out of touch with the beauty, magic, and health-giving properties inherent in the natural world. Many of us spend too much of our lives rushing about in a technological bubble—striving to make money, being everywhere but here, living life in fast-forward. We forget, at times, to focus on the parts of life that can bring us back into balance and harmony.

Still, the news is not all bad. People are still fighting to make us all more aware of the magical, beautiful things in the world.

In January 2001, for instance, the Vermont legislature became the first US state to pass a "Complementary and Alternative Health Care Act," and thus regulate the age-old techniques of herbal healers. The governor in Llewellyn's home state, the ultramodern politician Jesse Ventura of Minnesota, signed a similar bill into law, and it took effect in July 2001. No doubt other states are bound to follow suit in coming years as we continue to evolve and grow as a society.

In the 2003 edition of the *Herbal Almanac*, we pay tribute and homage to the ideals of magic and beauty and balance as they relate to the health-giving and beautifying properties of herbs. This may sound a bit far-fetched, but after all, it does not take much stretch of imagination to see that a French kitchen garden is a beautiful and magical thing, that natural herbal aphrodisiacs can help us grow in love with our partners, and that making paper and books from herbs only brings joy to our lives.

Herbs are the perfect complement to the power of the mind, an ancient tool whose time has come back around to help us restore balance in our lives. More and more people are using them, growing and gathering them, and studying them for their beautifying and healing properties. We, the editors and authors of this volume, encourage the treatment of the whole organism—of the person and of the planet—with herbal magic. One person at a time, using ancient wisdom, we can make a new world.

Note: Of course you must take care not to replace regular medical treatment through the use of herbs. Herbal treatment is intended primarily to complement modern health care. Always seek professional help if you suffer from illness. Also, take care to read all warning labels before taking any herbs or starting on an extended herbal regimen. Always consult an herbal professional before beginning any sort of medical treatment—this is particularly true for pregnant women. Herbs are powerful things; be sure you are using that power to achieve balance.

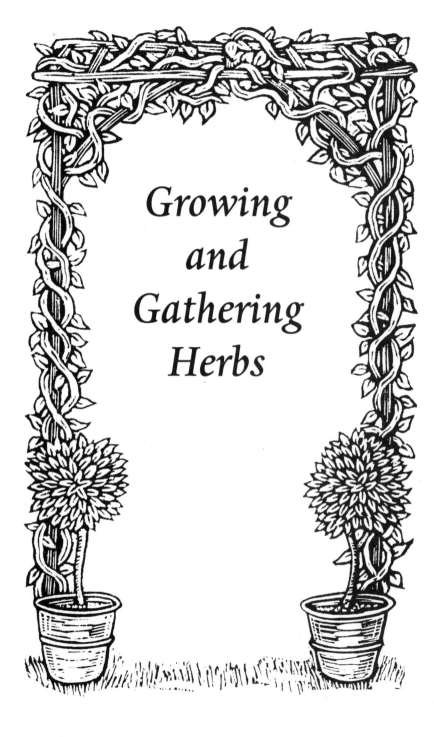

Growing
and
Gathering
Herbs

Growing Unusual Herbs in Containers

≫ by Scott Appell ≪

When it comes to cultivating herbs in containers destined for window ledges, patios, decks, rooftops, or window boxes, most people don't experiment beyond the garden center basics—sweet basil, oregano, rue, and lavender. This is a grave mistake, for whether we cultivate herbs for their magical merits, culinary importance, medicinal attributes, or ethnobotanical interest, really the only requirement necessary to grow all manner of herbs in any situation is a willingness to broaden one's own herbal horizons. In fact, it is very easy to grow unusual herbs, and so you can experience specimens that are rarely found in cultivation. Below are some basic tips to get you started growing your own rare herbs in containers.

Soil Basics

Many of the best-known herbs—sage, savory, thyme, rosemary, and lavender—prefer soils of good fertility, moisture retention, and impeccable drainage. In fact, overwatering is the primary cause of death for most containerized herbs.

So in order to make a good start with your herbs, be sure to purchase a good quality packaged soil, and to treat the soil so that it drains well in most cases. Nowadays, packaged soil must list its ingredients on the label. This in turn has finally guaranteed that buying prebagged soil is not a hit-or-miss affair. Though there are many good soils on the market, one of the best brands is Farfard, which is packaged in Canada but easily obtained from most large nurseries and garden centers. In general, a good soil contains organic ingredients such as compost, decomposed manure, guano (rotted bird or bat manure), horticultural charcoal, and ground oyster shells. To improve the drainage of any soil, you should add one quarter by volume sharp sand to the package. The addition of small amounts of New Jersey greensand, cottonseed meal, and bone meal will round out the mixture for long-term container plantings. Add the amounts listed with the package directions of each of these materials.

Note: Some herbs—such as basil, lemongrass, and stevia, for example—need soil that is relatively sand-free. They require instead the incorporation of more compost or peat moss in order to increase water retention.

Container Selection

With most garden hardscaping, or the assembling of the inanimate aspects of a living garden, we always work from the ground up. In the case of potted plantings, we begin with the container. The container we select is as important to the overall design scheme as the plants chosen to grow within it.

Anything that can hold soil can be used as a container garden. This, of course, expands our container selection into realms far beyond the standard terra cotta flower pot or ubiquitous drab-green plastic windowbox. When deciding upon a container, we may be as creative as we want, or we may choose to be traditional minded, innovative, daring, whimsical, or intriguing.

Also, we can cater to our individual financial budgets and be frugal by finding containers at the flea market, or extravagant by searching for a costly antique. It is all up to you.

Here are some suggested items you can use as herb containers: a discarded wicker basket, strawberry jars, recycled coal buckets, leaky soup tureens, milk crates, footed urns, authentic Ming vessels, Victorian chimney pots, and delicate antique ceramic and porcelain finds (Minton, McCoy, and Majolica, for example). Jardinieres, arborettes, jardinets, and cachepots are wonderfully unique containers—especially when they are overflowing with your favorite herbs. However, their fragility and expense warrants a sheltered and wind-free spot in the garden, as well as overwintering (in cold climates) in a frost-free cupboard or basement, emptied of plant material and soil.

Some Basic Containers

Strawberry Jars

Strawberry jars are very familiar containers, which were particularly favored by Victorian gardeners. They were so named because strawberry plants (*Fragraria* sp.) could be planted in the open mouth at the top of the jar and then trained to fill in the pockets below. Still, there is no rule that says a magical garden or a homeopathic herb collection cannot be cultured in the same fashion. Strawberry jars are available in a variety of materials; terra cotta, concrete, wood, and fine ceramic including blue Delftware. Their low center of gravity makes them practically tumble-free in wind storms, but you should always take care with fine ceramic vessels to protect them somewhat from the elements.

Strawberry jars need a particular planting technique to ensure success in growing. Because of their unique shape, inevitably there is a shaft of poorly drained, root-free soil running down the exact center of the interior. This constantly damp portion of the soil can allow fungal pathogens to prevail, and lead to the subsequent root rot of the plant material. To avoid this, a drainage column of a mixture of pea gravel (tiny pebbles), and horticultural charcoal must be installed. There is no exact recipe; but a general mixture of one-tenth charcoal by volume is excellent for this. Also, you should add a tube that is long enough to run the vertical length of the jar in the center of the soil. For example, a cardboard toilet paper tube may be the right height for a tiny, porcelain strawberry jar, and a cardboard paper towel tube may work for a pot of medium height. A length of plastic pipe, purchased and precut from the local hardware store, can be used in any size container.

The installation procedure for this is simple. Center and stand the empty tube upright on the bottom of the strawberry jar. Place a shallow layer of the pea gravel/charcoal mixture at the bottom of the pot and around the tube. Fill the tube with the pea gravel mixture as well, and keep the tube upright as you begin to fill the jar with your potting soil. Fill the pockets beginning with the lowest, and work upward to several inches below the brim of the jar. Gently give the strawberry jar a sharp rap on the table to settle the soil, then remove the tube from the soil, leaving the vertical column of pea gravel/charcoal behind. Finally, seed or place plants in the open mouth of the jar, and water the whole affair.

Jardinieres and Cachepots

These nineteenth-century glazed ceramic favorites were designed as pot covers. They were designed as attractive, time-saving devices, and they helped avoid the necessary horticultural housekeeping chore of scrubbing off the soluble salts, algae, and mold from the exterior surface of earthenware flowerpots. Remember, plastic had not yet been invented.

The difference between the two is a matter of size: jardinieres generally are wider than eight inches, while cachepots are smaller. There are several ways to use these in container gardens. Herb-filled plastic or clay pots can be slipped into them, but, in this case, due to a lack of drainage holes, the jardiniere or cachepot will fill up with water. Therefore, ideally, the inserted pot needs to be removed, watered, drained, and replaced each time—a very time-consuming chore. Though some clever gardeners utilize the lack of drainage in culturing aquatic herbs such as calamus (*Acorus* sp.), an alternative method would to drill drainage holes in the bottom of the vessel using a carbide-tipped concrete or porcelain drill bit. In this instance, the jardiniere or cachepot can serve as any freely draining decorative container.

Jardinets and Arborettes

Jardinets are glazed ceramic pieces designed to look like small, eight- to eighteen-inch-high, moss-covered tree stumps. Arborettes on the other hand are far more elaborate, taller, made of molded terra cotta, and shaped like trees with multiple jagged branches each with a planting hole at the end. Both are useful for their individual unusual features, placing plants at eye level in various situations. Though originally designed to hold forced spring-flowering bulbs, arborettes and jardinets work outdoors as well. Try them planted with any number of your favorite magical, culinary, or medicinal herbs. In areas with cold winters, these containers should be brought indoors.

Baskets

Baskets are by far one of the most beloved and familiar containers for planting herbs. Whether they are recycled curios, garage-sale gems, or dime-store finds, they make aesthetically appealing decorative containers rich with natural colorations and fibrous textures that offset the flowers and foliage of innumerable flora. The better a basket is protected from the elements, and from the effects of multiple waterings, the longer it will last. Treating valuable and collectible basketware with varnishes, polyurethanes, or other preservatives is beneficial. Being woven, of course, baskets have open spaces through which potting soil can fall or plant roots be exposed. To combat this, the basket must be lined prior to planting. The needed tools include sheet moss (easily procured from florist supply houses), clear or black sheet plastic (available from hardware stores), and potting soil. Line the selected basket with the moss, decorative side out. Re-line the basket, over the moss, with the plastic, being sure to punch drainage holes in it at regular intervals using an ice pick or other tool. Fill with soil, and plant in the usual fashion. To prolong the life of the basket in winter, it should be emptied of soil, and stored in a cool dry area with the lining removed.

Overwintering Procedures for Cold Climates

Unless you garden in higher USDA Zones (areas that are mild or frost-free during the winter months), winterization techniques become an integral part of culturing herbs in containers. Be sure to try new fiberglass, terra-cotta-look-alike containers, or else wooden ones, as these are durable and crack-resistant in cold climates. Pots containing annual herbs can be emptied of their plants and soil and stored in a frost-free garage or work shed. Urns, tubs, or planter boxes planted with perennial herbs should be placed on pot feet to allow for better drainage, thus avoiding perpetually soggy roots. Move plants close to a west-, south-, or east-facing brick wall or fence, which will act as a windbreak.

Before you do begin growing, however, you should know something about the United States Department of Agriculture (USDA) Hardiness Zones. The USDA has set up an easy-to-follow guideline for potential outdoor growers of plants, which I refer to below. The various categories, called Zones—which range from USDA Zone 1 to USDA Zone 11—reflect the annual winter temperature lows for a typical year in specific geographical locations within Canada, the United States, and points south. Basically, the higher the number of a USDA Zone, the warmer the winter clime. For example, USDA Zone 1 is in midcentral Canada, and USDA Zone 11 lies in the Florida Keys, Hawaii, and the Caribbean.

USDA Zone 1:	Below 50°F
USDA Zone 2:	-50°F to -40°F

USDA Zone 3:	-40°F to -30°F
USDA Zone 4:	-30°F to -20°F
USDA Zone 5:	-20°F to -10°F
USDA Zone 6:	-10°F to 0°F
USDA Zone 7:	0°F to 10°F
USDA Zone 8:	10°F to 20°F
USDA Zone 9:	20°F to 30°F
USDA Zone 10:	30°F to 40°F
USDA Zone 11:	Above 40°F

Herb Selection

Although herbs can be divided into three basic horticultural groups—annual, perennial, and biennial—I prefer to distinguish herbs by whether they prefer moist soils or drier conditions. When planning your herb garden, don't mix these two different types. Such mixed plantings will not succeed; inevitably only one type of plant will flourish. In a mixed planting that is kept moist, the drought-loving herbs will rot. Conversely, in a mixed planting that is kept drier, the moisture-loving herbs will wither. Plant like herb with like herb to guarantee success.

A Gallery of Unusual Magical Herbs

Lion's Ear (Leonotis leonurus) (*Family:* Lamiaceae)

This east and south African small shrub makes an unusual and beautiful addition to a sunny, drought-tolerant, mixed container planting. Considered both a magical, aphrodisiacal, and medicinal herb in Africa (particularly Kenya), lion's ear is consumed by males of certain tribes prior to festivals that involve amorous alliances and lion hunts. It purportedly endows the men with a lion's bravery and sexual prowess—that is, when lions mate, they do it dozens of times over a twenty-four hour period. In fact, this plant's scientific name is quite remarkable: the genus *Leonotis* is composed of the Latinized Greek "leon," a lion, and "otis," an ear—thus, "lion's ear." The fuzzy flowers look somewhat like a lion's ear. The species name, *leonurus,* is composed of "leon" and "ouros," or tail—therefore, "lion's tail." It is a herb with very leonine attributes.

The taste and texture of lion's ear is pleasantly spinachlike. These very woody annuals can withstand frost with no ill effects and are hardy to USDA Zone 9, where they can become quite shrublike and grow up to four feet. Lion's ear is a perfect butterfly and hummingbird plant, as their wonderful whorls of orange, tubelike flowers (produced late in the season) are impressive to behold. They make terrific cut flowers, and a series of potted specimens will make a unique potted annual in garden rooms or as a seasonal containerized hedge.

Mandrake (Mandragora officinarum)
(Family: Solanaceae)

Although mandrake is one of the botanical backbones of a magical garden, most people purchase desiccated roots from the herb store to incorporate into their spellwork, charms, fetishes, and talismans. Because of this, few of us have ever actually seen mandrake growing in a garden. Considering its celebrated history of magical use in European witchcraft, as well as its medicinal uses, mandrake is extremely rare in cultivation—even in botanic gardens and arboreta.

Because fresh is best, I recommend including this infamous herb in your magical garden. Keep in mind that mandrake's fame comes from the hallucinogenic hyoscyamine, atropine, and scopolamine content, which makes it lethal to man and beast alike. It must be cultivated in a toddler- and pet-free zone.

Mandrake is native to northern Italy, westward through the Balkans to Turkey, and southward to Greece. The twelve-inch-long foliage is slightly pubescent, or fuzzy, and it grows in a rosette shape. The leaves are at first upright, then later, they lie flat on the ground. They have wavy or crenelated margins, and the entire plant reminds one of a fuzzy, flattened head of romaine lettuce. The flowers, which are produced in early spring, are upright facing, tubular bell shaped, and greenish white in color. The deep-yellow, smooth-skinned fruit is ovoid, and has a pineapple-like fragrance. Often called Satan's apples, they too are fatally toxic. Although the plant is quite unassuming in appearance, it is the vaguely human-shaped roots—which are very similar in appearance to the unrelated ginseng root—which have endowed the mandrake with eminent mystery and power.

To grow, mandrake requires a moderately fertile, impeccably drained soil (that has additional sharp sand and turkey grit added) and full sunlight in order to flourish. They dislike winter wetness, thus their containers should be placed on pot feet. Move them near a stone wall for hibernal warmth and protection. Once planted, they dislike being disturbed. Place mandrake in long-term containers such as half whiskey barrels or strawberry jars. The plant is hardy to USDA Zones 5–8.

Sweet Flag or Calamus (Acorus calamus) (Family: Araceae)

Acorus calamus is a hardy, rhizomatous, perennial, swamp or bog plant native to Europe and the United States. It is araceous, meaning that it belongs to the arum family *(Araceae)*, and therefore is related to such familiar plants as calla lilies, philodendrons, and Jack-in-the-pulpits. Sweet flag bears spicy-scented, flattened, sword-shaped foliage that grows to two or three feet in length. The creeping rhizomes are covered with a brownish-red bark and creep over the surface of the soil.

Because of its pleasant smell, calamus was once considered a treading-herb; and was strewn upon the floors of churches and private houses to perfume the air when walked upon. This tradition still practiced at Britain's Norfolk Cathedral on important festival days. Acorus has proven insect-repellent properties as well, and was once thought to fend off the plague. It has been used for centuries as a medicinal herb, and the active ingredients are asarone and beta-asarone. The rhizomes are considered to possess antispasmodic, gas-expelling (carmative), and worm-expelling (anthelmintic) properties. It was also used to treat epilepsy, chronic diarrhea, mental ailments, and kidney and heart ailments. American colonists employed it to treat colic.

Although sweet flag has long been employed in European witchcraft, its use in American Hoodoo is far more fascinating. In Louisiana and other southern states such as Alabama and Georgia, Voodoo, and its variant among black Americans, Hoodoo, is still widely practiced. Voodoo is the American interpretation of Haitian *vodou*. Hoodoo, on the other hand, is folkloric magic handed down through oral traditions and practiced primarily in New Orleans. They both share some similar attributes, such as healing practices and strong Catholic roots, but they are not the same doctrine. Hoodoo uses Voodoo dolls, conjure bags (both *mojo* and *gris-gris*), potions, oils, incense, sachets, powders, floor washes, and herbs. In fact, the herbal inventory of Hoodoo comprises nearly two-hundred separate species. Part of the mystique of Hoodoo is the ability for a practitioner to conjure snakes, spiders, or other living creatures into the body of an enemy. Sweet flag is used to rid the body of these unwanted creatures—to do so, one must chew on a piece of the root and bathe in water containing potassium nitrate (saltpeter) for nine mornings.

Sweet flag prefers an aquatic lifestyle, and makes a wonderful herb for containers without drainage holes: jardinieres, cachepots, soup tureens, buckets, basins, and pickle crocks. It requires a water depth of four to six inches and full Sun to succeed. It is cold resistent, and hardy to USDA Zone 3. It is a exuberant grower, and will need division every three or four years.

A Gallery of Unusual Culinary Herbs

East Indian, or Tree Basil (Ocimum gratissumum) *(Family:* Lamiaceae)

Although basil can hardly be called unusual, this particular rare species is worth locating. *Ocimum gratissumum*, East Indian, or tree basil, a native of west and tropical Africa, has pungently clove-scented foliage up to six inches long. Depending on your palate, the foliage can stand in for any of your favorite recipes. Additionally, as this basil develops thick woody stems, there are uses for this plant that are not possible with the more familiar sweet basil (*O. basilicum*). For instance, try using the freshly cut shrubby stems as flavor-imparting skewers for vegetable brochettes. Or use them as trussing needles for poultry and fish, or throw the stems onto charcoal to impart a smoky-basil flavor to grilled food. This plant, like other basils, prefers full sunlight and evenly moist soil. Seedlings are particularly sensitive to overwatering. Tree basil is hardy to USDA Zone 10.

Stevia, Sweet-Herb of Paraguay, Sugar Leaf (Stevia rebaudiana) *(Family:* Asteraceae)

Although stevia was once uncommon in cultivation, it has become increasingly more available thanks to the work of large commercial herb growers and savvy home gardeners. The leaves contain stevioside, a substance three hundred times sweeter than sucrose. These Brazilian and Paraguayan varieties, which are hardy to USDA Zone 9, grow to several feet tall on woody stems similar to their cousins the asters and chrysanthemums. The foliage is slightly fuzzy, toothed (dentate), or with wavy edges (crenelate). The leaves may be dried and ground as a sweetener, or soaked in water, and the resulting liquid used to make teas, preserves, or health aids. Try using the foliage as a sweetly edible garnish for fruit salads and baked goods. Stevia prefers an evenly moist soil and can be overwintered indoors in cold climes.

Perilla, or Beefsteak Plant (Perilla frutescens) (Family: Lamiaceae)

Aficionados of Japanese cuisine know this plant as *shiso*, the aromatic fresh or pickled accompaniment to plates of sushi and sashimi. The foliage of this annual herb, native from India to Japan, makes an excellent addition to raw salads, or an edible garnish to all types of Asian cuisine. It prefers a sunny exposure and a rich, evenly moist, but not soggy, soil. Perilla is also an important medicinal plant in the Chinese pharmacopeia, where the leaves are reccommended to stimulate gastric activities, treat coughs and influenza. Perilla is hardy to USDA Zone 8, and grows quickly to two to three feet in height.

Cuban Oregano, Spanish Thyme, or Mexican Mint (Plectranthus amboinicus) (Family: Lamiaceae)

Once a common Victorian bedding and conservatory plant, *Plectranthus* disappeared into obscurity in this century but has recently enjoyed a horticultural renaissance. The common names are quite misleading—*Plectranthus* is native of tropical to southern Africa—and undoubtedly came to the New World through the slave trade. The thick and hairy leaves have a distinctly oregano-like aroma and flavor, and the plant resembles a furry, creeping coleus. Hardy to USDA Zone 10, it relishes fertile, well-drained soil and full sunlight, and it is very drought-resistant. Its decumbent (trailing on the ground) growth habit lends itself to hanging baskets and windowboxes. In Cuba, the plant is used to flavor goat or fish dishes. In India, the leaves are used to flavor beer and wine. The Vietnamese use the foliage to flavor their famed sour soup. The foliage is a little thick and too furry to be enjoyed raw in salads, but it makes an excellent addition to cooked dishes—from frittatas, to chiles, ragout, and tomato sauces. They are easy to overwinter on a sunny windowsill.

Rosemary Arp (Rosemarinus officinalis, cultivar)
(*Family:* Labiatae)

Rosemary is another herb that needs no introduction. Its needle-like foliage is light-green and lemon scented, and it is used in cuisines around the world. Rosemary flowers are light-blue; the plant has an overall open growth habit, and can attain a height of five feet under ideal conditions. The straight species is native to southern Europe and North Africa. All rosemary prefer a very sunny position, and fertile, but flawlessly drained, soil. Make sure you add plenty of sharp sand and horticultural charcoal to the potting mixture. Winter's soggy soils are a menace to rosemary. Place the containers on pot feet to avoid excess moisture. In fall, move the container to a southern-facing brick or stone wall, if possible, to aid as a heat-retentive windbreak. Remember the woody twigs can be used as skewers for lamb or chicken shish-kababs, or thrown on the charcoal grill to impart their aromatic smoke to other grilled foods. Rosemary makes a soothing, incense-like addition to kindling for indoor fires as well.

A Gallery of Unusual Medicinal Herbs
Cardamom (Elettaria cardamomum)
(*Family:* Zingiberaceae)

The deliciously aromatic seeds of this tropical relative to ginger are ground and added to Dutch and Danish pastry doughs, to curry powder recipes, cordials, gingerbread, bitters, sausages, and pickles. A native of India, cardamom is therefore hardy to USDA Zone 10, though it rarely blooms in northern latitudes. Cardamom seeds are chewed after meals to sweeten the breath, and the young shoots can be eaten raw, steamed, or roasted. Add a whole leaf or two to basmati rice prior to cooking to impart a wonderful fragrance and taste. Included in the Chinese *Materia Medica*, cardamom seeds are used medicinally to stimulate gastric activity, increase menstrual flow, and treat premature ejaculation, involuntary discharge of urine, and stomach ache. Like ginger,

Elettaria has a creeping rhizome that produces shoots in two rows of broad, dark-green leaves. It prefers a semishady spot and soil that is rich and water retentive, and it can be overwintered indoors on a windowsill or in a greenhouse.

Balsam Apple (Momordica charantia)
(*Family:* Curcurbitaceae)

The balsam apple, a cousin to the bitter cucumber popular in much Asian cuisine, is a medicinally important plant. A member of the gourd family, there are about forty-five species in the genus *Momordica*. Balsam apples are native to tropical Africa eastward through Indo-malaysia, where they are cultivated for food. Similar to other gourds, they grow as rambling, twining vines. Balsam apples produce oblong, highly textured fruit, which are matte green when young, and yellow or orange when mature. Upon ripening, the fruits burst open into a star-like configuration revealing glossy, red-coated seeds. These species have been introduced into North America, where they are considered a noxious weed of roadsides, hedgerows, and vacant lots.

Balsam apple gourds have medicinal value as they contain a substance similar in effect to insulin. In fact, balsam apples are still an important part of the Chinese *Materia Medica*. The fruit of the plant cool the body's systems, and act as a tonic and purgative. The seeds are utilized to treat fever, chest complaints, liver and spleen disorders, hemorrhoids, malaria, and bruises and swellings. The indigenous peoples of Costa Rica use the balsam pear in a number of medicinal recipes to fight gastritis and diabetes. Juice from the leaves and fruit is used to treat colic and worms. It is also used to combat some rather unusual afflictions as well, including chilblain, leprosy, and malaria. *Momordica charantia* has many uses in Puerto Rican folk medicine as well—combating skin fungus as a tincture. To make this medicine, fill a bottle with fresh balsam pear leaves, and cover it completely with a mixture of three-parts cooking oil and one-part rubbing alcohol. Let it steep for several days until the liquids absorb the color of the botanical. Apply to the infected area as often as needed. Alternately, you can boil up some foliage in water until it becomes deep green. Apply the resulting decoction to the skin for dermatological problems.

Balsam apples have been cultivated in European gardens since the seventeenth-century. They prefer full sunlight, and a rich, moisture-retentive soil. *Momordica* requires a trellis, obelisk, pergola, or other structural plant support on which to climb.

Bear's Breech (Acanthus mollis)
(*Family:* Acanthaceae)

Originally from the west Mediterranean, bear's breech was introduced into Britain during the Middle Ages. Although rarely encountered in the wild today, it is an integral part of European herb gardens. Its beautiful broad dark-green leaves and spikes of tubular white and mauve flowers are easily recognizable. The plant's genus name *Acanthus* comes from the Latinized Greek, *akanthos*, meaning "spine"; the specific variety *mollis*, meanwhile, translates as "soft," and indeed, the leaves of the plant are covered with soft hairs and spines.

Dioscorides, the classical physician, included bear's breech in his book *De Materia Medica*. The plant contains mucilage, tannins, glucose, and pectin-like substances, and was used as a healing herb for soothing burns, and in cases of gout. It prefers a compost-rich, well-drained soil, and is hardy to USDA Zone 6. Further north, it makes a handsome greenhouse or conservatory plant.

Belladonna, or Deadly Nightshade (Atropa belladonna)
(*Family:* Solanaceae)

Belladonna is a perennial, herbaceous herb native through western Europe northward and across Central Asia to the Himalayas. It grows to five feet, and bears simple, dark-green leaves similar in appearance to its relative datura. The plant produces drooping dark-purple flowers June to August, followed by shiny black berries. Its roots are thick and whitish. The whole plant has an unpleasant smell when crushed and is rare in cultivation, due to its fatally poisonous character.

In classical Greek mythology, there were three sisters, the daughters of the goddess of night, Nyx, who supervised the fate of every individual using spindle, fiber, and knife. They were depicted as three crones—Clotho, the spinner who spun the thread of life; Lachesis, the drawer of lots who measured out the thread of life; and Atropos, the inevitable, who cut the thread short. It is the name of the third sister, Atropos, that has given the lethally noxious belladonna its genus name, *Atropa*. The species variety, *belladonna*, translating as "beautiful lady," recalls the use of the juices of the plant to dilate the pupils of the eyes of the courtly ladies of Renaissance Italy. It was believed that the dreamy, intoxicated stare that this produced was the height of fetching beauty. Oddly enough, social anthropologists today understand that dilated pupils reveal sexual interest, and so this ancient practice makes some sense.

Alternately known as sorceror's cherry (an allusion to its small, shiny fruit), witch's berry, devil's herb, and dwaleberry (derived from a Scandanavian word for "trance"), this plant is laden with tropane alkaloids, including atropine, scopolamine, and hyoscyamine. This endows the herb with great hallucinogenic attributes when taken in small doses, and death in larger amounts. It was during the Middle Ages in Europe that belladonna achieved its greatest status in witchcraft and magic. As far back as 1324, it was an integral ingredient in flying ointments and necromancial elixirs.

Despite its highly poisonous nature, deadly nightshade has been valued as a medicinal plant for centuries, and was widely cultivated in medieval herb gardens. Atropine extracted from the roots and leaves is used in modern medicine as a narcotic, sedative, and diuretic. It is employed for disorders of the nervous system, and as an antispasmodic in ailments of the stomach, intestine, and bile duct. It is also used to treat whooping cough, asthma, and fevers. Externally, it relieves gout, neuralgia, and rheumatic pains, and has been effective in the treatment of Parkinson's disease. It has been proven that tiny doses of belladonna tincture even offered protection from scarlet fever. Please take care: belladonna should never be used without express supervision by your homeopathic healer or a general practitioner. It goes without saying that it must be cultivated in a child- and pet-free area.

Atropa prefers a semishaded area and rich compost-laden soil. It requires slightly alkaline soil, which can be achieved by adding a little prepackaged lime to the site. Because of its fleshy taproots it dislikes being disturbed, therefore grow only in a long-term garden. It is hardy to USDA Zone 6.

May Pops, or Apricot Vine (Passiflora incarnata) *(Family:* Passifloraceae)

Herbalists requiring an exquisite profusely-flowering ornamental vine with important medicinal properties, as well as large quantities of perfumed fruit, should consider *Passiflora incarnata*. Commonly known as May pops, or apricot vine (because of the taste of the ripe fruit), it is the hardiest of all passion flowers, and is known to survive in walled conditions as far north as USDA Zone 5. As a hardy vine, this plant can be used to create a stunning visual effect in a garden by placing a potted vine at the base of four support beams. It will twine up the supports through the season. Lovely, sweet-scented, white-to-lilac or mauve flowers are followed, in late summer, by two-and-a-half-inch lime green to yellow fruit. The fruit is delicious, and best eaten fresh or made into conserves, granitas, or sorbets. The vines will die back to their large fleshy roots every autumn. This herb tolerates surprisingly lean soils, but demands a well-drained site. A sunny location with average soil pH is satisfactory for success.

This plant too has a distinctive pharmaceutical and ethnobotanical history. The Cherokee people in western North Carolina and northwestern Georgia employed the plant for a number of maladies. A compound infusion of the roots was applied to boils, and the pounded roots were used to treat thorn and briar scratches. An infusion of the roots was given to babies to assist in weaning. This liquid was also employed to combat earache and liver problems. The crushed fruit was strained to make a social drink, and mixed with cornmeal to make a porridge. Young shoots and leaves were boiled or fried. The Houma people in Louisiana used an infusion of the roots as a blood tonic. In the nineteenth century, the flowering and fruiting shoots were recognized as having mild sedative and hypnotic properties and used to relieve insomnia and soothe nerves. It is currently employed in homeopathic treatments for nervous insomnia, complaints of the heart or stomach, and nervous disorders connected with menstruation and menopause.

Lemongrass (Cymbopogon citratus) *(Family:* Poaceae)

Not many people bother to grow this tropical, lemon-scented grass, preferring instead to purchase it from the green-grocer. Homegrown plants, of course, are more aromatic and succulent than packaged plants as a rule, and lemongrass is no exception. Its upright grassy foliage perks up a potted herb garden, and the basal portions of this plant's shoots are useful when chopped and used to flavor fish, soups, sauces, teas, yogurt, and curry. It is used commonly from Greece eastward to Thailand. The chopped foliage is tough to chew and is generally removed from dishes prior to serving. In China, the plant is boiled, and the water used to cure various ailments, including coughs and colds. Lemongrass is native to India and Sri Lanka, and is hardy outdoors to USDA Zone 9. Many gardeners are unaware that lemongrass can attain a height of five or six feet, and that the plant's graceful and nodding summer flowers add an unusual beauty to gardens. The plant in general appreciates a rich, moisture-retentive soil mixture and a sunny location. In addition to its culinary and magical attributes, lemongrass can be added to hot bathwater to impart a lemony fragrance, or can be strewn over burning charcoal prior to grilling fish or fowl.

Landscaping with Threatened Plants

≫ by Paul Neidhart ≪

American native plants are a valuable asset to our landscape. The value of wild plants is underestimated by our society. One only needs to consider how great a role plants play in our daily lives to realize the importance of conservation. Plants provide food, shelter, medicine, fuel, and clothing, and their byproducts are crucial to sustaining life on Earth. The beauty and aesthetic value of colorful plants please and soothe the minds of millions. There is a wealth of knowledge in every plant.

As wild areas decrease in size every year in America, populations of native plants need to be conserved more than ever. It is estimated that five plant species disappear from the wild each day. At this rate of loss no one really knows the long-term impact on the biosphere and on societies. Loss of habitat due to a variety of human

activities will dramatically affect the fate of plants and animals around the world. It is in our national interest to conserve natural areas and set aside more wild lands for future generations. Not only do we protect species by this, but we also create future banks of natural resources.

Landscaping with Threatened Plants

With the current rate of plant loss, we may soon find ourselves dealing with an irreversible decline in the planet's biodiversity. Landscaping with threatened plants provides one way to take positive action against this loss. That is, a great opportunity exists to bring native plants into our personal landscapes.

Every American is very familiar with the lawn, a plant space that is found primarily in suburban residential areas. In the past five decades, lawn space has spread drastically, and at a much faster rate than the spread of natural wild areas. Today, there is more than twenty-five million acres of turf grass in the United States. In order to preserve native plants amidst this spread of this single-species plant space, we need to roll back the carpet of grass now blanketing the nation.

Traditional lawns are relatively sterile landscapes. Mowed grassy areas do provide useful recreation and comfort for many, but with so many acres devoted to relatively few plant species we are underutilizing the land, our most precious resource. Consider that the lawn landscape is high maintenance, requiring large amounts of energy. Noise, water, and air pollution are the byproducts of growing lawns on such a large scale. It is estimated that ten times the amount of chemical inputs including herbicides, pesticides, and fungicides are used on lawns than in agriculture in the United States. In some major cities some estimate that over 40 percent of air pollution leading to smog problems is caused by mowing and trimming lawns.

With today's energy problems, the time is right to encourage low-maintenance landscapes that utilize our unique American plants. Property owners of both large and small plots can create areas for native plants. A perennial bed as small as five by five feet can support up to twenty species of native plants. An acre planted from seeds can support 100 to 350 species of native plants. If you want to cut down on mowing and increase diversity of your landscape, native plants can play a major role.

Every plant species across America has some value. Many people are interested in plants for their flowers, edible leaves or fruit, their medicinal qualities, or for their aesthetic appeal. When landscaping with threatened plants there are many other factors to consider: your bioregion, site exposure and soil conditions, availability of plant stock, how much time you want to put into it, and scale of project. When one speaks of a threatened plant, botanists and other scientists will generally agree that at least one in three species is threatened in the wild. From those numbers it is safe to say that there are plenty of species available to the homeowner for landscaping.

Growing Native Plant Species

When getting ready to provide space for threatened plants in your landscape use nature as your model. You can start by researching the bioregion of your area if you are not already aware of it. Visit a local state park and national forest to see the flora. Go to a local botanical garden for useful ideas for plant selections. A naturalist in the area may provide information and recommendations for species at risk. Contact the department of natural resources for a plant listing for your state. Nearly every major city or town across America has a native plant society. Join the local chapter to become involved in their work. These groups are out there to promote native plants and bring awareness to them. Many folks involved have native landscape gardens and will be eager to share valuable tips. Understanding plant communities local to your region will assist in designing your own garden. There are excellent books on the topics of native plants. Botany field guides, herbal publications, landscaping books, and ethnobotany guides are some sources of printed information.

Again when gardening with threatened plants mimic nature as closely as possible.

The use of companion planting is also a healthy way to create a vigorous landscape. Companion planting incorporates species that grow well together and complement each other's attributes. In general, start small and expect to build upon your basic foundation over a number of years. Site exposure and soil conditions will determine a large part of your plant selection. Growing a wetland plant in dry soil will not work, of course; it is important to match plants with their preferred soil conditions. This is also true for exposure of plants in the landscape. Full-sun species perform poorly in the shade and vice versa.

Soil is, generally speaking, the foundation of any garden or landscape. If a healthy soil is present, you can save yourself a lot of work in the future. If possible, you should take soil samples to university extension offices for testing. They will make recommendations for any supplements the soil may need.

A healthy soil will create healthy plants. As a rule, incorporating organic matter is one of the best ways to improve existing soil conditions. Healthy soils contain microbes that sustain plant growth. Compost from yard waste and composted manures make excellent soil additions. Leaf compost provides many micronutrients. On the other hand, chemical fertilizers should be avoided since they are a quick fix for plants and encourage sickly soil conditions. If the soil is healthy, plants will need little if any fertilization.

Soil conditions vary greatly across the country. The general categories of soils include dry, moist, or wet. A dry soil is typically sandy or rocky and well drained. Moist soils are what most people associate with a good garden soil. Wet soils hold moisture for most of the year. In nature, these soil conditions exists in varying degrees. Many plant species will adapt to particular soil conditions naturally. For example, a wetland plant does well in moist soil, though a dry land plant might also do well there. In some cases plants have adapted to all three soil conditions.

Aside from soil considerations, you should consider various options for the plant materials you wish to grow. "Threatened" does not mean impossible to get. It is possible to obtain rare and threatened plants without damaging wild populations. The cheapest way to source plants for gardens is to go to plant swaps held by garden clubs and native plant groups. In these events, gardeners from all levels of experience get together to trade plants and seeds. Also, plant rescue projects from areas to be developed often provide plant species that are hard to find and difficult to propagate. Keep in touch with local highway departments, construction outfits, and land development companies, and let them know that you are interested in digging up plants before a swatch of land goes under development. Take care though: You should not remove plants from the wild without permission of a property owner first.

Native plant nurseries are becoming more popular as gardeners seek out new species and the market grows. These outfits are excellent in providing sources of seeds and plants for local plant species. Most bioregions have several such nurseries now. Many of them offer landscape design and installation services. Seeds of threatened plants can also be found in many catalogs. Seed banks make many rare seeds available to the public—some catalogs advertise more than five hundred species.

Conservation through propagation can do much. Growing your own plants from seed provides you with hundreds and thousands of cheap plants. It is rewarding to start flowers, herbs, trees, shrubs, and vines from seeds. A greenhouse is handy for propagation but not necessary. A small nursery propagation facility in the backyard can consist of just a raised bed or a few nursery flats. However large or small the propagation is, there are many books on plant propagation on the market that you can refer to. Using the proper techniques, you will find this activity fun and rewarding; you might even learn something new about plant life cycles.

As botanists, gardeners, and horticulturalists experiment with growing threatened species, more and more information on wild plants is made available. Deciding what plants to use in the landscape will be determined by what is available. You may chose to grow your own herbal medicine from threatened plants in your garden. In this case, be aware that there are many native plants have been grown and harvested for medicinal use throughout the centuries. You may also decide to create gardens from threatened plants to provide habitat for local wildlife for butterflies, hummingbirds, and many species of rare birds. This kind of garden will provide enjoyment for kids and adults as flowers bloom and animals collect seeds and pollen from these rare plants. Keep in mind too—with a little planning, you can design a garden with various species that bloom all season.

Recommended Rare Species

The following is a partial listing of some recommended rare plant species and families that you can grow in your garden. Many of the plants have been used historically as medicinal herbs. Today, some are still found in commerce in the natural products industry. Many of the plants below are available through native plant nurseries.

The milkweed family *(Asclepiadaceae)* contains over 2,000 species, mostly perennial herbs. This family is named after Asklepios—the Greek god of healing—and contains many medicinal plants. Butterfly weed *(Asclepias tuberosa)*, also known as pleurisy root, is an excellent landscape plant for the full-sun meadow. Its bright-orange flowers attract many species of butterflies. It is drought tolerant and requires little care. Common milkweed *(Asclepias syrica)* has a long use as a wild edible—though it should be cooked before eating. The flowers produce a heavenly scent and are pollinated by monarch butterflies and bees. Give it plenty of room in the full-sun garden. The pods produce a wonderful silk-like material that was used during World War II as a stuffing for life preservers.

The *Berberidaceae* family contains blue cohosh *(Caulophyllum thalictroides)*, a woodland plant that is one of the first to emerge in spring. This important herb grows well in the shade-garden-provided rich soil. Mayapple *(Podophyllum peltatum)*, and Oregon grape *(Mahonia* spp.) are also worth a place in the garden. This family of plants gets its name from berberine, a bitter alkaloid.

A landscape without a member of the *Asteraceae* family would be incomplete. This large plant family contains many well-known plants. The sunflower *(Helianthus* spp.) has many wild species across the United States. Most are perennial herbs and grow large and produce showy displays of yellow flowers. Seeds of wild sunflowers are a preferred food of many songbirds. Arnica, boneset, chamomile, blazing stars, and echinacea are just a few of the other herbs in this family.

Goldenseal *(Hydrastis canadensis)* and black cohosh *(Cimicifuga racemosa)* are in the buttercup family *(Ranunculaceae)*. Goldenseal is considered a native herbal treasure. Used by Native Americans for a variety of medicinal and cosmetic purposes, it grows well when provided shade and rich soil. Black cohosh adapts well to perennial gardens. Provided ample moisture, this woodland herb will grow in full-sun conditions. Its tall, white, flowering spike will bloom for several weeks. Gold thread *(Coptis)*, columbine *(Aguilegia* spp.), larkspur *(Delphinium* spp.), marsh marigold *(Caltha)*, and pasque flower *(Anemone)* also belong to this family.

If more people grew American ginseng *(Panax quinquefolius)*, they would likely save this threatened plant. American ginseng seeds are available for planting in many specialty nurseries. This medicinal herb, used in many Asian herbal traditions, likes moist, well-drained soil in a rich woodland setting. It needs at least 70 percent shade to grow. Ginseng is in the *Araliaceae* family, which contains many threatened species of herbs. Information on ginseng cultivation is abundant.

Trillium is in the *Liliaceae* family, which is made up of over 3,600 species worldwide. More than forty species of trillium itself occur throughout America. Trillium species generally have beautiful flowers, and they prefer rich, moist, well-drained soils. Many trillium species are threatened, mostly due to wild collecting.

Orchids *(Orchidaceae)* represent a large family of plants that have unusual and beautiful flowers. There are over 285 species of orchids in the U.S. Most are rare and need protection. Lady's slipper orchids *(Cypripedium* spp.), for instance, are magnificent, though it can take up to eight years for a lady slipper to bloom for the first time from seed. Many lady slipper orchids have been dug out of the wild to plant in gardens. They do not transplant well and often die, thus stressing the native population.

Slippery elm is a member of the *Ulmaceae* family, which contains about 150 species widely distributed in temperate and tropical regions. Also known as red elm, this tree can be found in most of the eastern United States and southern Canada. Slippery elm has distinctive bark, foliage, and twigs. The leaves are rough; the bark is gray and less coarse than American elm. The inner bark occurring next to the sapwood is the material that makes the tree popular—it is used as food and medicine. It has a sweet earthy taste when eaten fresh. It is commonly used as a mucilage—for sore throats, irritated respiratory systems, ulcers, and other irritations of the mucous membranes. There are a wide variety of products containing slippery elm bark. Opera singers use throat lozenges of slippery elm for its soothing action. The quality of slippery elm varies significantly on the market. The wood of the slippery elm is used for flooring, siding, agricultural implements, wagons, and furniture. Seasoned, it makes great firewood, producing little ash and burning completely through. Occurring mainly as scattered individuals, slippery elm trees can grow to sixty feet in height, though it is becoming hard to find healthy older trees of this size. Currently all of the slippery elm on the market is from wild sources. When the bark is harvested from the tree, despite all efforts the tree more than likely will die, as harvesting makes the tree more susceptible to disease. As with American elm, red elm is being attacked by the Dutch elm disease. This fungus arrived from Europe about seventy years ago and has caused extensive death to our native elms. On the other hand, by cultivating this wonderful tree we can help produce organic supplies of inner bark, keeping down the amount of harvesting occurring with threatenened wild populations of the tree.

Future of Plant Conservation

Thousands more plants are suitable for us to cultivate in our landscapes and gardens. This list given here only represents a tiny fraction of plants needing conservation.

To do your part in these efforts, check with local native plant nurseries and your state department of natural resources of lists of threatened plants. Be sure you know your nursery's original source for plants—some nurseries offer plants dug from the wild, which of course only adds to the problem of habitat destruction.

Landscaping with threatened native plants provides food, medicine, beauty, shelter, fuel, and wildlife habitat for native species. Planting a medicinal garden using strictly native plants will surprise many people who are unaware of the diversity of plants growing in North America. Landscaping with native plants will help conserve America's unique flora. The future of native medicinal plants is in the hands of the people willing to make this extra effort to preserve this heritage.

And finally, imagine how much you will learn about your own living space by discovering the plants meant to grow there naturally.

For Further Study

Bormann, Herbert. *Redesigning the American Lawn.* New Haven, New Jersey: Yale University Press. 1993.

Epels, Thomas. *Botany in a Day.* Pony, Montana: HOPS Press, 1996.

Gladstar, Rosemary. *Planting the Future.* Rochester, Vermont: Healing Arts Press, 2000.

Johnson, Lady Bird. *Wildflowers Across America.* New York, New York: Abbeville Press, 1988.

Mohlenbrock, Robert. *Where Have All the Wildflowers Gone?* New York, New York: Macmillan Publishing Co., 1983.

Phillips, Harry. *Growing and Propagating Wildflowers.* Chapel Hill, North Carolina: University of North Carolina Press, 1985.

Stermer, Dugald. *Vanishing Flora.* New York, New York: Harry N. Abrams, Inc., 1995.

Wild Edibles

by Roberta Burnes

Nature is filled with everything we need in order to live a generous existence—from food and medicine to clothing and shelter. There is a simple pleasure in knowing the world provides us with this sustinence in its fields, meadows, and forests. Unfortunately, most of us have lost the knowledge that our early ancestors had about wild plants and how to use them. A basic knowledge of some of the more common wild edibles is more useful than we can imagine; not only is the food free and abundant, but many of these wild edibles are packed with vitamins and minerals that store-bought produce are lacking.

In today's world of heavy packaging and prefabrication, many people approach wild edibles with a measure of disdain or suspicion—as if these plants must surely taste awful because

they don't come from the supermarket. Perhaps this is because many of these plants are considered pests or weeds that must be banished from the garden. Or perhaps it is simply a fear of the unknown. This aversion is so accute that I even occasionally have to disguise these edibles in my meals to get my husband to eat them. On the other hand, my two-year-old, who hasn't learned this modern aversion to the natural, will happily eat anything he has helped me "harvest" from the garden, regardless if we planted it there ourselves or if was dropped there by the hand of old Mother Nature.

Here is a truth each of you should take to heart: Even if you live in a city, you are surrounded by wild plants that can be utilized for food, medicine, cordage, and dye. In fact, many common lawn weeds—the violet, dandelion, plantain, and chicory—are both very edible and very medicinal. Common milkweed not only attracts butterflies, but its stem contains fibers that can be twisted into rope and its young pods are edible when boiled in several changes of water. Common mullein, often found in fields and along roadsides, is used medicinally for its ability to quell coughs and treat asthma. Flowers of many species, both wild and cultivated, are edible. This includes such diverse species as yucca, day lily, violet, nasturtium, and squash. Hedgerows are often full of edible treasures like elderflower, rosehips, and common sumac (whose berries can be made into a thirst-quenching "lemonade"). Even the thorny thistle has a crunchy, water-filled stem that can be peeled, albeit carefully, and eaten raw like celery.

Bless the Innocence of the Child

As mentioned above, I often gather wild edibles with my son. I find it amazing, and somewhat heartening, that even a two-year-old can learn how to identify plants. It gives me hope for humanity that our confused relationship with nature today is not necessarily a natural thing; it is rather a misguided social construct that can we can counteract with our children. Though of course, I don't need to warn you that you should always remind children never to eat a plant without first checking with you.

In general, this is how it seems to work. Once we've chosen one species to harvest, I let my son do the picking and preparation. Then we both share in the feast. As a rule, children are often much more willing to try something that they have helped to harvest and prepare. If you are able to instill this love of naturally harvested plants early in a child, perhaps you will be doing your part to counteract the biases of modern societies, which favor mechanized and processed foods.

The following are a few of the easiest and tastiest wild edibles to find and prepare. Keep in mind that there are hundreds of useful and delicious plants in the world. Many of these plants have multiple uses including food, fiber, and medicine.

In my list, for obvious reasons I've avoided plants that have poisonous look-alikes—such as those in the nightshade and carrot families. Nevertheless, it is always wise to consult a good plant guide such as *Peterson's Guide to Edible and Medicinal Wild Plants*. Do not attempt to eat anything that you cannot positively identify as being edible. You should also avoid collecting plants within fifty feet of any major road, as plants can concentrate lead and other harmful materials that may be present due to run-off.

Purslane

You've probably encountered purslane *(Portulaca oleracea)* if you have a garden; it's considered by many to be nothing more than a troublesome weed. Yet this is one weed you'll want to welcome to your garden—and to your dinner table! In fact, purslane is one of the tastiest and most nutritious herbs you'll find anywhere. Purslane has been cultivated for centuries in the Middle East and Europe, where it is used as a potherb in soups, stews, and salads. It is also popular in Mexico where it's sold as a staple vegetable in farmers markets.

Purslane grows abundantly across North America in gardens, waste areas, and even sidewalks. It seems to prefer poor, dry soil. Purslane's dark, shiny green leaves are arranged alternately on succulent, creeping branches. The leaves are paddle shaped and fleshy. Both leaves and stems are edible and have a sweet, lemony flavor that my son loves. The inconspicuous yellow flowers mature to produce tiny seed cups filled with hundreds of fine, black seeds. I've heard that the seeds can be ground into flour, but this seems like more work than it's worth!

You should harvest purslane from June until the first frost. I usually find it as I'm weeding the garden, so I pull the entire plant up by the roots. Break off the roots and wash the plants thoroughly. The tender growing tips can be used whole, but otherwise I usually strip the leaves and discard the tougher stems. Eat them raw or steam them like you would asparagus (the flavor is very similar). Purslane doesn't cook down the way some greens do, which means you'll wind up with about as much bulk after cooking as you started with. Try adding the tender, raw tips of the plant to fresh salads. The stems and leaves can also be pickled.

As an added bonus, purslane is packed with powerful nutrition. A 100-gram serving of raw purslane contains 21 grams of protein, 2,500 milligrams of thiamine, 103 milligrams of phosphorus, and measurable amounts of calcium and vitamin C. Purslane is also rich in omega-3 fatty acids.

Note: You should avoid purslane if you are pregnant or have digestive problems.

Lamb's Quarters

Lamb's quarters (*Chenopodium album*) gets its name from the whitish fuzz that appears on the young leaves of the plant. Lamb's quarters is one of the most common weeds in the garden; in fact, it's likely you'll find it growing almost anywhere it can get a bit of sunlight, and therefore you will likely consider it quite a pest. Still, lamb's-quarters has been used as a potherb for centuries both in its native Europe and in Appalachia, where it is often called "wild spinach" due to its similar taste.

A prodigious self-seeding annual, lamb's quarters can be harvested throughout the spring and summer. Choose the tender growing tips or pick whole plants before they enter the flowering stage. Strip the leaves off and eat them raw, or cook them as you would spinach. Lamb's quarters leaves contain large amounts of iron and calcium, and are rich in beta-carotene as well. Try adding the herb to a vegetable soup with onions and potatoes; purée the soup in batches once the vegetables are cooked through. Whenever I go out to weed the vegetable garden, I gather whatever lamb's quarters I find and steam them up for a quick, green snack. A little garlic and olive oil complement the spinach-like flavor very well indeed.

Pokeweed

This wild edible should be harvested and eaten with care, as the entire plant is considered toxic. That said, young pokeweed shoots are actually considered a delicacy in the South. With proper harvesting and preparation, you can enjoy them too.

Pokeweed *(Phytolacca americana L.)* is a common weed across most of North America. It often grows in disturbed areas like construction sites, but it will happily take up residence in your garden if you forget to weed it. Pokeweed is spread by birds who eat and deposit its dark-purple berries along hedgerows and woodland edges. The berries have been used for dye (though it's not very colorfast, especially when exposed to sunlight), and the root has traditionally been used for problems concerning the lymphatic system. Pokeweed can reach heights of thirteen feet and has thick, purple stems and droopy, green leaves.

As a rule, pokeweed should only be harvested in the very early spring, just as its first shoots appear above the ground. When it's in this stage, the leaves of this plant are stiff and rounded at the tips, pointing straight up from the ground. Snap off the shoots at ground level when they are five inches high or shorter; this is the only stage in which the plant is considered safe to eat.

Pokeweed must be cooked properly before eating, as the plant contains powerful alkaloids that can cause severe gastric upset. Wash, rinse, and boil the greens twice, in two changes of water, for at least five minutes each time. Rinse the greens well again, then season and enjoy. If you want to enjoy the Southern delicacy known as "poke salet," as mentioned in the old song "Poke Salad Annie," fry the boiled and rinsed greens in a little bacon grease for a few minutes. Finally, add some scrambled eggs and cook until the eggs are done. As we say down South, it sure is "good eatin'"!

Fiddlehead Ferns

These succulent beauties are at the top of my list of wild edibles. The first time I tried them, I knew I was in love. Fiddleheads are actually the young shoots of the ostrich fern (*Matteuccia struthiopteris*). They appear in the spring along moist bottomlands from the Great Lakes north and east into Canada and New England. Many young ferns have this spiral shape, but true fiddleheads are a dark, shiny green color with a deep U-shaped groove on the inside of the stem. Young fiddleheads are surrounded by a papery brown "onion skin" husk that falls away as the frond unfurls. They are best picked when less than three inches high and still tightly spiraled.

After I first discovered fiddleheads, I didn't pay much attention to which fern species I was collecting from. If it looked like a fiddlehead, I picked it! Several of my fiddleheads turned out to be bracken ferns—distinguished by their brown, furry stems. At the dinner table we soon realized there is a HUGE difference in flavor (and digestibility) between these two plant species. Unlike the mild, pleasant flavor of ostrich fern fiddleheads, bracken fern is extremely bitter tasting. Although used medicinally by the Cherokee for various ailments, bracken fern is a known carcinogen if consumed in quantity. Needless to say, I quickly learned how to tell the difference between these plants.

Look for fiddleheads in the spring, breaking them off just an inch or so beneath the tight little coils. Winnow the papery covering off by tossing and shaking them in a brown paper bag, then wash well in a sink full of water to remove all traces of sediment. Fiddleheads should be cooked before eating, as raw ones can cause nausea and have a slightly bitter taste. Once cooked, they have a delicate, nutty flavor that's reminiscent of asparagus and spinach. Prepare them the same way you would any firm green vegetable. That is, you can steam them, stir-fry them, add them to soups, or blanch and marinate them in olive oil and balsamic vinegar and add them to pasta salads. For flavor and pure elegance, you can't beat these gourmet treats from nature.

Stinging Nettles

Believe it or not, few plants in the forest or fields can match the stinging nettle *(Urtica dioica)* for medicinal and nutritional value. Don't let the name scare you; stinging nettle is perfectly safe to eat when cooked; though it is somewhat tricky to get to that stage. Indeed, despite its sting the plant has a rich flavor that I find even more palatable than spinach.

Stinging nettle grows to three feet in height and is covered with stinging hairs. The "sting" is caused by the presence of formic acid and histamine, but both of these chemical agents are neutralized through the cooking or drying of the herb.

The leaves of stinging nettle are bright green, heart-shaped, and toothed along the edges. Its flowers, which are also green, appear throughout the summer. As a rule, stinging nettle prefers moist bottomlands, and so it often appears along woodland creeks and rivers.

Stinging nettle contains a wealth of minerals—including iron, calcium, magnesium, and potassium. It also contains high amounts of vitamins A, B, C, and K. Stinging nettle has numerous applications in traditional herbal medicine; a complete list would fill pages, so I won't go into it here except to mention that it is particularly useful in treating anemia, and its astringent nature makes it valuable in treating internal or external bleeding.

Nettle tea is traditionally drunk as a tonic and blood purifier. Also, I have known several people who actually sting themselves with nettle as a localized treatment for arthritis pain. After the stinging sensation wears away, the arthritis pain is often relieved for several hours or more.

Stinging nettle can be prepared as a tea, tincture, salve, or compress, but my favorite way to consume nettle is to eat it. The best time to gather it for food is in the springtime, when the shoots are still tender. Wear gloves when handling nettle, and snap off the top six to eight inches of each plant. Steam them gently until bright green and wilted, about three to five minutes. Chop and serve with butter or margarine. The texture is coarser than spinach, but the flavor is unbelievably delicate and fresh. Stinging nettle is also great when added to your favorite soup and stew recipes.

Urban Herbal Gardening

✎ by Ellen Dugan ✎

Hello faithful readers! It's your down-to-earth, neighborhood Garden Witch back for another year to help with your urban gardening questions and challenges.

Over the years—while working in the nursery industry and recently while lecturing as a master gardener—I have had many people ask me about growing plants and herbs in a city environment. Is it possible? Can I really do it? The answer would be: Of course you can! Container gardens are taking the gardening world by storm. Lush city gardens are sprouting up on balconies everywhere. Fragrant, flower-filled courtyards and rooftop gardens are all making their way into the lives of the city gardener. Sunny decks are crammed with edible herbs and produce, even as we speak. Secret shady gardens thrill their owners in alleys behind apartment buildings and dainty window boxes add enchantment to many a metropolitan windowsill. And you too can achieve this without much extra burden to your busy lifestyle and your checking account.

Growing a Variety of Plants

Plants of every variety and description can flourish in pots and containers. It is possible to grow just about anything in a pot—including veggies, flowers, and herbs. The best part about container gardening is that you have a lot more control than with ordinary gardens—over weeds, the size of your plants, and your color combinations. Container gardens are mobile, adjustable, and suited to everyday life. If you grow tired of the arrangement you can easily shift things around. With container gardens, urban gardeners have the opportunity to create a private natural space all their own in which to dream and relax.

Making a city herb garden is a creative process of trial and error. City living can be stressful on plants. They have to manage pollution and an artificial habitat. Design your own garden with plants that will thrive on the strengths, weaknesses, and quirks of your particular growing conditions. Experienced urban gardeners know that they have to find a balance between having the plants they want and those they can successfully grow.

But let's face it, not all of us are pros at this sort of thing. So to help you with urban herbal gardening, here are some pointers that will help you achieve growing success.

Choosing a Site

The site where you choose to create your container garden will be your own small mini-climate. A mini-climate concerns such things as the amount of sunlight and shade your plants receive, moisture levels, and wind exposure. The trick to discovering your site's mini-climate is observation. Keep a sharp watch on how much light your balcony or deck receives and at what time of the day, if any, that you have shade. Shade and light are key. If you have early morning shade and full sunlight from noon on, your site probably faces west. This will be a sunny garden and will require sun- and heat-tolerant plants. One must also take into consideration that neighboring buildings can affect light and shade patterns by cutting off sunshine or reflecting more light and heat back to you due to light-colored walls.

In fact, there are also varying degrees of shade—full shade, dappled shade, and part shade. To try and ease confusion, here are some basic rules for determining what sunlight exposure or type of shade that you do have.

• Draw out a simple diagram and, at various times of the day, mark where the shade hits with dashed lines. Note the time on your drawing. This will take you all day, but it is critical information; stick with it because it can be a important tool in helping you to choose plants.

• If there is less than two hours of sunlight, this is a full-shade garden. Among the plants you can grow are: bugle, columbine, dead nettle, ivy, lily-of-the-valley, monarda, mints, periwinkle, Solomon's seal, tansy, and the violet. Consider that light-colored walls will help to reflect sunlight and warm up your shady garden.

• If your garden gets between two and six hours of sunlight, it is a partial shade garden. These plants should thrive here: angelica, black cohosh, blue cohosh, betony, cat-mint, foxglove, heliotrope, lady's mantle, mallows, mints, soapwort, and sweet woodruff.

• If it receives six to twelve hours of daily sunlight, this is a full-sun garden. Look for heat-tolerant plants such as: rosemary, lavender, sunflowers, santolina, and scented geraniums. You should have great luck with culinary herbs and roses if you don't allow them to dry out. Exposed sites such as rooftops, penthouses terraces, and balconies often receive this much sunlight each day.

All right. No need to panic at this point. After finding out how much shade or sunlight your garden will receive, next check out the direction that your site is oriented to—using a compass if necessary. An easy directional plant list follows, with annual and perennial plant suggestions for color and structure. These are a general rule of thumb only.

- South-facing gardens receive sunlight all day. You should have success with a wide selection of plants and culinary herbs. Try annual purple fountain grass, sunflowers, roses, geraniums and petunias.

- East- and west-facing gardens receive six hours of sunshine daily, but in the morning and evening respectively. In east-facing gardens plant hydrangeas, day lilies, impatiens, and azaleas; in west-facing ones, geraniums, coreopsis, coneflowers, morning glories, and sunflowers.

- North-facing gardens can get as little as two hours of sunshine. Plant begonias, hostas, and rhododendrons.

Generally speaking, too much of a good thing may create challenges in any site you choose for your garden. Full sunlight and steady winds can cause growing problems for plants. Strong summer heat tends to bake plants. Excessive winds strip moisture out of plant leaves—this is known as transpiration. Overall, there are four factors that affect transpiration: light, temperature, relative wind, and humidity. Adding mulch to your soil helps, as does figuring out how to provide a little shade—with awnings, trellises, pergolas, or other features—or a windbreak for those full-sun gardens. The next time that it rains, you will also want to keep an eye on how any precipitation falls on your chosen site and how the water drains. Some spots may stay completely dry, some areas may not take in much water at all, and others may receive a good soaking, so plan accordingly.

All of these growing conditions—shade, sunlight exposure, and rainfall patterns—taken together will help you determine what you can and cannot achieve in your urban garden. No matter what your sunlight exposure, make the most out of the space you have by arranging containers in groups that complement each other. When placing large containers on balconies or rooftop gardens, check the strength of the structure. Find out if your building has weight limits or rules about heavy objects on balconies. Containers filled with soil can be very heavy. Conversely, small containers may be easily blown away. Find yourself a happy medium—try an intermediate size of container. Or use window boxes and fasten them safely down. You can also make use of hanging baskets. Remember as you set up a container garden, you should make use of two inches of gravel or small rocks at the bottom of the container to aid in drainage. Work with a good quality potting mix, and add lots of sterile compost to enrich your soil. Invest in some fertilizer, a watering can, and get ready to garden.

Below, I have included various annuals and perennials in these mixed-pot planting schemes that consider color, height, and scent, as well as site conditions. As you assemble your garden, be sure to place taller plants either in the back or middle of your pot. Then plant the medium sized ones in front of those with the shorter varieties around the outside edges. Add trailing plants to complete your containers. A trick that we professionals use when designing pots and containers for sale is to plant them very full. Don't scrimp on the plants! But remember to coordinate the shade or sunlight tolerances of the plants. Here are some combinations that I have conjured up, just for you.

Practical Magic Pot Combinations

Moonlight magic garden (for part shade): Artemesia, nicotiana, betony, mugwort, white petunias for scent and nighttime sparkle. Tuck in some white zinnias to attract the butterflies.

Culinary herb garden (for full sunlight): Fennel, lavender, catmint, chives, dill, thyme, rosemary, sage, scented geraniums, nasturtiums, pineapple sage with its bright-red flowers, and sunny marigolds.

Fragrant fascination garden (for full to part sunlight): A standard tree rose, lavender, alyssum, sage, catmint, coordinating shades of begonias and petunias for color, and spicy dianthus (pinks) for texture and scent.

Shady spot garden (for full shade): Pansies, violas, ivy, and mints. Plant the variegated-type ivy to add some visual interest to this pot. As the pansies fade in the summer heat, replace them with a colorful nonedible shade annual such as begonia or impatiens.

Hanging-basket magic garden (for various conditions): Look for prostrate varieties of herbs such as rosemary and thyme. Nasturtiums make a nice trailing plant, as do ivy and periwinkle. The ivy and periwinkle require shade. The other trailing herbs mentioned will thrive in sunlight. All of these will spill nicely over the sides of your baskets and tall containers. Ivy is a great trailer. Although not an herb, strawberries make great hanging-basket plants. They will require full sunlight. Try an ever-bearing strawberry that will produce fruit for a longer season.

Herbal enchantment garden (for full to part sunlight): Rosemary, dill, parsley, bronze fennel, wooly thyme, tricolor sage, and yarrow. Use a large container and plant the yarrow in the middle and the other herbs in a circle around it. Or use a strawberry pot. Plant the yarrow in the center and tuck the other herbs in the outside pockets.

Something else that is entertaining to try involves arranging your containers according to the four elements—earth, air, fire, and water. You can create combinations of annuals, ornamentals, perennials, and herbs that are attuned to the elements.

Earth garden (for shady garden): Should include green plants with lots of foliage, including ferns, lady's mantle, sweet potato vine, green varieties of coleus, licorice plant (heliochrysum), mint, and monarda.

Air garden (for full sunlight): Choose shorter varieties of sunflowers for the center of the pot. Around it plant yellow cockscomb, marigolds, lemony colored snapdragons, golden-yellow calendulas, yellow zinnias, and santolina. Plant variegated vinca vine or prostrate rosemary to fall gracefully over the edges of the container.

Fire garden (for sunlight to part shade): Plant pineapple sage, red New Guinea impatiens, bright-red annual sage (salvia). Add annual vinca vines to trail over the edges of your container. Try adding Japanese blood grass to the center of this container for visual interest. In the fall add scarlet mums to the container, or place in separate containers and group around the other plants.

Water garden (for shade): Plant heliotrope, red variegated coleus, streptocarpella to hang over the sides, blue lobelia, purple sage, betony, and forget-me-nots. Top this off with blue delphiniums in the center or back of the container. Add variegated ivy to spill over the sides. Start the container out in the spring with blue pansies and violas. As the summer progresses replace the faded flowers with purple impatiens.

In general, you should always start small and experiment. See what grows successfully for you. Add more containers as you go along. All containers will need drainage holes and a thin layer of mulch to protect from drying winds. You can make your garden bird and butterfly friendly by adding a shallow saucer of water for them to drink out of. Butterflies are attracted to parsley, zinnias, monarda, coreopsis, coneflowers, and salvias. Parsley is a butterfly nursery plant. The caterpillars eat the parsley and then go off and lay their eggs. If you are feeling adventurous try growing buddleia, the butterfly bush, in a large container on a sunny site. Remember, if you want to attract wildlife such as birds, bees, and butterflies don't use any pesticides. If damaging insects become a problem, I recommend using a natural pyrethrum spray, selectively.

Windowsill Herb Garden

For those of you who don't have a deck or balcony, here are some suggestions for a windowsill herb garden. Herbs that are grown indoors add a fresh aroma to your home, and because they are close to hand they encourage you to make use of them for seasonings and in food preparation.

To thrive, herbs need a sunny growing area, water, air humidity, and protection from drafts and extreme temperatures. Turn your pots occasionally to encourage even growth.

Bay: Add a leaf to chili or stews.

Borage: Use these pretty, blue flowers to garnish food and beverages.

Chives: Cut off the flowers for improved leaf production. Use chives to season potatoes, eggs, salads, stews.

Marjoram and oregano: May be added to salads, egg and cheese dishes.

Nasturtiums: The flowers are edible. Toss them into salads for a peppery bite.

Parsley: Used as a spice, garnish, and breath freshener. You should always have plenty on hand.

Rosemary: Great with chicken and beef. Don't overwater this plant.

Sorrel: Lush, green leaves may be used as a substitute for spinach.

Sweet basil: Great indoor plant. Pinch off the flowers to encourage leaf production.

Tarragon: These thin, aromatic leaves have a distinctive flavor.

Magic of Plants

Plants add enchantment to our lives every day and in many ways. So go on, try creating your own urban garden. You never know what lessons these plants may teach you.

To add a further twist to this task, below I have added a list of the magical associations of the plants that I have been mentioning. Many blessings on your herb gardening!

Shade

Begonia: Helps with premonitions

Bugle: Health and healing

Columbine: Courage and love

Ferns: Fairy magic and invisibility

Hosta: Mystery, health

Lily-of-the-valley: Happiness and wisdom

Mint: Prosperity

Solomon's seal: Protection, banishing unwanted spirits

Tansy: Vigor and long life

Violet: Fairy magic, love, protection from enchantment

Part Shade and Sunlight

Angelica: Inspiration, protection

Artemesia: Moon magic, women's mysteries

Betony (lamb's ears): Protection, children's magic

Catmint: Cat magic, affection, beauty, cheerfulness

Cohosh: Love, protection, courage

Foxglove: Fairy magic, protection

Heliotrope: Invisibility

Lady's mantle: Love, romance

Monarda: Success, prosperity

Mugwort: Moon magic, psychic powers

Nicotiana: Moon magic, healing, cleansing

Soapwort: Cleansings

Sweet woodruff: Protective charm for athletes

Full Sunlight

Borage: Courage, psychic abilities

Calendula: Health

Cockscomb: Protection, healing

Dill: Protection, prosperity

Fennel: Health, purification

Lavender: Counteracts the evil eye

Morning glory: Power, protection, love, banishing

Petunias: Power and cheer

Rose: Love, adds energy and speed to any spell

Rosemary: Remembrance, cleansing, love, and health

Sage: Wisdom

Strawberries: Perfection

Sunflower: Affluence, grandeur

Thyme: New projects

Yarrow: The all-purpose Witches' herb

Zinnia: Friendship

Winter Activities for
Herb Lovers

⤛ by Dallas Jennifer Cobb ⤜

Though often considered a time of discontent, winter, a time associated with dormancy and death, can actually be a productive and fruitful time for herb lovers and gardeners. All it takes is some careful attention to some gardening basics, and a general shift in attitudes to this underappreciated season.

As the seasons shift, the earth moves through a cycle of descent into regeneration, a veritable slumber through the cold months. The herbal gardener also shifts from the summery joy of planting, blossoming, and fruition to the autumnal energy of harvesting, storing, and putting up the herb garden's abundance. After the harvest we tuck in our garden beds, prepare the herbs for their hibernation through winter, and then we wait. While they sleep in their beds, there is much that we can do.

In the summer, with long days of light and warmth, many gardeners are loath to go indoors. But in the winter, the long, drawn-out darkness and the fierce cold weather are incentives to stay indoors. The lack of outdoor light and warmth can be conducive to undertaking herbal creations indoors. While winter can be a time of hibernation, of sorts, for the gardener, it does not have to be an unproductive time. We can make herbal oils and vinegars, create herbal healing salves and balms, and dry herbs to use as teas, spices, scent sachets, and treats. Gardening can stay with us through the wintry months through the pleasures of taste and scent, and the whimsical thoughts of herbs that we will invite to our gardens anew in the spring.

Tucking in the Garden Bed

As the autumn chill urges us to gather warm sweaters around us, and the bite of the wind on our cheeks turns our skin red and slightly dry, we bundle up warmly, and with gloved hands put our garden to sleep for the winter. As the leaves fall, we work with nature's cycles to prepare our garden beds for hibernation. We clean up the yard, and till leaf mulch into the garden for aeration. The compost bin is ready for harvesting, and we spread a thick layer of rich compost over the garden to provide revitalizing nutrients. Finally, we cover the beds with a good layer of straw for warmth, taking special care with more delicate perennials like sage *(Salvia officinalis)* and lavender *(Lavandula augustfolia)*, fluffing straw around their root bases and among their remaining branches. The straw provides vital air space needed to insulate against the cold, and to keep physical space between the plant matter and the snow or ice.

When spring arrives and the last threat of frost is over, the straw can be raked off the herbs, removing the warm blanket and gently waking up the garden. In Zone 5 or colder areas, straw can be removed gradually, initially exposing just the top of the plant to sunlight while still protecting the root base. In case of a nighttime dip in temperature, the plant's root base is safe, enjoying the benefits of daytime exposure to sunlight and nighttime cold protection. Straw can be left in the garden year round. In the spring it can be raked into the depressions between raised beds, onto the pathway through the garden, or stored in a well-ventilated containment. The heat of drying straw can cause combustion though, so always ventilate it well, and refrain from storing it inside a shed or garage. If you don't already spread straw on your pathways, consider doing this. Harness the heat of the drying straw to facilitate budding, and for the shade and water conservation it provides in the heat of summer. Straw is like a blanket that we pull over our beds in the fall, then pull back gradually in the spring to help with summer awakening.

Who Sleeps Indoors?

Many tender perennials need to come indoors to survive winter. Even with a protective layer of straw, lemongrass (*Cymbropogon citratus*), rosemary (*Rosmarinus officinalis*), and Spanish lavender (*Lavandula latifolia*) will die from exposure if left outdoors. Consider using planters or containers for these herbs so they can easily move from garden or patio into the house. Many gardeners keep only annuals or tender perennials in pots, so they know in the fall exactly what has to come indoors.

Pots of herbs can be kept in kitchen windows or sunny spots throughout the house so you can enjoy their fragrance, taste, and healing properties year round. Treat them as you would flowers, watering them regularly, giving them as much sunlight as possible, and fertilizing them before major transitions. In the fall, add fresh compost to top up the pot, and in the spring repot, moving up a size, and putting compost in the bottom and top of the pot. This will provide nutrients and energy, needed by the herbs, to smooth these major transitions.

Garden Planning

Many gardeners are like their gardens. With the move indoors, inside our homes for the winter, there is a journeying into ourselves, into a deeply meditative state. In this state, we work on our gardens, with our minds, hearts, and spirits, while the garden beds lay dormant and sleeping. We can dream of, and plan, our gardens for the spring to come. To do so, choose a notebook and keep notes of your dreaming and planning. Sketch your garden plans. Draw small diagrams of your beds and plan where to relocate, plant, or cull new herbs.

Why not design a theme herb garden? A healing garden containing goldenseal *(Hydrastis canadensis)*, echinacea *(Echinacea angustifolia)*, lemongrass, calendula *(Calendula offinalis)*, and comfrey *(Symphytum officinale)* is beautiful, fragrant, and contains the essentials for remedies to cure many common ailments. It is also a good combination for welcoming butterflies and humming-birds to your garden.

A fragrance garden can bring joy to both garden and home. Herbs such as lavender, lemon balm *(Melissa officinalis)*, and berg-amot *(Monarda didyma)* evoke good feelings and make a lovely potpourri combination. Lavender stalks can be braided and then hung in a bedroom or closet for a lovely fragrance and to protect from clothing moths.

A tea garden can be created in containers or pots to control such prolific herbs as lemon balm, peppermint *(Mentha piperita)*, spearmint *(Mentha spicata)*, and chamomile *(Chamaemelum nobile)*. Together or separately these herbs make tasty herbal teas that bring the scent of the garden alive in the midst of winter's chill. Dry herbs in the fall to use throughout the winter. Package them separately in airtight containers or Ziploc bags, and when you are ready for tea, mix the herbs to your liking.

Near the kitchen door plant a culinary garden with favorites like parsley *(Petroselinum crispum)*, sage, rosemary, and thyme *(Thymus vulgaris)*. Add flavorful accents with basil *(Ocimum basilicum)*, coriander *(Coriandrum sativum)*, lovage *(Levisticum officinale)*, and dill *(Anethum graveolens)*. Color the garden with edible flowers such as nasturtium *(Tropaeolum majus)* and calendula. Culinary gardens can get very specific; try a "spaghetti" garden: oregano *(Origanum vulgare)*, basil, garlic *(Allium sativum)*, and chives *(Allium schoenoprasum)*. The combinations for theme gardens are endless: a child's garden, a pet garden, a lemon garden, or a dye garden. Envision the magic of an alchemist's or Witch's garden. Decide on your theme, dream, plan, and design through the winter.

The Fruits of our Labors

There are many ways to preserve herbs and store them for use throughout the winter—oils and salves made from herbs that bear their healing energy; dried herbs that flavor your cooking or make a calming cup of tea; herbal vinegars that are rich in the fragrance of the herbs. To choose herbs for any of these creations, think of the herbs you enjoy for their many properties.

Making Herbal Vinegars

To make herbal vinegars, start with a wide-mouthed jar with a lid. Choose the herbs you want to use, and make sure they are dry. Fill about one-quarter of the jar loosely with herbs, and then pour in vinegar until the jar is full. Screw on the lid, and store the jar in a dark place for at least six weeks, and up to a year. The flavor becomes more concentrated as time passes. If you are making vinegars in the summer and can stand the jar in a sunny spot outdoors, the time can be shortened to three weeks. If you think of it, turn or shake the jar a few times every now and then.

To decant the vinegars, use cheesecloth or muslin to strain out the herbal particles. Squeeze the cloth to release all the vinegar and discard the used herbs in the compost. Pour vinegar into ornamental bottles, and label them with the date and herb. Use throughout the winter in salad dressings and marinades. Experiment with different kinds of herbs and vinegars to get different taste combinations.

Combinations for Herbal-Infused Vinegars

- Chilies, garlic, and oregano in cider vinegar

- Sage, parsley, and shallots in red wine vinegar
- Mint, honey, and cardamom seed in white vinegar
- Dill, garlic, and nasturtiums in cider vinegar
- Oregano, chives, and garlic in balsamic vinegar

Making Herbal-Infused Oils

Infused oils can be made easily at home and used for cosmetic or culinary purposes. For cosmetic use, choose base oils of almond, coconut, or olive oil or some combination of these three. For culinary oils, almond and olive oil are popular choices, though you can also use neutral-tasting safflower, sunflower, or soya oil, or tasty walnut or toasted sesame oil.

Almond oil is a light oil that is easily absorbed into the skin. It is scentless, mildly flavored, and light in color. It is ideal for both culinary and cosmetic infusions, but can be fatal for people with nut allergies. Be sure to label your oils with their full ingredients. Coconut oil is a rich emollient oil. It is heavier in texture, clear in color, and wonderfully rich in scent. Coconut is best used with complimentary scents or tastes, both in culinary or cosmetic oils. Olive oil is excellent because of its versatility, but should be used only for cold infusions. It is widely used for culinary purposes and gaining popularity in cosmetic products. Olive oil is dark green in color, and has an olive scent to it. For cosmetic products, use olive oil only in products with earthy scents, and not as a base for a lightly scented perfume product.

Infused oils can be made in two ways, hot or cold. Cold infused oil takes longer, but is very easy and sure not to deplete herbs of their vital energies by heating. Fill a clean and dry wide-mouthed jar with your chosen herbs. Cover the herbs with oil, and seal the jar. Label the jar with the date and the ingredients, and store in a cool, dark place for six weeks. Decant as with vinegars.

To make hot-infused oil, use a double boiler saucepan with water in the bottom and oil and herbs in the top. Keep a secure lid on the pan, and bring the water to a boil. Then lower the temperature to a simmer for two hours. After two hours take the pans off of the heat, and allow them to thoroughly cool before straining and decanting the oils following the directions above.

Store your infused oils in ornamental bottles labeled with their ingredients and the date of bottling. Use a dark bottle when storing the oil away from sunlight in order to protect the vital energies of the herbs.

Combinations for Culinary Herbal-Infused Oils

- Garlic and chives in olive oil (great for making zesty garlic bread)
- Basil, chili pepper, and garlic in olive oil
- Rosemary and orange peel in toasted sesame oil
- Lemon verbena, lemon balm, and lemon thyme in walnut oil
- Basil and oregano in olive oil

Combinations for Cosmetic Herbal-Infused Oils

- Comfrey and calendula in olive oil (for making healing salves)
- Mint and orange peel in almond oil (for making Luscious Lip Balm)
- Chamomile and lavender in almond oil (for making Sleepy Time Relaxing Rub)
- Basil, rosemary, and grapefruit peel in walnut oil (for making Visionary Oil)
- Jasmine flowers, rose petals, and coconut oil (for making Caribbean Island Bath Oil)

Making Healing Salves and Balms

Making herbal salves, ointments, and balms is easy when you have infused herbal oils. Beeswax is used to set the oils, thickening their consistency. If you prefer thicker ointments use more beeswax than recommended. If you prefer a lighter consistency use less beeswax. Do not substitute paraffin wax for beeswax in these recipes, as paraffin is a fire hazard in warming.

Luscious Lip Balm

Infuse peppermint and orange peel in almond oil for 6 weeks. Strain and discard the herbs. In a saucepan, melt 1 ounce of beeswax, then slowly add 1 ounce of infused oil. Mix slowly and remove from heat. Pour into a small container and allow to cool completely. Label fully. For use, apply a dab to your lips when you are going out into cold weather, or when the skin feels dry.

Dry Skin Healing Ointment

Infuse comfrey and calendula in olive and almond oils for 6 weeks. Strain and discard the herbs. In a saucepan melt 2 ounces of beeswax, then slowly add 1 cup of infused oil and 1 ounce of Vitamin E oil. Mix slowly and remove the mixture from the heat. Pour into a clean container and allow to cool completely. Label fully. Rub ointment liberally into skin when it feels dry. This is especially useful for preventing dry hands and cracked heels.

Gardeners' Hand Salve

Follow the directions above for Dry Skin Healing Ointments, except increase beeswax to 3 ounces. Add 1 ounce of lavender infused oil or 10 drops of lavender essential oil. Add 2 ounces of cocoa butter or lanolin. Have Gardeners' Hand Salve on hand when spring arrives, and make gifts of it to your gardening friends in the dead of winter.

Sleepy Time Relaxing Rub

Infuse chamomile and lavender in almond oil for 6 weeks. Strain and discard the herbs. Pour into a clean plastic bottle with a squirt top. Label fully. For use, warm the oil in the palms of your hands and massage into the back, feet, and hands. Chamomile and lavender promote relaxation and will bring on a peaceful sleep. This oil is gentle and safe for use with children, infants, the elderly, and the frail. It can even be used by pregnant women to soothe their belly and back.

Visionary Oil

Infuse basil, rosemary, and grapefruit peel in walnut oil for 6 weeks. Strain and discard the herbs, pouring oil into a clean jar. A few pieces of dried grapefruit peel or dried rosemary look nice floating in the jar. Label fully. If you have been working at the computer for a period of time, reading, or doing any concentrated activity which has strained your eyes, pour a small amount of Visionary Oil in the palms of your hands. Rub them until they are warm, then place your hands over your tired eyes. Feel the warmth, and smell the rosemary reviving you.

Caribbean Island Bath Oil

Infuse jasmine flowers and rose petals in coconut oil for 6 weeks. Strain and discard the flowers. Pour the oil into a clean plastic bottle with a squirt top. Label fully. For use, squeeze two or three generous squirts under the faucet as you run your bath. As you soak in the rich emollient coconut oil, close your eyes and smell the Caribbean surrounding you. Be sure to clean the bathtub thoroughly after using a bath oil to prevent bath mishaps.

Herbal Abundance

Winter wealth from your summer herb garden doesn't end here. Consider the variety of teas that can be made from your tasty and aromatic herbs. Mix and blend the herbs and try out old favorites and invent new tastes. With each new blend, write down the recipe for the combination you have made and later jot a short note on how you enjoyed the tea combination. Then, when you create a favorite, you can recreate it again and again. Herbs can be dried and stored for use as spices, combined with cooking and baking to enhance the flavors of your meals and treats. Try lavender shortbread and fresh basil pesto.

Lavender Shortbread

Add 3 tablespoons of dried lavender to 1 cup cold butter (do not use margarine) and 2 cups all-purpose flour and ½ cup powdered sugar in a large bowl using a pastry cutter. Then mix quickly with your hands, and press into an ungreased 9-by-9-inch pan. Prick all over with a fork. Bake at 300°F for 50 to 60 minutes until golden brown.

Fresh Basil Pesto

1   cup of fresh basil leaves
3   tablespoons of pine nuts or walnuts
3   tablespoons of grated Parmesan cheese
3   large cloves of garlic
    Olive oil

Purée the ingredients in a food processor. Slowly add just enough olive oil to make a smooth paste. Pesto is great for use on pasta, fish, vegetables, or bread.

When winter comes to your garden, don't lament. Put on your warm clothes, put your garden to sleep, and retreat indoors to use the herbs you harvested in the summer and fall. Though the garden sleeps, herb lovers stay devoted through the cold times and enjoy the fruits of their labors and love year round.

For Further Study

Britton, Jade, and Tamara Kircher. *The Complete Book of Home Herbal Remedies*. New York, New York: Firefly Books, 1998.

Culinary
Herbs

Alchemy in the Kitchen

≫ by Jonathan Keyes ≪

This past spring, I helped a friend start a small garden in his back-yard. Along with an assortment of vegetables and flowers, we grew a patch of culinary herbs that we could pick easily and add to our meals. Each of these herbs not only adds flavor to our cooking, but also has medicinal properties that can treat a wide variety of ailments. By cultivating these herbs in our back yard, we get the freshest, most vital and chemical free herbs that we can find.

For most people, kitchens are the centers of the household—the place where we cook and nourish ourselves. The kitchen therefore can also be the most magical place in the house. It is here that we act as alchemists, melding different ingredients and then using heat, the element of fire, to cook the food, the element of earth. The heat causes evaporation, or the element of water, and creates an aroma, or the element of air. The food is magically transformed into sustenance and nutrition for our mind, body, and soul.

Use of Culinary Herbs

Culinary herbs act as synthesizers, flavoring the various ingredients we have integrated in our food, and emphasizing the natural taste and aroma of the food. Understanding the properties and beneficial healing powers of each of the herbs we use helps us to know when we should use them and how much to add. Choosing the right combination of herbs is a cornerstone of good cooking. If you have ever added too much black pepper or too much salt, then you know how important it is to be careful and mindful in preparing a meal. Viewing cooking from this angle, the entire process becomes an art form, a chance for us to perform a healing ritual everyday in our own kitchen.

Culinary Herbs in History

The use of herbs in cooking goes back thousands of years. Ancient Egyptians valued garlic and onions above all other herbs as valuable, and tasty, healing remedies. Around 3000 B.C., the famous Chinese herbalist Shen Nung wrote that fresh ginger "eliminates body odor and puts a person in touch with the spiritual realm." In the third century B.C., Hippocrates, the father of Western medicine, prescribed the common culinary herb fennel for colic and digestive complaints.

Herbs have played a role in many important events and trends throughout history. For instance, after the fall of Rome the trade for spices between Asia and Europe slowed, and spices were deemed incredibly precious. In the late 1200s, it was the drive to find an easy source of spices that led Marco Polo to travel to China. Slowly, old spice routes began to be reestablished, changing and opening up the world at the time. When the Ottoman Empire closed the trade routes to the east in the 1400s, European merchants sought new avenues for reaching valuable

Asia. This is one of the main reason Europeans sailed west to find a new passage to India and China; of course we all know the story of Christopher Columbus and his eventual landing in America in 1492.

Though Columbus was mistaken in his belief that he had reached India, he did bring new culinary herbs such as cayenne and allspice back to the Old World. Later, New World explorers brought back chocolate, tobacco, and tomatoes. As Europeans began to colonize North America, they continued to bring over new culinary herbs to plant in Europe. Many of these herb gardens included herbs familiar to many of us today—lemon balm, basil, caraway, dill, fennel, garlic, marjoram, mints, parsley, rosemary, sage, tarragon, and thyme.

Six Great Culinary Herbs
Basil (Ocimum basilicum)

Background: Basil is native to Asia and Africa and has been indigenous to the Mediterranean regions for thousands of years, yet it was only traded to Northern Europe after the sixteenth century. Astrologically, basil is associated with the sign of Scorpio. Basil is a sacred herb in India where it is associated with the gods Vishnu and Krishna. In many cultures, basil has been used to purify sacred spaces. As John Gerard wrote in 1597: "The smell of basil is good for the heart and for the head, that the seede cureth the infirmities of the heart, taketh away sorrowfulnesse which cometh of melancholy, and maketh a man merry and glad."

Taste and Energetics: Basil has a very aromatic quality and imparts a pleasing flavor when added to a meal. Basil is very stimulating and heating; its spicy flavor can help reduce stagnation and counteract damp conditions in the body.

Medicinal Properties: Basil has numerous volatile oils and tannins that assist the process of digestion and also seem to lift the spirits and allay fatigue and depression. Basil primarily works to relax the stomach muscles so that food can be properly assimilated, and indigestion can be avoided.

In Cooking: Basil can be used in a wide variety of meals and is especially useful in combination with ingredients such as garlic, tomatoes, and onions. Basil often goes well with Italian and Thai style meals. In Italian cooking, it goes well in pizza, pasta, and calzone sauces as well as in pestos. In Thai cooking, it adds a delicious aroma to stir-fry.

How to Grow: Like tomatoes, basil is a sensitive plant and should only be planted after the first frost is over. Basil needs plenty of sunlight, but watch out for overheating when it is very young. Basil likes nice rich soil so add potting soil, peat, and compost to the hole where you plant it. Make sure you give it plenty of water, or it will dry out. Be sure to pinch out the flowers when they appear so that the herb gets leafier.

Garlic (Allium sativum)

Background: Garlic has a rich and ancient history. Egyptian rulers gave copious amounts of garlic and onion to slaves who built the pyramids. Greeks called the Egyptians "the stinking ones" for their love of this bulbous herb. The Egyptians were also known to swear on a bulb of garlic in the same way that many swear on a Bible today. India's ancient healers prescribed garlic for leprosy as well as cancer. In medieval times, garlic was thought to ward off evil and would often be hung on front doors. We see the modern equivalent of this in kitchens where people hang garlic braids. Peasants of the Middle Ages had a special fondness for this herb and ate it as a regular staple in their diet. Garlic has been used as an herbal remedy since antiquity. As recently as World War I, garlic juice was used to treat infected battle wounds. As famous English herbalist Nicholas Culpepper wrote: "Garlic is a remedy for all diseases and hurts . . . it helpeth the biting of mad dogs and other venomous creatures, killeth worms in children, cutteth tough phlegm, purgeth the head. . . and is a good remedy for any plague."

Taste and Energy: Garlic has a hot and spicy flavor when raw, but is sweet and mellow when cooked. Garlic helps move stagnant energy, promotes the circulation of blood and chi, and alleviates cold conditions.

Medicinal Properties: Garlic has numerous medicinal properties that make it a valuable herb to add to one's diet. Garlic has antibacterial and antiviral abilities due to its high content of alliin. Alliin breaks down into allicin, which acts as a type of antibiotic for infections, colds, and flus. Garlic also has the ability to reduce cholesterol, lower blood pressure, and diminish blood clots that lead to strokes and heart attacks. Garlic also acts as an antioxidant, reducing the cell damage that often is a precursor for cancer. Garlic helps to stimulate the immune system, which also helps ward off cancer. Finally, garlic lowers blood sugar levels and therefore is a helpful remedy for diabetes.

In Cooking: Garlic should always be bought fresh and not bought in powder or salt form, where its medicinal and energetic value is lessened. Garlic adds a delicious flavoring to most any type of cuisine. It is used in meat dishes such as braised lamb, seafood dishes, and casseroles. It can be added to soups, stir-fry, and in raw form to salad dressings. When cooking garlic, be careful not to overheat it as it will add a strongly bitter, burnt flavor.

How to Grow: Garlic is easy to grow by breaking off cloves from a bulb and then planting them in the spring. Plant them in rows six inches apart and two inches deep. They are ready in the late summer. Another way to grow them is to begin in the fall and wait until the following summer to cut down the stalk so all the energy goes into nourishing the bulb. Make sure you store garlic in a cool, dry place.

Cumin (Capsicum annuum)

Background: This wonderful-tasting herb belongs to the *umbelliferae* family—home of coriander, dill, fennel, and parsley. This distinct herb distinguishes itself as a necessary ingredient in Asian curries as well as Mexican chili dishes. Originating in the

Upper Nile, cumin found its way to Asia via the ancient spice trade routes. The Moors introduced cumin to Spain where it found its way to the New World in the 1500s. Research has found that Pharisees in Biblical times paid their taxes partially in cumin seed. In Greek and Roman times, cumin was viewed as a symbol of greed and miserliness. But during the Middle Ages, cumin gained a reputation as a token to keep lovers faithful to each other. Cumin is mentioned in the Bible, in Isaiah 28: "For the fitches are not threshed with a threshing instrument, neither is a cart wheel turned about the cumin; but the fitches are beaten out with a staff, and the cumin with a rod."

Taste and Energy: Cumin has a distinct assertive taste, and it is slightly bitter and heating with a pleasantly stimulating quality.

Medicinal Properties: Cumin contains from between 2.5 and 4 percent volatile oils. Such oils have a stimulating effect on the digestive process, and help one process food better. It is said to relieve flatulence and to calm the nerves. It can be helpful for tension headaches and premenstrual pain.

In Cooking: It is not necessary to use too much cumin in one's meals—a little goes a long way, usually no more than a quarter to half teaspoon for a meal for six. It is used often in curry dishes that include lentils, peas, and vegetables, and adds flavor to rice and couscous dishes. It is often found in the cuisines of Mexico, the Middle East, North Africa, and India. Use it as an ingredient along with chili powder to make a good chili. Add it to black bean soups that need a flavoring agent. Here is a quick rundown of the main ground spices used to make curry powder: coriander (6 parts), turmeric (4 parts), fenugreek (2 parts), cumin (2 parts), cinnamon (1 part), cardamom (1 part), ginger (1 part), black pepper (1 part), cloves (1 part), cayenne pepper (1 part).

How to Grow: Cumin tends to grow best in hot climates so if you live in the temperate regions of North America or northern Europe, it may be difficult to grow this herb. Luckily, it is easy to find this herb in most stores. If you live in a warmer climate such as southern California, Arizona, New Mexico, and parts of the South, you can sow the seeds directly into the ground six inches apart. Harvest the seed heads just before they are ripe and hang them up in a warm, breezy area until they are dried.

Peppermint (Mentha piperita)

Background: Originally, spearmint was used regularly in cuisine and as a medicine. Eventually, peppermint evolved as a natural hybrid and is more commonly used today. One famous mythological story about mint comes from the Greeks. In this story, Pluto, god of the underworld, fell in love with a nymph named Menthe. Pluto's wife, Persephone, was so jealous that she turned Menthe into a mint plant. Pluto could not reverse the process but did give her the sweet aromatic odor that defines mint. Mint came originally from the Mediterranean region and eventually spread to northern Europe and then North America. Mint is used to treat coughs and headaches, as well as to bring good luck. John Gerard wrote of mint in the sixteenth century: "The savor or smell of the Water Mint rejoyceth the heart of man, for which cause they strew it in chambers and places of recreation, pleasure, and repose, and where feasts and banquets are made."

Taste and Energy: Peppermint has a spicy and slightly bitter flavor and is also cooling.

Medicinal Properties: Like most culinary herbs, the volatile oils in peppermint assist digestive problems. Menthol and carvone specifically have an antispasmodic effect and soothe the lining of the stomach wall. Peppermint oil has anesthetic properties, which make it useful externally to heal toothaches, headaches, and muscle aches. Peppermint has been noted to have antibacterial and antiviral properties and is helpful for healing colds, flus, bronchitis, and viral infections such as herpes. Finally, peppermint can help stimulate a slight sweat, which helps cool down the body if it has been overheated.

In Cooking: Mint has been used for thousands of years in Middle Eastern dishes such as couscous, cracked-wheat salads, and lamb dishes. Mint varieties have cooling properties that make them useful to balance hotter spices like cayenne and curry. Because of this, mint is used often as a garnish in Thai, Indonesian, and Ethiopian food. Mint is a wonderful addition to carrots, potatoes, beans, and peas. Peppermint can be infused in juice or alcohol to add a spicy, pungent aroma to a drink.

How to Grow: Mint is very hardy and often grows as a weed in the corner of some gardens. It enjoys direct sunlight and needs to be pruned regularly to increase growth. Watch out, though, because this herb can take over. One trick I know is to sink peppermint into a big bowl and plant the whole thing in the ground. This ensures that the roots can't spread. Place the peppermint roots about three inches into the earth.

Rosemary (Rosmarinus officinalis)

Background: In Latin, rosemary means "dew of the sea," likely because it grows wild on the Mediterranean coast. Rosemary was used in ancient times as a preservative to wrap meats. Greek scholars believed that rosemary helped preserve memory, and they would wear garlands of this herb to help them in their studies. Rosemary became a popular herb in Tudor England where it was frequently grown as a potted plant. Rosemary has been associated with marital fidelity and as a way to ward off evil witchcraft and bad dreams. Sir Thomas More said of rosemary: "I let it runne all over my garden walls, not onlie because my bees love it, but because it is the herb sacred to rememberance, and therefore, to friendship."

Taste and Energy: Rosemary has an uplifting, aromatic quality that reminds one of pine trees, with a hint of citrus fruit.

Medicinal Properties: Rosemary has a number of useful properties, and, like most culinary herbs, it helps stimulate proper digestion and relaxes the stomach lining. This antispasmodic effect also helps relieve menstrual cramps. Rosemary helps stimulate the circulatory and nervous system as well.

In Cooking: Rosemary has a strong and piercing flavor, and therefore has been used traditionally for cutting through the heaviness of meat dishes. A few leaves of rosemary go well with foods such as legumes, potatoes, squashes, carrots, and yams. Rosemary can be added as a garnish to salad dressings, fruit dishes (sparingly), and in honey to give it an aromatic flavor. Rosemary has been added to wines and ales as an uplifting spice.

How to Grow: Find a sheltered spot in your garden that gets a good dose of afternoon Sun and is well drained and sandy. Grown from seed, rosemary should be transplanted when the seedlings are about two inches tall. Plant it in the late spring, and trim often every fall to encourage new growth.

Thyme (Thymus vulgaris)

Background: Thyme is a native of the Mediterranean lands and has spread throughout Europe and North America. Thyme has a long history as an herbal condiment, a medicine, and for magical purposes. Ancient Romans sprinkled thyme on sacrificial animals to make them more worthy of the gods. The ancient Greeks made offerings to the gods by burning thyme. The name of the thymus gland has its origins in medieval times, when anatomists believed it resembled the thyme plant. John Parkinson wrote of thyme: "To set down all the particular uses whereunto thyme is applyed were to weary both the writer and the reader... we preserve them with all the care we can in our gardens for the sweete and pleasant sents they yield."

Taste and Energy: Thyme has a slightly peppery aroma, is mineral-rich, and strengthens the entire system like a tonic.

Medicinal Properties: One of the most prized substances from the mid-nineteenth century to World War I was thymol, an extract from the thyme plant. Thymol was used as an antiseptic for infections and as a disinfectant in operating rooms. Thyme's volatile oils helps soothe the digestive tract and prevent flatulence and dyspepsia. A few drops of thyme oil can be placed in hot water to breathe for alleviating deep-seated coughs and bronchitis. Infusions of thyme can be used as a gargle for sore throats and laryngitis. Thyme's antispasmodic effects help alleviate women's menstrual cramps as well. Thyme has a high degree of iron—up to five milligrams per tablespoon (dried).

In Cooking: Thyme works well as a harmonizing influence, bringing the taste of different spices together. If you are using strong and pungent herbs such as garlic, rosemary, or cayenne, try adding some thyme to mellow and balance them. Make sure to add just the leaves, as the stem is tough. Thyme can flavor stocks for soups and casseroles. It also helps strengthen and bring out the taste of root vegetables, fish, and poultry dishes. Thyme can retain its flavor even if it has been cooked at a high heat.

How to Grow: There are numerous ornamental types of thyme, so make sure to get the culinary type. Plant the thyme ten inches apart in abundant sunlight. Thyme enjoys being planted near other aromatic herbs such as lavender and rosemary. In the summer, prune thyme back to encourage new growth.

In Conclusion

Spices have been a treasured part of cooking since antiquity. Whereas once only the very wealthy could afford herbs, we are blessed today with access to most any herb we desire. We also can easily grow a variety of herbs in our own gardens. If at all possible, grow or buy your herbs fresh so that you have a direct relationship to how they smell, touch, taste, and feel. With this direct relationship comes a deeper connection to our food, to our nutrition and health.

Each culinary spice has a flavor and an energy that makes it unique and potent. By spending a little time with just a few herbs, we get to know them like they were a good friend or family member. They truly become wonderful allies as we stir them into our pots and sauté them in our pans. Herbs help transform our lives and bring us greater joy and health.

Herbal Tea Parties

≫ by Cindy Parker ≪

W hen I was a child, my grand-
mother often made tea for
me. As soon as the kettle
whistled, she poured boiling water
over the Lipton tea bag nestled in my
cup. After a few dunkings, the brew
would turn a beautiful amber color—
almost ready to drink, but not quite; it
still needed grandma's special touch—
a red-and-white-striped hard peppermint candy. I'd wait for her to drop it
into the hot liquid, then I'd watch as it
dissolved into nothingness. This is my
earliest and fondest memory of taking
tea with my grandma.

Most of us, if we glance into the
past, have some memory of taking tea.
Maybe it's a favorite cup that comes to
mind or the aroma of the brew itself. It
might be a simple sweetcake that we
remember eating with tea—perhaps
cinnamon toast lovingly prepared by
dad or a scone baked by mother.

Cradling a warm cup of tea between your hands while inhaling the fragrant steam conjures feelings of comfort whether alone or in the company of others.

History of Tea

Tea itself is steeped in history and tradition. Legend credits the first liquid consumption of tea to Emperor Shen Nung in 2737 B.C. This health-conscious ruler of China was reputed to always boil his water before drinking it. One day a gentle breeze deposited a branch of the *Camellia sinensis* plant into his cauldron of hot water. He was so delighted with the heady aroma that he couldn't resist tasting the resulting infusion. He was most impressed, and thus began the drinking of tea.

In the Orient, tea has long been popular among the monks as an aid to meditation. The ceremony that accompanied its use became a respected ritual among not only the spiritually inspired, but also among dignitaries and common people. Taking tea was time for participants to enter a peaceful space. Its ability to heighten alertness was scientifically validated with the discovery of the plant's stimulating constituents.

When tea traveled to Europe, it was used from a slightly different point of view. After its arrival in England, it took on a more culturally elite role with greater emphasis on proper etiquette and manners as the means of showing gratitude and respect. Anne, the Duchess of Bedford, was founder of the afternoon tea party tradition. At that time, it was customary to hold dinner until the men returned from hunting. The hunger pangs that stemmed from such a long wait between meals led this royal maiden to request finger foods during the late afternoon. She soon began inviting other women friends to join her. In time, tea became a prized commodity in England. Of course, this was true in early America as well, though because of the symbolic protest known as the Boston Tea Party—wherein rebels dumped crates of tea in Boston Harbor to protest high taxes—the colonists began drinking liberty tea that was brewed from local herbs.

Today in America, herbal brews are again gaining popularity. Their delicate flavors and medicinal properties enhance the ancient ritual of taking tea in an atmosphere of peace and tranquility.

Herbal Tea Time

In general, tea time is the perfect opportunity to escape from the daily grind and renew our bodies, sharpen our minds, and honor our spirit. This may be done in solitude, or it may prompt invitations for others to join the party. Either way, herbs can make perfect brews for modern tea time. Their use began as an act of rebellion, but today their inclusion is a conscious choice. They not only provide tasty beverages but may also be used to flavor foods and add interesting garnishes.

There are various elements associated with the traditional tea party that may be adapted to modern-day schedules and time restraints. It's okay to make scones from a mix or even purchase them from a local bakery. A picnic can be spread out on a blanket rather than served on a coffee table or in a formal dining room. If you don't have enough matching dishes to serve all your guests, celebrate the fact that mixed cups and saucers reflect the uniqueness of each individual. Have fun, be creative, and always emit a calm presence, as peace is essential to any tea party.

Making Herbal Tea

The most obvious way to incorporate herbs in a tea party is in the tea itself. I like to serve a hot tea that contains some *Camellia sinensis*, either black, green, or oolong tea, along with a herbal blend that is completely caffeine free. It's also nice to include a cold beverage such as iced tea or lemonade. There are many plants to choose from when brewing a herbal tea, but for beverage blends, the more mild, fruity, or minty plants are best.

When mixing tea blends, I use volume to define parts. That is, each part is whatever measure is chosen depending upon the quantity desired. Simply combine the various herbs in a bowl, toss together to distribute evenly, and store in a glass jar. To brew, use 1 teaspoon of the blend for every six ounces of water. You can place the herbs loose in a cup to strain later or use a tea ball. Bring the water to a boil and pour over the herbs. Cover and steep fifteen to twenty minutes. Remove spent herbs, and serve. Here are a few of my favorite blends; common garden herb mixtures are usually best served hot.

Garden Wisdom Tea

3 parts chamomile

2 parts peppermint or spearmint

1 part rosemary

½ part sage

½ part thyme

Tranquility

This tea calms and relaxes both children and adults.

3 parts each of chamomile and lemon balm

2 parts each of linden flowers and rose petals

1½ part lavender

1 part hops

Indian Summer

This can be served as a refreshing iced delight.

3 parts of a mixture of lemon balm, lemon verbena, and/or lemongrass

2 parts chamomile

1 part each of spearmint, hibiscus, and rose hips

½ part mixture of lemon and orange peel

Tea Breads and Munchies

Munchies are always better when served with tea. A buttery English muffin oozing with raspberry mint jam makes a satisfying dish with tea. Quick breads such as zucchini spice or the favorite family nut bread become absolutely delicious. And there is no more perfect food with tea than the famous scone.

The scone is a biscuit that uses simple ingredients, requires no special equipment, and is easy to make. It also lends itself to infinite possibilities. Cheese, bits of smoked ham or bacon, or culinary herbs like sage or even pesto may be added to make a more hearty, savory scone. The traditional sweet scone may include fruit, nuts, or chocolate chips. The diversity is endless; they are best served fresh from the oven.

Lavender Scones

⅔ cup milk

1 tablespoon dried lavender buds

2½ cups flour

1 tablespoon baking powder

1 teaspoon salt

1 stick butter

½ cup sugar

Heat milk and lavender almost to a boil. Allow to steep and cool. Strain and add enough milk to make a full ⅔ cup. Sift together flour, baking powder, and salt. Cut in butter with pastry blender. Toss in sugar, and stir in milk with a fork to form a soft dough. Knead 10–12 times on a lightly floured board. Roll out fairly thick and cut into rounds. Bake at 425°F until lightly browned, about 12 minutes.

Savories

The healthiest, least fattening foods at a tea party are the savories. Dainty sandwiches are the standard fare but just about any main-course food falls into this category—appetizers, soups, salads, pasta, casseroles, meat pies, and veggies. The dainty cucumber sandwich is probably the most traditional savory selection. But the sandwich provides much room for creativity. Open- face sandwiches may be garnished with fresh slivers of veggies or sprigs of herbs. Egg salad is perfect with dill or salmon pâté with fennel. The bread may be cut into shapes with cookie cutters or cut diagonally into triangles, or horizontally and vertically into small squares. If one slice of white bread and one of whole wheat is used for each sandwich, they may be served with alternate sides showing, creating a checkerboard effect.

Some sandwiches may be made ahead of time, wrapped in plastic, and chilled. To make striped sandwiches, stack and fill several layers of bread and wrap. When ready to serve, simply slice and serve sideways to display the multiple layers. I also make pinwheels several hours in advance. After removing the crusts from two pieces of bread, zap them in the microwave for ten seconds to moisten. Immediately overlap them along one edge and use a rolling pin to press them together into one long piece of bread. After spreading this with filling, roll it up, wrap it tightly in plastic wrap, and chill. To serve, cut into rounds.

There are many fun things to do with sandwiches. You may want to apply a thin layer of mayonnaise to the sides and dip them in finely chopped green herbs or crunchy nuts and seeds. When hosting a children's tea party, it's fun to set out a variety of cookie cutters, peanut butter and cheese spread, and a variety of cut-up fruits and veggies so they may create their own artistic sandwich. The following are some recipe ideas for savory tea snacks.

Herbed Cucumber Sandwiches

8   ounces cream cheese

2   cucumbers, seeded (or use the English variety)

2   tablespoons sour cream

1   tablespoon lemon juice

2   tablespoons herb mix (I suggest 4 parts dried basil, 2 parts dried onion flakes, 1 part dried thyme)

Slice cucumbers very thin, either peeled or unpeeled depending on your preference. Some people soak them in salt water too, but I don't find this necessary. Mix the rest of the ingredients to make a filling. Spread bread with filling and top with a thin layer of cucumbers. Another piece of bread may be added or they may be served open-faced. For a wild food version, a layer of tender chickweed or dandelion leaves may be added.

Flower Sandwiches

Spread bread with strawberry cream cheese. Serve open faced garnished with edible flowers such as Johnny-jump-ups, dianthus, violets, or borage. These may also be made into pinwheels or stripes and can be quite colorful.

Chutney Pear Sandwiches

8   ounces cream cheese

½   cup peach or mango chutney

Dark rye bread

2   fresh pears

Lemon juice

Spread cream cheese and chutney on dark rye bread. Brush pear slices with lemon juice and place on filling.

Nettle Quiche

1   cup fresh nettles

½   cup chopped onion

1   clove fresh garlic, minced

½   cup grated cheese of choice

1   premade pie crust

3   eggs, beaten

1   cup milk

Place nettles in a pot of boiling water. Cook several minutes, strain, and chop. Sauté cooked nettles with onion and garlic. In a pie crust, layer cooked veggies with grated cheese. Mix eggs and milk, and pour over pie. Sprinkle with calendula petals. Bake at 375°F for 35–40 min, or until golden brown and firm.

Desserts

What would an herbal tea party be without a dessert dish to add a finishing touch? Confections are capable of etching luscious memories in the mind, especially when chocolate is involved. Biting into a juicy strawberry covered in chocolate never fails to stimulate the senses, just as a rich chocolate cake with raspberry filling soothes and comforts the soul.

Offering several desserts allows guests to choose what satisfies them. Simple fruit parfaits layered with yogurt and granola are obviously more healthy than ones made with ice cream and gooey fudge, marshmallow, or caramel. A tray of cookies allows your visitors to take pleasure in a tiny piece of sweetness.

Ma Parker's Coriander Cookies

2   cup flour

½   cup butter

1   cup sugar

3   tablespoons ground coriander seeds

1   egg, slightly beaten

1   tablespoon milk

1   teaspoon vanilla

Cut butter into flour with a pastry blender till crumbly. Add sugar and ground coriander seeds. Mix remaining ingredients, and add to flour mixture. Mix until a soft dough forms. Roll dough into ½-inch balls and place on cookie sheet. Flatten with a cookie stamp or the bottom of a glass. Bake at 400°F for 6–8 min.

Trifle

Trifle is historically served at tea time. It is made by arranging several layers of cake, filling, and fruit, though variations come from different geographical areas. Regardless of choice of ingredients, however, a trifle should always be visually appealing. It is usually made in a clear glass bowl or in parfait glasses.

Pound cake, angel food cake, or lady fingers may be drenched with a bit of liquor such as brandy or schnapps for added zip, with alternating layers of a filling such as Jell-o, pudding, or yogurt followed by a layer of fruit. I like to stack berries in between pillars of cake on the outer side of the bowl. Top with whipped cream and garnish with fruit and mint leaves.

Pawpaw Trifle and Other Cake Suggggestions

Pawpaws are a Midwestern fruit that tastes something like a banana, but looks like a small mango. I cut them open and squeeze out the flesh, which simultaneously mashes the fruit while removing the skin and seeds.

Cut a pound cake into squares. Mash pawpaw fruit and mix with vanilla yogurt. Combine fresh raspberries with sliced peaches. Layer all of the above in a clear glass bowl at least twice. Top with whipped cream.

A very simple dessert suggestion is gingerbread topped with cream or a lemon sauce. Use herbs such to flavor desserts—peppermint with chocolate, pineapple sage with peaches, rosemary with fruit, and scented geraniums with cake. A very simple, healthy dessert may be made by drizzling round slices of fresh oranges with honey and sprinkling with cinnamon.

Serving Suggestions

Now that we've covered what to serve at a tea party, let's discuss how they should be served. Foremost, the most important element of a tea party is an air of calm tranquility. You should never appear to be hurried or hassled. Always respect proper etiquette and manners at your tea parties. Take care that everyone is polite and on their best behavior. This ambiance will be enhanced through the harmony of people present, through the food, the dishes, the table setting, and so on. When hosting a tea party, select a focus to build the event around and make it sparkle with purity.

The traditional afternoon tea party, steeped in formal elegance and propriety, occurs usually in the dining room, at a large and beautifully arranged, linen covered table. Cups and saucers with matching plates are laid out along with linen napkins and appropriate eating utensils. The centerpiece usually embodies artistic elements from nature—blooming daffodils in the spring, a bouquet of colorful garden flowers in the summer, a cornucopia of gourds in the fall, or an arrangement of dried flowers and grasses in the winter. The food should be attractively served in a way that displays a variety of offerings at different eye levels. Tiered plates is the key here. Each level may contain a sampling of the various types of food—desserts on the top, savories in the middle, and breads on the bottom for instance. Larger platters are then used to serve the main bulk of the entrées. Special serving dishes such as trifle bowls and cake stands provide different heights that further enhance eye appeal and visual interest.

If these dishes are not part of your kitchen cupboards, don't panic. Maintain that air of calm tranquility by creatively utilizing whatever you already have in accordance with the occasion. If it's an outdoor tea, a simple checkered tablecloth with paper napkins will do just fine. Don't get hung up on rules but rather celebrate adaptability. One of my favorite ways to solve the problem of supplying enough tea cups when I do classes is to ask everyone to bring their own favorite cup and saucer. This adds another dimension to the festivities as participants are encouraged to share stories about the cups they brought.

Tea may be experienced in so many ways. The possibilities are endless and require little more than hot water and the plant material to pour it over. Of course, it may be embellished as extravagantly as one desires. This simple ritual is rich in tradition but also provides a medium for unique expression. May the information provided here be your springboard to many wonderful encounters not only with tea, but with fellow human beings as well.

An Herbal Meal
for the One You Love

≫ by Sheri Richerson ≪

G rowing herbs in your garden
can be very rewarding, but
have you ever wondered if you
were making full use of the herbs?
Besides making potpourri, wreaths,
and other craft projects, you can also
use them to make a full meal for the
one you love.

Herbs are not only easy to use in
cooking, but if pure and fresh they add
something unique to your meal.
Although you may substitute store-
bought or dried herbs, I suggest you
use the freshest possible ingredients. I
grind my own pepper from green and
pink peppercorns, and I always try to
pick my herbs as I use them.

These recipes have been created
and tested in my kitchen with excellent
results! The only caution with using
herbs is that you don't want to overdo
it. Using too many herbs or using them
in every dish of a meal is a sure-fire way

to ruin your guests' appetite. As a rule of thumb, I will use herbs in two dishes. If I decide to use herbs on my meat then I will also use them on my vegetables or potatoes, but definitely not both.

Furthermore, the well-known health benefits of herbs make using herbs to season your culinary creations good for mind and body as well as spirit.

Appetizers

Herbal appetizers can be a great starting point for any meal. They help to prepare the guests for what lies ahead by tempting their taste buds. Appetizers also make fantastic finger food for a tea party or get-together of any kind.

Dilled Cottage Cheese

This appetizer is easy to fix, and also very pretty. To start, scoop out one spoonful of a carton of cottage cheese with an ice cream scoop. Place the cottage cheese in the center of a saucer and place parsley around its bottom edges. Sprinkle some chopped fresh dill, salt, pepper, paprika on top, and serve.

Lemony Chicken Wings

24 chicken wings

2 large cloves of garlic

½ cup olive oil

½ cup minced lemon verbena

⅛ cup lemon juice

Salt and pepper to taste

Preheat the oven to 350°F. Bake the chicken wings for a half an hour in a 13-by-9-inch pan. While the chicken is baking, mix the remaining ingredients. Remove the chicken from the oven after the first half hour and baste it with the mixture. Return the chicken to the oven for another half hour. Baste approximately every ten minutes with the drippings.

Kevin's Toasted Cheese

1   baguette or other fresh crusty bread
    Colby cheese
1   tablespoon fresh oregano
1   tomato

Slice the bread, and place thin slices of colby cheese on top of the bread. Add the tomato slices to the top of this and sprinkle with oregano. Broil directly on the oven rack until the cheese melts. Serve warm.

Salads

Preparing a salad can take the place of an appetizer and will prepare your guests for what lies ahead. With a bit of creativity you can make a very colorful and tasteful salad that will have your guests talking for weeks.

Tangy Flowered Salad

Take a head of lettuce and chop it up as you normally would. Add cheese, tomato, and whatever other salad ingredients you would normally use. Then add about a tablespoon of fresh chopped dill weed and mix. Once the salad is mixed, arrange fresh edible flowers, such as scented marigolds and nasturtiums, on top as a garnish.

Herbed Potato Salad

3   sprigs thyme, lemon thyme, summer savory,
    or oregano
4   large basil leaves
2   tablespoons snipped chives or garlic chives
3   cups potato salad

Add these herbs to your favorite potato-salad, either homemade or store-bought.

Main Dishes

The most important part of the meal is the main dish. I try not to rush my meat when it is cooking. There is simply no comparison to meat that has been slow cooked over open coals. Be sure to use a meat thermometer to ensure you are cooking at the proper temperature. You may choose to put herbs on the hot coals, instead of directly on the meat, allowing the smoke to flavor the meal.

Sheri's Herb Chicken

4   boneless, skinless chicken breasts

1   stick butter

    Garlic and/or seasoning salt to taste

    Freshly ground pepper

½   cup flour

1   beaten egg

1   tablespoon chopped parsley

½   teaspoon each pineapple sage, rosemary, and thyme

½   cup white wine

Flatten the chicken and coat with one-half of the melted butter. Season the chicken with above spices. Put the chicken in a Ziploc bag with flour and shake, then dip in the egg. Remove the chicken and place it into a baking pan with the remaining melted butter. Top with the herbs. Bake at 350°F for 30 minutes. Baste with the butter in pan during cooking. I usually try to baste it every 10 minutes during this time. Remove from the oven after 30 minutes and pour the wine over the chicken. Bake another 20 minutes. Sometimes I baste the chicken further with the butter and wine mixture from the pan.

Herbed Turkey

1   turkey breast, ten pounds or less

2   teaspoons parsley

1   teaspoon sage

1   teaspoon fennel seed

1   teaspoon salt

Poultry seasoning to taste

Garlic and/or seasoning salt to taste

½   cup white wine

2   tablespoons lemon juice

1   stick butter, melted

Mix the above ingredients except the wine, lemon juice, and butter together. Pour the wine and lemon juice over the turkey. Melt the butter and then pour it over the turkey. Sprinkle the other ingredients on top. Bake as normal according to the directions for your specific turkey, basting approximately every half an hour. This turkey is tender and juicy!

Pork Chops in Raspberry Sauce

1½   tablespoons butter

4   lean pork chops

1   cup flour

Worcestershire sauce to taste

1   cube chicken bouillon

1   cup water

8   fresh pineapple sage leaves

1   teaspoon each of rosemary and thyme

6   tablespoons raspberry vinegar

Garlic and/or seasoning salt and pepper to taste

Melt the butter in a pan over medium heat. Rinse the pork chops in water and dust with flour. Put the pork chops in the butter, add a few drops of Worcestershire sauce, and brown on both sides. Reduce the heat, add the water and bouillon cube to the pan. Stir until dissolved. Top the pork chops with fresh herbs and pour the vinegar on top. Cover and simmer until done, approximately forty-five minutes. Add salt and pepper to taste.

Herbal Roast

2   tablespoons butter

3   tablespoons olive oil

1   beef roast, 4 to 6 pounds

6   tablespoons red wine

¼   cup A-1, or other, steak sauce

1   bay leaf

1   teaspoon thyme

2   tablespoons each sage and parsley

1   tablespoon chives

    Garlic and/or seasoning salt and pepper to taste

Preheat the oven to 350°F. Melt butter in skillet, and add the olive oil. Add the roast, turning to brown on all sides. Once the roast is browned, put it into a baking pan, being sure to scrape all the drippings from the skillet into the pan. Add water to the pan until it is approximately half-full. Pour the red wine and steak sauce on the top of the roast. Add the herbs to the top of the roast and the seasonings to taste. Cook approximately an hour and a half, or until the meat is tender (an internal thermometer will read 145°–160°F when done, depending on how rare you like your meat). I like to baste my roast approximately every twenty minutes. You can also add some potatoes and carrots to the roast if you like. I usually do this at the beginning and sprinkle the herbs and seasonings over them too.

Vegetables

Herbed Vegetables on the Grill

Various vegetables, such as corn on the cob, eggplant, squash, onions, and so on

1 tablespoon butter

2 teaspoons lemon juice

½ teaspoon each dill, marjoram, thyme, basil, savory

Salt and pepper to taste

This recipe can be used either on a grill or indoors on the stove. To cook on the grill I put my vegetables in a foil packet that I make myself out of aluminum foil. Though with fresh corn, I peel the husk back, remove the silks, then wash the corn and spread the above mixture on the corn before covering it back with the husks and wrapping it in foil. Fresh corn on the cob should be laid directly on the coals and be turned every 15 minutes for an hour. Otherwise, I add all of the above ingredients to the foil pouch and seal it up. I cook this on top of the grill for about half an hour. If you're cooking indoors just add everything to the pan and cook as usual.

Potato Wedges on the Grill

If you're like me and prefer to cook your meals outside in the summer, try this variation on potato wedges. You may also cook them in an oven at 350°F for about half an hour.

Cut your potatoes into wedges. I use between four to six medium-sized potatoes. Rinse, boil for 5 minutes, and put into a foil packet. Drizzle potatoes with 3 tablespoons oil and sprinkle with oregano and thyme (approximately half-teaspoon each). Seal the packet and put on top of the hot coals. Turn about every 15 minutes so the potatoes don't burn. Top with the cheeses of your choice.

Herbed Fried Potatoes

4 tablespoons butter

4 large potatoes

Garlic salt and pepper to taste

1 teaspoon oregano and chives

Melt the butter in a pan over medium heat. Slice potatoes and add to pan. Add garlic salt and pepper to taste. Add herbs, stirring until potatoes begin to brown. Reduce heat, cover, and cook about an hour or until potatoes are tender.

Pasta
Sheri's Spaghetti Sauce

This recipe is my own creation, as I'm too picky for store-bought sauces. Leftovers can be frozen.

½   cup olive oil

1   pound ground beef

4   strips finely chopped bacon (you can substitute a tablespoon or two of bacon bits)

4   cloves garlic

3   tablespoons parsley

    Oregano, thyme, and rosemary to taste

    Black and cayenne pepper to taste

2   ounces red wine

1   16-oz. can tomato sauce

1   8-oz. can tomato paste

1   dash Worcestershire sauce

    Seasoning salt to taste

1   teaspoon or so sugar

    Parmesan to thicken sauce

Cook ground beef and bacon in olive oil, then drain the fat thoroughly. Place meat and other ingredients in a slow cooker, and let it simmer all day—about 6 to 8 hours—tasting it on occasion. Sometimes I will cook it one day, let it sit refrigerated overnight and reheat the next day. I especially like this over lemon-pepper spaghetti. It's a good lasagna or pizza sauce too.

Breads

Hot Herb Garlic Bread

1   loaf of any type of bread
    Butter
2   teaspoons each fresh parsley, dill, oregano
    Garlic salt to taste
    Grated Parmesan cheese

Slice your bread and butter it. Sprinkle lightly with the parsley, dill, oregano, and garlic salt. Sprinkle with cheese and bake at 400°F for approximately 10 minutes or until cheese melts.

Herbal Bread

You can add fresh or dried herbs to any bread recipe. Experiment with adding small amounts of herbs to the dough. Some of my personal favorites are lavender, rosemary, and an Italian mixture of rosemary, thyme, and oregano.

Herbal Butter

If you don't want to make bread yourself, try an herbal butter to top your bread with. These are very easy to make. Just add herbs to your store-bought butter, and blend. Refrigerate the mixture so the herbs can blend. That's all there is to it. I also like to put a scoop or heart-shaped patty of this butter on a dish and surround it with parsley. I usually sprinkle a dried herb on top.

If I make a heart-shaped patty, I shape it by hand being sure to keep my hands moist. Then I run a butter knife under warm water and over the top of the butter to smooth it out.

Desserts

Scented Geranium Cream Cake

1   cup heavy whipping cream
1   cup sugar

2   eggs

1½ cups flour

2   teaspoons baking powder

1   teaspoon vanilla extract

Fresh rose or mint pelargonium leaves

Whip the cream until it is stiff. Add sugar and beat until blended. Add the eggs one at a time, beating each time until blended. Add the flour and baking powder and mix again. Add vanilla extract while continuing to mix.

Butter two 8-inch cake pans and line with pelargonium leaves. Pour the batter into pans. Bake at 375°F until the cake is golden brown on top, about 30 minutes.

Cream Frosting

4   rose or mint pelargonium leaves

2   cups confectioners' sugar

1   egg white

1   teaspoon lemon juice

1   drop vanilla extract

Small pelargonium leaves for garnish

Macerate the four leaves in a mortar and pestle until the fibers are broken, then add to the confectioners' sugar. Beat egg white with a whisk until frothy. Add the egg, lemon juice, and vanilla to the sugar mixture. Whip until smooth.

Spread the icing on the cooled cake and garnish with additional leaves. This is a fantastic recipe that will have people asking over and over again for the recipe.

Quick And Easy Herbal Ice Cream

This is so easy it's almost like cheating, but you can say you made it yourself!

1   gallon of your favorite ice cream, partly thawed

Chopped mint (any variety you prefer)

8 ounces chopped nuts (optional)

Mix in the mint with the ice cream until you are satisfied with the taste. Experiment with this; the more you add the stronger the taste. Add in the optional nuts if you wish, and mix thoroughly. Pour the mixture into a freezer container and refreeze. Serve topped with sprigs of mint or drizzled with chocolate.

Beverages
Herbal Tea Favorites

Brewing a cup of herbal tea or making a pitcher of herbal tea is as easy as 1-2-3.

For 1 cup of tea add about a teaspoon of fresh or dried herbs to 8 ounces of boiling water. Steep for five to fifteen minutes, depending on how strong you like your tea, and enjoy.

To make a gallon of herbal tea, choose your herbs (lemon balm, mints, chamomile, and so on) and add approximately forty fresh leaves or flowers, adjusting the amount to your individual tastes.

Spring Herbal Tea

10 fresh pineapple sage leaves

16 fresh lemon balm leaves

12 small mint leaves

6 cups boiling water

Add leaves to a pot and pour in boiling water. Allow to steep for 10–20 minutes. This is a delicious tea! I make it every spring as soon as I have enough herbs to do so.

Special Herb Seasonings

If you don't want to pick fresh herbs every time you cook, or if you live in a place where it isn't possible to grow fresh herbs year round, you can hang them to dry. Be sure to allow for proper air circulation by placing them in an airy spot such as an attic or workshop with windows. If you do not have a place to hang them they can be dried in an oven, microwave, or dehydrator. Another little-known trick for preserving herbs is to freeze them. If you are going to use herbs in a soup or other culinary creation where a bit of water is not harmful, you can freeze your fresh herbs in ice cubes. Then you just add the ice cubes to the recipe.

For storing dried herbs, you can use old spice jars or even buy special jars to put your dried herbs in. Be sure, though, that the herbs are completely dry before packaging. If you are drying individual herbs, place them whole into the containers, as this allows for the best flavor results. If you are making an herbal blend, you will have to crumble them when placing them into containers. Make only small amounts of these blends at a time to make sure you always have the freshest flavor.

Here are some of my favorite herbal combinations.

Basic Herb Blend

4   tablespoons dried oregano

4   teaspoons dried marjoram

4   teaspoons dried basil

4   teaspoons dried savory

2   teaspoons dried thyme

2   teaspoons dried rosemary

1   teaspoon dried sage

Be sure to use crumbled herbs when you are measuring them out. This mixture tastes great on meat, fish, or vegetables.

Fine Herbes Blend

Equal parts parsley, chives, French tarragon, and chervil

This is a fantastic mix for Italian dishes. Combine equal parts of each of these herbs together. Make sure they are dried and crumbled before assembling.

Herb Decorations

Herbal Candles

What's a romantic dinner without candlelight? You don't need to spend a fortune to create a fantastic candle. Follow these simple steps for a great homemade candle.

Gather:

1   pillar candle

    Various pressed, dried herbs and flowers

1   votive candle (should be the same color as the pillar candle)

1   grapevine wreath, candle holder, or freshly picked flowers

1   glue gun

1   paintbrush

    Old pan for melting wax

Melt the votive candle for use as a "glue" to attach the pressed flowers and herbs to the pillar candle. Use the paint brush to dab the wax onto the candle, and then quickly place the pressed material onto the spot before the wax dries.

Once your candle is decorated, seal it by brushing a layer of melted wax onto the candle. If you are doing a large number of candles you can quickly dip the candle into melted wax and then add the flowers and herbs to each.

Use the grapevine wreath as a candle holder and glue fresh or dried flowers and ribbons on it. The only drawback is that fresh flowers will wilt fairly quickly.

You can also make an elaborate centerpiece with taper candles on either side—just make additional small wreaths that match the main bouquet to cover the candle holder or even add some herbs or flowers directly to the taper candles.

Herbal Centerpiece

If you decide to make a flowered centerpiece many herbs such as tansy, mints, dill, and lavender make wonderful additions to typical flowers in the above directions. One favorite centerpiece of mine is made with peonies and tansy. I like the tansy because it has a fern-like appearance and helps to keep the ants away from the peonies.

Good Luck

I hope you will enjoy the recipes and craft projects I've included here. It's easy to create different versions by adding your favorite herbs, using an herbal butter instead of regular butter, or marinating with an herbal vinegar.

Decorating with herbs is also easy. It is festive and a far cheaper way to go than purchasing an expensive bouquet from a floral shop. It also allows you to have more control over the final design. Enjoy your time with the one you love.

Bhang: The Sacred Drink of Shiva

by Magenta Griffith

On the night of *Maha Shivratri*, the major holiday of Shiva worship, devotees prepare and drink an intoxicating beverage called *bhang*. Traditionally, this is made from cannabis, almonds, and milk; devotees sing songs in praise of their god, and dance to drums. Offerings of bhang are poured out before or on statues of Shiva. This celebration would be incomplete without this herbal beverage.

Shiva, the Destroyer

Shiva is one of the three great gods of India—which include Brahma, the Creator; Vishnu, the Preserver; and Shiva, the Destroyer. He is considered by many to be the most powerful god of the Hindu pantheon. Known also by many other names—Mahadeva (the Great God), Mahayogi (the Great Yogi), Nataraja (Lord of the Dance)—Shiva is perhaps the most complex of

Hindu deities. Shiva is the patron god of mystics, ascetics, and yogis. To some of his devotees, Shiva is both creator and destroyer. In one story, he opens his third eye, and his gaze destroys the world. He then dances the world back into being. One mystical doctrine states that he has done this innumerable times, but since he recreates the world perfectly, no one knows it has been destroyed and re-created.

Shiva is also called *Bhole Shankar*, one who is oblivious of the world. By this name, he is worshipped by yogis and other ascetics, including wandering holy men called *sadhus*. Bhang is certainly part of the practices of some sadhus, and sharing bhang with a holy man is considered obligatory if offered, even if one does not otherwise use cannabis.

Bhang

Bhang refers to the lower leaves of the cannabis plant, which is considered the mildest of the three grades of the plant. *Ganja* is the flowering tops only, and is usually smoked, and *charas* refers to the resin, which is also called hashish. Botanically, cannabis is considered to be a member of the same family as hops, which is used in making beer. In India, it was used extensively in folk medicine. It was believed to lower fevers, induce sleep, improve appetite, and cure dysentery. India is not the only place it was used medicinally; Chinese herbalists prescribed it to treat, among other things, malaria, rheumatic pains, and "female disorders," likely menstrual cramps. The use of cannabis preparations goes back at least several hundred years in India, to as early as 1000 B.C. At one time it was theorized that *soma*, the ancient sacred drink mentioned in the *Rig-Veda*, was bhang, though the descriptions of soma ultimately differ from contemporary bhang in appearance. It is possible that bhang was later substituted for soma in rituals, and soma was made from a now-extinct plant.

Bhang is thought by some in India to bestow supernatural powers on the users. Cannabis preparations may have been used as part of Tantric rituals; one of the properties ascribed to it is as an aphrodisiac. As such, it makes sense that this herb is sacred to Shiva, since he is the patron of Tantra, and often is worshiped in the form of a stone lingam, or phallus. Offerings are made to the Shiva lingam, which can be anywhere from a few inches to a few feet high, by pouring milk, bhang, or other sacred drinks over it; flowers are left at the base, usually in the form of a wreath encircling the lingam.

According to legend, bhang originated when Shiva was dancing the destruction of the world. Since all the other gods were afraid he would completely destroy the world, they went to his wife, Parvati, and begged her to do something. She thought for a while, then told the various gods, "You, bring me milk; you, bring me the leaves of this plant; you bring me the bark of that tree; you, bring me almonds," and on through all the needed ingredients. She put them together, and cooked them, and strained them with her sari, and put the first batch of bhang in a jar. She took the jar to Shiva and said, "Here, destroying the world is thirsty work, have some of this." So he drank it, and continued to dance, but more slowly, and then he drank some more, and stopped altogether, and told Parvati, "That was good, do you have any more?" So she gave him more bhang, and he said, "I'll destroy the world some other time." This is why we don't drink bhang every day, just on special occasions.

The following recipe is one version used in India. Since cannabis is illegal in the United States, I cannot recommend using this recipe, authentic as it is.

Original Recipe for Bhang

4   cups whole milk

½   ounce cannabis, finely chopped

2   tablespoons almonds, blanched and finely chopped

⅛   teaspoon cloves

¼   teaspoon cinnamon

¼   teaspoon powdered ginger

1   dash cardamom

½   teaspoon rosewater (optional)

¼   cup sugar

Put milk in a pan, add cannabis, and stir while heating over a low fire. Gradually add other ingredients, continuing to stir. Heat until it begins to steam, and keep simmering; never allowing it to come to a boil. Keep stirring, if not continuously, fairly often, chanting "Om nama Shivaya" while stirring. Cook for about a half hour. Strain through fine strainer or cheesecloth and chill.

American Recipe

4   cups milk, whole or 2%

2   tablespoons almonds, blanched and finely chopped

¼   teaspoon cloves

½   teaspoon cinnamon

¼   teaspoon nutmeg

½   teaspoon powdered ginger

1   dash cardamom

½   teaspoon rosewater (optional)

¼   cup sugar

Put milk in a pan and heat over a low fire until it begins to steam. Gradually add the rest of the ingredients, continuing to stir. Keep stirring continuously, chanting "Om nama Shivaya" while stirring. Cook for about ten minutes. Strain through fine strainer or cheesecloth and chill. If you wish to use this preparation for another deity, be sure to use an appropriate chant.

Garnishes and Gremolata

≫ by K. D. Spitzer ≪

I f you are nervous about herbs and want to feel comfortable in using them in your daily life, a good tip is to grow them yourself. A strawberry jar by the back door, a window box on the deck railing, or a tiny plot by the kitchen door can make you comfortable with these plants, and in turn influence your cooking in many ways. When fresh herbs are just a step away from your kitchen counter, you're more likely to pause to grab a handful to throw into any dish. Tossed on takeout or dusted over frozen dinners, fresh herbs add a special flavor and a personal touch.

Don't worry about the particulars in using herbs. They don't need to be minced finely just because the recipe calls for it—all you really need to do is pinch the leaves off with your fingers and drop them in whole. There are no set rules—just do what works for you.

Some Herbal Ideas

It is fairly common now to find fresh herbs in the grocery store, which is a great boon in the winter months. When you bring them home, pick them over and rinse in cold water. Shake or spin dry, wrap loosely in a paper towel, and then secure with plastic wrap or tin foil. They should keep for a couple weeks preserved in this fashion. If you are new to growing herbs in pots, you need to be aware that plants in pots dry out very quickly. Here in New England, I often have to water every day in July and August. It's best to water in the morning. The reward, of course, is fresh herbs, practically at my fingertips.

There are too many varieties of herbs to count, so perhaps this is a stumbling block for most people. But do not be worried—the key is just to make a start, trying various herbs and making notes on what you do and do not enjoy. Experiment a little! If you find you like thyme, then try lemon thyme or other varieties of the herb. Put whole sprigs of herbs you think you might like under the skin on the chicken you're roasting. Sprinkle the fresh leaves on goat cheese. Try it on sliced tomatoes. Use it along with rosemary to infuse your olive oil. Wrap sliced sweet potatoes, thinly sliced onion, minced garlic, and whole sprigs of lemon thyme in tin foil; drizzle with olive oil and secure tightly. Bake at 350°F for an hour or so—the time depends upon how large the packet is. See what happens. With herbs, the possibilities are just about endless.

Plant spearmint in a pot with a large diameter, and keep the pot on the door step. This will make it readily available and also prevent this invasive herb from taking over the garden. Pinch off a stem or two, and put the leaves in your salad. This is a wakeup flavor that will impress your family and guests. Put several sprigs in a water pitcher along with slices of lemon or lime, and let sit in the fridge for an hour or two before serving. In the springtime, freeze yellow forsythia or red quince blossoms inside ice cubes, and toss them into the pitcher along with the mint and lemon or lime before serving. The flowers are edible as well as showy. In winter months, substitute thin slices of fresh ginger for the mint.

Toss whole basil leaves in your salad. Chervil's feathery leaves have been ignored far too long in favor of the ubiquitous cilantro. Once you have tasted this versatile French-lineaged herb, you will happily add it to salads, eggs, and fish. Using it often will keep a pot of it pinched back and bushy. The more you use it, the happier it is. This is true of most herbs, actually,

Don't overlook pungent herbs with fruit. Poach slightly underripe pears and peaches with bay leaves and peppercorns. Garnish with nasturtiums for additional peppery punch, and a touch of class. Spearmint or pineapple mint are delicious with mango or papaya; drizzle with fresh lime juice.

Gremolata

The Italians created a garnish for soups, stews, and roasts that elevates homely comfort foods to a real taste sensation. Ordinarily paired with osso buco, gremolata is very versatile and can be changed to include what's available. There are just three basic ingredients: garlic, parsley, and lemon zest. Sprinkle this mixture on your entrée just before serving. This can really wake up a pot roast or a slow-cooking stew. It's also delicious on grilled fish. Start with the following recipe, and choose the proportions to suit your own taste buds.

Basic Gremolata

2 tablespoons chopped, fresh flat leaf parsley

3 garlic cloves, minced

1½ teaspoon grated lemon zest

Mix together and drop a spoonful on each portion of what you're cooking. Flat leaf parsley provides flavor and vitamin C; it's available year round and you should always have some in the vegetable crisper. (Note: Curly parsley is really only good as a garnish. Don't waste your money on it.)

Here's a simple and effortless soup that can be served anytime; most of the ingredients can be found in your pantry. Served to company, it has an impact that belies its simplicity. Fennel bulbs are sold in most grocery stores under the name "anise," which reflects its flavor but not its actual place in the vegetable kingdom. If you haven't discovered this herb/vegetable, do so soon. Remove the stalks and save for a vegetable broth. Add the feathery fronds to scrambled eggs, salad, or even gremolata. Cut the bulb in half vertically, remove the center core, and then thinly slice to add to salads for a burst of freshness on the tongue. Poach gently in chicken or vegetable broth to serve as a side dish.

Tomato Fennel Soup

2	tablespoons olive oil
1	fennel bulb, finely chopped or shredded
1	garlic clove, minced
1	28-ounce can of whole Italian tomatoes
3	cups chicken broth (or two cans)
¼	cup lemon juice
	Sea salt and freshly cracked pepper

Using a heavy kettle, drop in the olive oil and add the fennel bulb and garlic. Saute for 10 minutes, but do not let the vegetables brown—they just need to sweat and become translucent. Drain the tomatoes and add them to the pot. Let warm for about 5 minutes, then add the rest of the ingredients, including the drained tomato juices; cover and simmer for 15–20 minutes. Remove the pan from the heat, and puree the soup in a blender or food processor. Return to heat, and season to taste with salt and pepper. At this point the soup can be refrigerated for 24 hours before serving. Add the feathery fennel fronds to the basic gremolata recipe above, and sprinkle a spoonful onto each serving of the hot soup. This recipe will serve 4.

Note: Olive oil for cooking does not need to be extra virgin. A good quality pure olive oil is acceptable. Canned Italian tomatoes are a great buy during the ten months that fresh tomatoes are out of season. Drain them well and slice for sandwiches and salad.

Hazelnut Gremolata

A nut gremolata can be dusted over grilled vegetables or portabello mushrooms, sprinkled on a baked potato, or spread on bruschetta to serve on an appetizer. Add some olive oil and serve on pasta.

 1 cup hazelnuts, finely chopped
 2 tablespoons fresh thyme leaves
 2 tablespoons flat leaf parsley
 1 cup extra virgin olive oil
    Salt and pepper to taste

Add a few tablespoons of water to the herbs and oil so that the mixture will blend into a paste.

Walnut Gremolata

Here's a less expensive version to use on pasta for a late night supper with bread and wine.

 1 cup walnuts, finely chopped
    Juice and zest from one lemon
2–3 cloves garlic, minced
 1 cup flat leaf parsley, chopped
 ¾ cup extra virgin olive oil
    Salt and pepper to taste

Blend ingredients until a paste forms. This can be refrigerated and will keep for a couple of weeks.

For a quick pasta supper, cook capellini to serve no more than 4. Add ¼–½ cup water to thin the paste, and toss with the capellini.

Mint Gremolata

Getting tired of salsa and the whole chili pepper thing? To add a Greek or Moroccan flair to your meals of grilled lamb chops or leg of lamb serve them with the following mint gremolata. Also, you may use this gremolata to season a sliced orange salad—just add the zest of one orange to the recipe. Or just sprinkle on a tabbouli-stuffed tomato.

Zest from one lemon

¼ cup spearmint, chopped

2 tablespoons flat leaf parsley, chopped

3 garlic cloves, minced

½ cup Parmesan or romano cheese

Mix ingredients together. Follow serving suggestions above, or simply put it into a small dish to pass at the table.

Gremolata Salad Dressing

Salad dressing can be jazzed up with gremolata. Toss this recipe with fresh greens or pour over hot potatoes for a refreshingly different potato salad.

¼ cup flat leaf parsley, chopped

1 clove garlic minced

2 tbsps extra virgin olive oil

2 teaspoons Dijon mustard

Juice and zest, minced from one lemon

1 tablespoon of cold water to thin

Salt and freshly cracked pepper to taste

Mix ingredients and stir well. This will make about ½ cup of dressing. You may want to double it for potato salad.

Lovely Lavender

≽ by Chandra Moira Beal ≼

L avender is my favorite herb. It
reminds me of my mother, of
her lavender steam facials, and
of old-fashioned perfumes and hard
candies. Lavender can be found growing all over the world—in royal gardens
and in high-rise patios, in common
gardens and in the gardens of French
chefs. A recent trip to a lavender festival,
where a vast array of lavender products
was on display, inspired me to think
about this herb's wide range of uses.

There are at least twenty-eight distinct varieties of lavender, all of which
are used for perfume, cosmetics, potpourri, and flavoring. Lavender is so
versatile it can be used in linen drawers,
or on the body, as an insect repellent. It
can be added to a bath, burned as
incense, mixed with beverages, and
even eaten.

Lavender easily grows in pots or
gardens, and you may find the dried

petals in most health-food stores. Lavender oil is also readily available and generally inexpensive, as are an endless array of lavender perfumes, soaps, and toiletries.

History of Lavender

Lavender comes from the Latin verb *lavare*, which means "to wash." The herb was popular among Romans for use as a bath scent, and it was also used in perfumes in ancient Phoenicia. Solomon used lavender wands to sprinkle holy water and purify the temple.

Lavender has long been treasured for its medicinal qualities as well as its cosmetic applications. It was mentioned in the thirteenth century *Book of the Physicians of Myddvai* as helpful "for the panting and passion of the hart and for them that use to swoune much." Salmon recommended using lavender in his 1710 *Herbal* against "the bitings of mad dogs and other venoumous creatures." In fact, lavender is considered a protector of snakes or goddesses with snake totems, and can be used to invoke Hecate and Saturn. Culpepper noted that Mercury rules the herb, and that the herbs carries his effects very potently. He also recommended steeping lavender in wine (see recipe below) to "help them to make water that are stopped or are troubled with the wind or colic."

Like Mercury, lavender attracts energy of a high vibrational nature, making it a good tool for meditation and increased awareness. Lavender's scent brings a sense of inner calm, peace of mind, and freedom from stress—all helpful qualities in times of quiet reflection. It can be used as a tonic during times of concentration, such as when studying for extended periods of time. Lavender serves as an aid in visualization and clairvoyance, and can help make magical work more permanent. And finally, lavender can aid in sleep and brings a sense of tranquility to the wearer.

Useful in traditional Midsummer incenses, lavender makes a popular choice in handfasting rituals, and is sometimes used in aphrodisiacs and love spells. It has also been used in childbirth rituals, for welcoming a newborn into the world and encouraging serenity and peaceful awareness in the child.

Cooking with Lavender

Cooking with lavender is somewhat of a lost art. The flowers can be used in appetizers, entrées, and desserts to impart a complex taste that is sweet, herbal, and spicy at the same time. Generally you can use fresh and dried lavender interchangeably in recipes, but fresh lavender is stronger than the dried form. If you are infusing a liquid with lavender, taste it often, and remove the petals when the flavor is strong enough. Too much lavender can be unpleasant.

Try these recipes to start your experiments with lavender:

Lavender Cream

1   tablespoon dried lavender blossoms

1   cup heavy cream

Crush the lavender blossoms to release their scent and mix them into the cream. Cover and chill for three hours. Strain out the blossoms and use in place of regular cream in baking, coffee, or tea.

Lavender Sugar

1   pound granulated sugar

½   cup fresh or dried lavender blossoms

Mix the sugar and the lavender, and store in an airtight container. Before using, sift out the lavender. The sugar will become more infused with lavender scent the longer it sits. Use in place of plain sugar.

Lavender Honey

2 cups clover honey

½ cup fresh or dried lavender blossoms

Combine the honey and lavender in a stainless-steel pot and bring to a boil. Remove from heat, and let it steep for 30 minutes. Strain out the blossoms, and store the leftover honey in a tightly sealed container. This honey can be used in cooking or tea, or even spread on toast or drizzled over fruit.

Lavender Wine

Pick eight to ten corollas (the purple blossom) from a fresh sprig of lavender, and float them across a glass of chilled white wine. Alternatively, place a whole lavender sprig in the glass. Enjoy.

Cooking with Magical Intent

≈ by ShadowCat ≈

I once made a cherry tart in the shape of a heart and fed it to my lover. He loved me forever and ever, which was far longer than I could bear.

Anonymous

Be careful what you ask for, said the wise man once, or you might get it.

Cooking is a sacred, magical art. To prepare and serve food is to nurture life, to actually feed that divine spark within us that sustains us. To serve others is to serve the gods. That said, it is clear why feasting is part of a vast array of religious holidays in almost every cultures. Feasting is celebration of life and spirit. To be a cook is to be a priest of priestess— relegated to serving in the kitchen, but still serving up spirit, joy, and life.

Many years ago, I talked to Scott Cunningham about a book he was writing, now published under the title *Cunningham's Encyclopedia of Wicca in the Kitchen*. At the time, I had two

young children at home and a full-time job, so the cooking I did was mostly the easy kind—processed food mostly that could be warmed up and put on the table in fifteen minutes. I had no time for the magical aspects of cooking, or so I thought.

Scott told me of his culinary experiments in turning food preparation into spell work. He was excited about the magical properties of food and spices, and that one could cook and bake with magical intent. Nice idea, I thought, but I was too busy to use such magic in my kitchen.

Now, the children are grown and raising families of their own, and recently I picked up Scott's book again. Suddenly, something magical happened—I could now relate to his basic idea. Now that I had the time to really throw myself into learning cooking techniques and trying new recipes, I began to wonder: Is it possible to make magic in the kitchen? Since then, I have started paying more attention to my cooking, and I find I am now infused with magical intent when I am preparing food. Here is how you can be, too.

Magic in the Kitchen

The first thing to do in making your kitchen more magical is ritual cleansing. To do so, sweep your kitchen floor of any unwanted presences. Put your hair up and out of the way if it is long. Wash your hands well and make sure that all of your utensils are spotlessly clean. Wipe your countertops down, focusing on cleansing them to prepare for magical work. Now don your magical apron, which like a magical robe changes you from a mundane individual into a magical cook. You might even purchase a new apron, perhaps with symbolism special to you, particularly for the purpose of magical cooking.

One of the most important things I discovered as a cook is to be sure I use the correct utensils for the recipe at hand. For example, for years I made stew in a stainless-steel pot, cursing it for sticking and burning on the bottom. One day I was watching a chef on a cooking show make stew in a cast-iron, enameled

Dutch oven, and it struck me that I might try one. I went to the story and found a Martha Stewart equivalent (much cheaper than the French kind), and of course, the next batch of stew didn't stick or burn.

The lesson? Arm your magical pantry accordingly. Get rid of old pots and pans and habits. Throw out old flour and spices and start fresh. Buy only what you need, but exactly what you need. If you are making a stir-fry, get a real wok and season it well. The wok is one of the oldest and most versatile cooking utensils on Earth. I use mine for stir-fry, making an omelet, cooking noodles and corn on the cob, and for stirring up sauces and gravy. Seasoned regularly, the wok is the perfect nonstick surface on the range.

Now, examine the magical properties of the herbs and spices you use on a regular basis. You might want to eliminate some or make some changes in what you use to change your magical intent. Be daring with herbs and spices. More is not necessarily better, but being willing to try new herbs is a key to good cooking. You might even consider having your own organic herb garden. Mine grows right outside my kitchen door. Herbs don't need much space to flourish, and fresh herbs add fresh life to your food. Here are a couple examples of recipes useful for preparing food with magical intent.

Peace and Prosperity Pizza

1 prepackaged pizza dough (for prosperity)

1 jar or can pizza sauce (for prosperity)

1 teaspoon each: oregano (for peace); basil (for prosperity); marjoram (for peace)

1 small can black olives (for peace)

1 cup sliced mushrooms (for psychic awareness)

1 pound mozzarella cheese (for love)

½ cup Parmesan cheese (for personal power)

Altogether these elements create a peace and prosperity pizza, which may be prepared and consumed with magical intent. You might want to have a salad on the side, so try this one for peace and protection.

Peace and Protection Salad

Use amounts as desired for personal magical emphasis and taste.

> Lettuce, any variety (for peace)
>
> Tomato slices (for love and protection)
>
> Sliced black olives (for peace)
>
> Chopped green onions (for protection)
>
> Cucumber slices (for peace)
>
> Various herbs of your choice: basil, mint, and so on

Dressing

½ cup oil (for peace)

⅓ cup vinegar (for protection)

2 cloves finely chopped garlic (for protection)

1 teaspoon salt (for protection)

½ teaspoon paprika (for protection)

½ teaspoon sugar (for love)

Combine ingredients in a covered container and shake to blend. Pour over salad and toss. Sprinkle with coarse ground black pepper (protection) and grated Parmesan cheese (personal power).

When you have completed your food preparation, it is important to clean up your kitchen and put everything away. Wash the dishes, wipe down countertops, sweep the floor, and put your magical apron in the laundry. I encourage you to look at your favorite recipes to discover what you are really cooking up. Try new recipes. Invent your own. Cooking is magic.

Herbs for Health

Native American Herbal Healing Ways

by Marguerite Elsbeth

The earth is our mother. She should not be disturbed by hoe or plough. We want only to subsist on what she freely gives us.

Chief Joseph

American Indian cultures in general share the strong belief that all life is interrelated, and that the power of the world works through a sacred circle or hoop. The hoop represents the immediate environment surrounding the people—that is, stars, planets, mountains, deserts, forests, and waters. Ultimately, the hoop is a holy space allowing those inside it to be one with Earth and the sky. It holds everything together, and if any portion of the hoop remains open, good things can slip away from the community, or bad things from outside can enter.

Native people also believe that poor health comes from spiritual or energy imbalances; that is, evil or misguided spirits, people, and thought-forms generated by negative mental and emotional patterns and responses can cause an individual to be ill. Such imbalances cause lethargy, depression, and physical disease, along with a host of other ills, and they may endanger the welfare of the entire community in addition to the person who is sick. Consequently, it is necessary to reestablish peace and harmony among the people, the community, the environment, and the spirit world in order to restore good health.

Working with Nature

Like other ancient methods of treating disease, American Indian healing reflects a very old way of working with nature. Traditional American Indian healing is holistic, meaning it does not focus on symptoms or diseases. Rather, the healer considers the whole individual and his or her physical, mental, emotional, and spiritual well-being.

The particular methods of diagnosis and treatment are as diverse as the languages, landscapes, and customs of the approximately 500 American Indian nations that make up the indigenous people of Turtle Island—one of the original names of North America. Still, although American Indians have distinctive cultures, and use diverse methods and ceremonies to promote healing, they generally hold the same ideas about health, disease, and the cause and cure of illness. The following four steps are fairly common among all the tribes.

The Use of Medicine Men and Women

When energy imbalances occur, American Indian people often rely on the power of a medicine man or woman who is able to contact the spirit world to combat disease. Medicine people use their special abilities to appease the displeased or angered spirits that cause illness, and thus restore good health to the tribe.

Each tribe has certain individuals who are recognized as healers. These people receive special teachings. Some medicine people are also distinguished as holy men and women. The medicine bag in which they carry their herbs and other healing secrets is the symbol of their status and authority.

The healing methods medicine people use do not follow a particular set of rules. There are no written guidelines. Every healer works differently with each individual, using herbs, ceremonies, and spiritual gifts as they find it necessary. Each tribe uses its own spiritual knowledge and techniques. The techniques by themselves do not bring about healing; they are only steps towards becoming whole, balanced, and reconnected to the spirit. A healthy patient has a healthy relationship with his or her community and, ultimately, with the greater community of nature.

Ceremony

Ceremonies are used to contact the spirit world and engage its support in the healing. Healing might involve talking circles, the ceremonial smoking of natural tobacco, herbs, animal spirits, vision quests, or sweat lodges. The healing often begins with a purification ceremony.

Purification of the Body

Body purification is fairly common in American Indian healing. The sweat lodge, which is similar to a sauna, is a common healing and religious ceremony used for purification, spiritual renewal, and education. The lodge itself is a small structure made from a frame of saplings that is covered with skins, canvases, or blankets. A small flap opening is used to regulate the temperature. A depression dug in the center of the lodge holds the hot rocks. Sage or cedar is sprinkled over the rocks, and then water is poured over them to create fragrant steam. Those inside the lodge sing, pray, and sweat as a means to cleanse the body, mind, and spirit.

The Pueblos, Apache, Navajo, Paiute, Shoshone, Tewa, and Zuni peoples use sage or cedar as a gynecological aid, diuretic, emetic, and disinfectant for colds and coughs, and a cure-all for a variety of diseases. When the leaves and berries of this plant are burned on the rocks in the sweat lodge, the aromatic smoke carries the prayers of the participants to the Great Spirit, who is responsible for the creation of the world.

Herbal Healing Ways

Herbs play an important role in healing. Most American Indian people treat plants with respect because they believe that plants have supernatural powers, or may be inhabited by spirits. The Seminoles of Florida hold an annual purification festival called the Green Corn Dance. On the festival's first day, they take an herbal tea called the "black drink" that induces vomiting and purges the body of toxins. Those who do not drink the tea, it is thought, will become sick sometime before the year ends.

People who have the gift for curing with herbs spend considerable time gathering plants to prepare their medicines. However, not all American Indian people gather herbs in the same way. There are as many different methods for collecting botanical plants, as there are cultures, customs, and religious traditions. Some American Indian tribes grow medicinal plants, and others gather plants from forest, swamp, grassland, or desert.

People who live close to nature choose to purify themselves and propitiate the spirit inhabiting a plant before they partake of its medicine. For American Indians, it is customary to make an offering to the spirits before gathering medicinal plants. Otherwise, if the plant is not given proper reverence, the plant spirit may be offended, and the user deprived of its benefits.

Migrating peoples such as the ocean-faring Asians, Vikings, Celts, or other Europeans may have influenced American Indian herbal healing traditions, and Native plant knowledge came together as a mixture of fact, folklore, and superstition. For example, it is said when leaves looked like the liver, they could be used to treat that organ. Yellow plants were thought to be good for jaundice, a condition causing yellowish pigmentation of the skin, tissues, and body fluids. Red plants were used to treat the blood. The worst smelling and tasting herbs were used for healing.

People watched animals eating certain plants and then tried them too, as a common way of learning which herbs were good for particular conditions. This is, of course, very wise, as animals are closely in tune with nature; they do not think about the healing process, they just do what comes naturally—eating grass when their stomachs are upset, for example. Our perceptions may conclude that grass-eating causes regurgitation; therefore ingesting grass is bad because it makes the animal sick. However, regurgitation is nature's way of ridding the body of toxins in the system, so actually eating grass is a useful thing for animals.

Many of us are careful about what we choose to consume these days, but so were Native peoples. They knew what could cure them, and what could kill them. Consider that North and South American Indians have given modern society more than 200 drugs—including aspirin, painkillers, muscle relaxants, cures for scurvy and malaria, and so on. Much of the pharmaceutical remedies that are used today were in fact used by American Indian people in the form of natural herbal medicines many centuries prior to the arrival of Western civilization.

Valium, for example, a well-known drug used to relieve mild to moderate anxiety, was originally derived from valerian root, an herb used to treat nervousness, insomnia, emotional depression, and stress-related hypertension. Ear coning, usually associated with New Age healing, is another centuries-old way to relieve earache, fight infection, and remove toxins and wax from the ear. American Indians made ear cones of the herb yerba de buena. American Indian herbal medicine in fact is still evolving, even as modern medicine looks back to its traditions.

American Indian Herbal Healing Remedies
Ojibwa Tea

The Ojibwa, a Northern American woodland Indian tribe, use an herbal remedy that is trusted by many herbalists and their patients. More commonly known as *essiac*, Ojibwa tea helps move the body toward a state of integration and good health, boosts the immune system, cleanses and supports the liver and blood, and is useful in treating all autoimmune and allergic disorders and degenerative diseases such as cancer. (See warning at the end of this article.)

Ojibwa Tea

2   quarts distilled water

¼   cup burdock root

8   teaspoons sheep sorrel

2   teaspoons slippery elm

¼   teaspoon turkey rhubarb

In a stainless-steel, glass, or crockery pot, bring water to a full boil, cover, and continue boiling for 30 minutes. Add ingredients, and stir well. Boil for 10 minutes, uncovered, stirring occasionally. Remove from heat. Cover, and steep for 12 hours. Put the tea back on the heat, and boil briskly for 10 minutes. Remove from heat, pour through a strainer into boiled glass jars or jugs, and seal with sterile lids. Refrigerate.

Adults over ninety pounds drink 1 or 2 ounces of tea twice a day (morning and night) on an empty stomach. Serve hot or cold, or add brewed regular tea to taste. Do not eat for a half hour after drinking, so that the tea can work its way through your system. Use until the problem is eliminated. Children should be given only little amounts—no more than a half ounce per serving. Watch for indigestion or changes in bowel movements. Some sensitive individuals may be allergic to the herbs used in the tea, so it is best to experiment with very small amounts first.

Choctaw Tea

This herbal detoxification remedy is common to the Choctaw people, and some other American Indian tribes.

¼   teaspoon white sage

½   teaspoon red clover

¼ teaspoon pine needles

1 pinch of chaparral

Grind the herbs. Boil 1 quart of distilled water. Place the herbal mixture into a heat-resistant glass container. Pour water over the mixture, and steep for 20 minutes. Refrigerate. Drink ½ cup three times a day on an empty stomach. Note: Chaparral can cause serious liver/kidney damage, or tumor eruption in sensitive individuals. Consult your physician before using. Stop using if you experience passing tiredness, upset stomach, or nausea.

Native Herb Liver-Detoxification Tea

This basic recipe is a highly effective, natural way to cleanse the liver, and remove accumulated toxins from the body.

1 gallon of distilled water

4 teaspoons milk thistle seed

4 teaspoons red clover

4 teaspoons dandelion

2 teaspoons cat's claw

Brewing equipment: Coffee bean grinder; stainless steel, glass, or crockery pot; one 32-ounce glass jar with lid; one 1-gallon glass container; funnel; and strainer.

Grind the herbs to a fine powder in a coffee grinder. Place herbs in a 32-ounce jar. Bring approximately 24 ounces of distilled water to a boil, and pour over herbs. Cover and steep for a few hours. Place a funnel into a 1-gallon container, place the strainer over the funnel, and pour the tea into the container. Refrigerate. Sip 8 ounces of this tea throughout the day, every day, until symptoms are alleviated. Watch for passing tiredness, upset stomach, and nausea.

Individual American Indian Herbs

The following list contains some of the herbs used in American Indian healing traditions for a variety of ailments:

Black walnut: Including the kernel and the green hull, is rich in organic iodine, manganese, and vitamin B15. It also contains strong antiseptic properties, and is a good anti-fungal. Commonly used to relieve constipation, irregularity, and poor digestion, this herb also oxygenates the blood to cleanse the body of parasites. Its strong healing properties make it useful topically for bruises, skin rashes, fungal infections, herpes, warts, and ringworm. Occasionally, black walnut has been used orally to heal mouth and throat sores and restore tooth enamel.

Burdock: Inhibits the growth of bacteria and fungi in the body, and is administered mainly as a blood purifier and liver detoxifier. Some herbalists also consider it to be both a diuretic and diaphoretic. When applied as a poultice, burdock treats psoriasis, acne, and other skin conditions, as well as bruises, burns, knee swellings, and gout. Caution: Burdock may cause dry mouth, blurred vision, and even hallucinations in sensitive individuals.

Comfrey: Is used to heal bruises and ulcers. It is also useful for skin irritations from burns, bruises, cuts, and insect bites.

Cota: Is served as a beverage tea. It is also used to treat high blood pressure, mild fever, stomachaches, and is used as a stimulant. It is also known as Navajo tea.

Echinacea: Comes from the common coneflower, and may be used to shorten the duration and intensity of cold and flu symptoms, and to ease menstrual cramps. As an immune stimulant, blood purifier, and an effective antibiotic, it facilitates the wound-healing process. Use this herb to treat rheumatism, infections, bee stings, snakebites, tumors, syphilis, gangrene, eczema, and hemorrhoids.

Mullein: Is an old-time remedy for bronchitis and dry, unproductive coughs. Mullein is a good expectorant, and in the process of clearing out the congestion it also soothes irritation in the throat and bronchial passages. An antispasmodic, mullein can also relieve stomach cramps and help control diarrhea.

Osha: Also known as chuchupate, ligusticum, and bear root, this is a very strong healing medicine and natural antibiotic. It is useful for the early stages of sore throat, chest colds with painful breathing, and dry asthma. Osha stimulates the immune system and prevents secondary infections.

Red clover: Is a powerful blood purifier and immune stimulant. It has been used effectively in treating ulcers, stomach cancers, whooping cough, and various muscle and bronchial spasms. Combined with equal parts of blue violet, burdock, yellow dock, dandelion root, rockrose, and goldenseal, it is a strong remedy for cancerous growths and leprosy. (Warning: See your doctor if you suspect you may have cancer.)

Sage: Is used to relieve excess mucus buildup. It eases mental exhaustion and strengthens concentration. In a lotion or salve, it is useful for treating sores and skin eruptions, and for stopping bleeding. Chewing the fresh leaves soothes mouth sores and sore throats. Sage is good for stomach troubles, diarrhea, gas, flu, and colds. It treats dandruff. Sage combined with peppermint, rosemary, and wood betony provides a headache remedy. It can regulate the menstrual cycle, decreases milk flow in lactating women, treats hot flashes, and works as a deodorant. (Use this remedy with caution.)

Shepherd's purse: Is a common weed that may be used as a tea. It is considered to be one of the best treatments for stopping hemorrhages of all kinds—of the stomach, lungs, uterus, and from the nose and kidneys. It is a remedy for catarrhal conditions of the bladder and urethra, as well as in ulcerated conditions and abscesses of the bladder. (See your doctor if you suffer from any of these conditions.)

Slippery elm: Has long been used in traditional herbal medicine. It eases digestion, draws out body impurities and toxins, and assists with healing. It soothes irritated tissues of the intestines, colon, urinary tract, and stomach, and is beneficial in treating inflammation. This herb also nourishes the adrenal glands, gastrointestinal tract, and respiratory system, and helps the body expel excess mucus.

Thistle: Is used to protect the liver against toxins, and encourages the regeneration of new liver cells. It is beneficial for individuals, such as cancer patients, taking drugs that are hard on the liver, and is an excellent tonic for toxic chemical contamination, chronic hepatitis, and abnormal liver function in general. This herb will help the body to recover from any injury. (See your doctor if you suffer from any of the conditions.)

Willow: May be used to treat the common cold. Tea brewed from the bark of the willow tree contains salicin, now used in the form of aspirin. American Indians have long used willow bark tea to treat joint pain.

For Further Study

Native American Ethnobotany Database. http://www.umd.umich.edu/cgi-bin/herb/. University of Michigan-Dearborn.

Note

As mentioned in the Introduction to this book, you must take care not to replace regular medical treatment through the use of herbs. Herbal treatment is intended primarily to complement modern health care. Always seek professional help if you suffer from illness. Also, take care to read all warning labels before taking any herbs or starting on an extended herbal regimen. Always consult an herbal professional before beginning any sort of medical treatment—this is particularly true for pregnant women.

Ashwagandha: India's Superb Tonic

⇜ by Kevin Spelman ⇝

Withania *somnifera*, commonly known as ashwagandha, is one of the most revered of all the tonics of India. For thousand of years, this herb has been used traditionally to nourish and rejuvenate the debilitated and the convalescing.

According to Indian healers, the nourishing effects of ashwagandha affect all of the bodily tissues, so perhaps this is why this herb is considered on a par with ginseng *(Panax* spp.)—to which it is comparable in effect but not in its energy. In the ayurvedic pharmacopoeia, ashwagandha is classified as a rejuvenative—a classification that parallels ginseng's position in the Chinese pharmacopoeia. Though you may wish to note that, although equally beneficial, at the time of this writing ashwagandha is more affordable than ginseng.

The Use of Ashwagandha

Traditionally, pregnant women have used ashwagandha as a nutritive food in the form of a decocted tea. Milk cooked with a decoction of ashwagandha and ghee is used as a remedy for a variety of gynecological disorders and as a fertility aid to reduce the likelihood of miscarriage. The author has used ashwagandha in treating a number of prenatal women to strengthen and prepare the mother for the delivery and for her postpartum needs. Additionally the author managed a case where a combination of ashwagandha and cramp bark was used successfully to stop a threatened miscarriage.

As a rejuvenative tonic, *W. somnifera* is a specific treatment for the weakened, the elder, the young, and the convalescing. For children, ghee cooked with one-quarter part the amount of ashwagandha and pepper with ten parts milk is useful for treating malnourishment and emaciation. These ancient preparations cleverly made use of the chemistry of natural products by employing milk or ghee, lipid solvents, to extract the lipid soluble withanolides and sitoindosides in the herb. These constituents have been studied extensively and have led to the understanding of ashwagandha as an adaptogen.

The Adaptogenic Effects of Ashwagandha

Adaptogens are defined as any agent that increases the nonspecific resistance of an organism to stress and other detrimental environmental influences. Generally, this term is most commonly used now to refer to specific plants that when ingested are:

1) nontoxic,

2) normalize bodily processes, irrespective of the direction of pathological changes, and

3) create a nonspecific resistance to a very broad spectrum of harmful factors of different physical, chemical, and biological natures.

Adaptogens such as ashwagandha have shown marked activity in modulating the stress axis (also known as the hypothalamus, pituitary, adrenal axis), and decreasing the reactivity to stress. As a result of these effects, adaptogens promote regeneration of the body after stress or fatigue and rebuild strength as well as provide an enhanced response to physical, chemical, or mental stress. One proposed mechanism for these remarkable effects is through the metabolism of adrenal cholesterol levels, which are many times higher in animals given adaptogens than in their matched controls. This indicates increased tolerance to stress in general.

Ashwagandha has been thouroughly evaluated for its adaptogenic activity. In both human studies and animal models it has demonstrated significant anabolic effects. Young animals fed ashwagandha over eight months demonstrated weight gain of 227 percent compared to the control group's gain of 145 percent. When fed to pregnant animals, ashwagandha increased the weight of offspring 156 percent compared to a control group. In human children between the age of eight and twelve, the herb significantly increased body weight, plasma proteins, and mean corpuscular hemoglobin, and in adults promoted a stronger average strength. In male adults aged fifty to fifty-nine, parameters such as hemoglobin, red blood cell count, hair melanin, and seated stature improved when taking ashwagandha. Additionally, sexual performance was reported to improve in 71 percent of these subjects. Another research group reported effects on reproductive tissue as well. That is, an aqueous extract of ashwagandha promoted a notable increase in testicular weight, spermatogenesis, and an apparent increase in the diameter of seminiferous tubules and the number of seminiferous tubular cell layers in the testes of treated animals. Additionally, it was concluded that the extract had a testosterone-like effect.

Other effects of ashwagandha, which are typical of adaptogens, include a protection against metabolic stress in cold and immobilization models. In one such investigation, parameters such as blood glucose, creatinine, urea, and lactic acid were maintained in normal range among a stress-study group. This demonstrates ashwagandha's ability to normalize physiological functions regardless of stress. In other laboratory studies, the use of ashwagandha has provided significant protection for the heart and liver. Ashwagandha treatment also resulted in significant increase in blood coagulation time. The use of the herb also mildly offsets the increase of adrenal weight due to various stressors, a negative compensatory mechanism. In a swimming endurance test, considered a stress model, ashwagandha use increased swimming times in subjects by more than 290 percent over a control group. Ashwagandha's adaptogenic effects have repeatedly exhibited enhanced stress tolerance in a variety of models.

Much of this research has focused on ashwagandha extracts that were concentrated in withanolides, cortisol-like molecules. However, a group of clever researchers facilitated the elucidation of a general theme of herbalism—that the whole plant is the medicine, not just a particular group of constituents that show activity. These researchers used a withanolide-free aqueous solution of the roots. This extract exhibited significant antistress activity against a battery of tests such as antifatigue effect, swimming performance time, swimming-induced gastric ulceration and hypothermia, immobilization-induced gastric ulceration, autoanalgesia, and biochemical changes in the adrenal glands. This research implies that the additional cost of withanolide standardized ashwagandha products may not be necessary.

Another commonly observed property of adaptogens is their antioxidant properties. Although antioxidant properties alone cannot begin to explain all of the complex activity that an adaptogen elicits, antioxidant properties may explain in part some of the antistress, immunomodulatory, cognition-facilitating, anti-inflammatory, and anti-aging effects produced by ashwagandha.

Antioxidant research does show free-radical scavenging capacity and a protective effect on DNA.

In traditional ayurvedic medicine, ashwagandha is often not used alone. The herb is used traditionally often in formula in order to make use of the synergizing effects of other herbs. In a stress study on a formula containing aswagandha and holy basil *(Ocimum sanctum)*, shatavari *(Asparagus racemosus)*, gokshura *(Tribulus terristris)*, and shilajit (a black resin found flowing out from between fissures in rocks), excellent protective effects were demonstrated. The above ashwagandha formula was able to off-set these detrimental effects of spleen weight reduction and concentrations of adrenal gland ascorbic acid and cortisol often found in subjects under stress.

The Central Nervous System Effects of Ashwagandha

Ashwagandha is also used extensively in treating the central nervous system. Traditionally considered a central nervous system (CNS) rejuvenative, the herb calms and strengthens the mind and nerves, and it is effective as a sleep aid—inducing deep, restorative sleep. Both short-term and long-term memory, as well as other cognitive functional deficits, have improved with the use of ashwagandha—this may occur through an enhanced cortical muscarinic acetylcholine receptor capacity in various cortical regions. Additionally, the herb influences gamma amino butyric acid (GABA) activity, which may explain its effectiveness in treating anxiety and as a sleep aid. In one study, a formulation containing primarily ashwagandha was used to treat thirty-four diagnosed cases of anxiety neurosis. Complaints of anxiety were markedly decreased after twelve weeks of treatment.

In other sorts of central nervous system imbalance, ashwagandha also proves clinically useful. In cases of bipolar disorder and attention deficit disorder (ADD), for example, ashwagandha is helpful. In bipolar disorder, a tea of ashwagandha administered as an enema has demonstrated usefulness in the management of mood swings. In a case of ADD, the use of the tincture has been effective.

Ashwagandha has also helped to ease the development of tolerance to the analgesic effects of morphine, and it may suppress the development of dependence to opiates in general. This may, with further study, indicate promise in the treatment of addictions.

As previously mentioned, ashwagandha demonstrates antioxidant activity. In the case of the CNS, antioxidants such as ashwagandha have demostrated protective effects in various regions of the brain, particularly the frontal cortical and striatal areas. The activity stems from an induction of the enzymes superoxide dismutase, catalase, and glutathione peroxidase and is comparable to the effect of the drug deprenyl. These enzymes are key to promoting body resistance to inflammation and free-radical damage. Other researchers suggests that ashwagandha offers cytoprotective properties from stress to hippocampal neurons. These combined effects may be responsible for part of the restorative and rejuvenative activity of ashwagandha, and generally serve to reinforce the traditional use of ashwagandha in neurodegenerative diseases. In such diseases as Alzheimer's, multiple sclerosis, and Parkinson's, where inflammation is a major precursor to such disorders, ashwagandha may be helpful.

Anti-inflammatory Effects

The significant anti-inflammatory properties of ashwagandha make the herb useful in treating rheumatic swellings and in the internal treatment of respiratory disorders such as asthma. The root powder of the herb has shown efficacy in a variety of cases of acute and subacute inflammation. In asthma and arthritic conditions, preparations and extracts of ashwagandha have shown significant efficacy in certain studies. One researcher demonstrated an anti-inflammatory effect five times stronger than phenylbutazone and equal to hydrocortisone when using an isolated constitent of the herb, withanolide F, in an injection. Of course, this is not relevant to herbalists who buy ashwagandha products off the shelf.

Immune Effects

With the increasing toxicity of the planet and our food and water sources, immune weakness is becoming a common complaint among many peoples of the Earth. Cancer is on the rise; some scientists hypothesize that this increase may be explained by the increasing medical attention on the use of antibiotics in treating all manner of illness, as well as the increasing number of uniquely adapted microorganisms our immune systems face.

Immunomodulators, as a category of botanical medicine, show great promise in the treatment of the immune dysregulation induced by the increasing toxic environment. Ashwagandha, as an immunomodulating herb, may be helpful due to its ability to upregulate cytokines. Cytokines are peptide molecules that communicate to cells, especially white blood cells (WBC), during an immune response. These peptides are involved in infection, inflammation, cytotoxic reactions, division and differentation of cells, and so on. Ashwagandha enhances levels of a variety of cytokines, including IFN-g, IL-2, and GM-CSF. The herb also enhances stem cell proliferation and differentiation.

Through the action of these cytokines, immunomodulators have the abilty to normalize immune function regardless of whether the immune system is deficient or in excess. This is a remarkable trait of botanical medicines and a testament to the balancing effect of certain herbs. This also is a seeming paradox to pharmacologists who seek a simple, single-directional thera-peutic treatment. Ashwagandha demonstrates a remarkable ability to balance the immune system regardless of the direction of imbalance.

Ashwagandha has true immunomodulatory effects, both in immune-regulating effects—i.e., in the decrease of inflammatory response and in inhibiting delayed-type hypersentivity reaction—and immune stimulation—i.e., increased WBC counts, antineoplastic activity, immune protection from irradiation, and stimulation of IFN-g, IL-2, GM-CSF.

The protection of the immune system by ashwagandha against immunosuppressive drugs is impressive. Studies have shown ashwagandha offers protection from azathioprin, cyclophosphamide, paclitaxel, and prednisolone. These effects include the reversal of bone marrow suppression, low white blood cell counts, and low platelet counts. This makes ashwagandha an excellent treatment in ameliorating the side effects of chemotherapy in cancer treatment. Unfortunately, it may take three weeks before patients feel measurable changes.

Similiarly, ashwagandha provides protection from radiation, radiosensitizing activity, and antineoplastic activity, further suggesting the herb as a treatment in cancer. And to round out these extraordinary influences on the immune system, in terminal infections ashwagandga has been shown to prolong survival time. This is probably due to increases in phagocytosis and intracellular killing of peritoneal macrophages.

These immunomodulatory effects are not unusual in the world of herbal medicine; astragalus and the polysaccharide-rich mushroom varieties of reishi, maitake, and shiitake have similar activity and have been used for thousands of years to care for the ill. The traditional ayurvedic use of ashwagandha has led modern researchers to verify the efficacy of its tonic, adaptogenic, and immunomodulating properties. Further studies will certainly continue to validate the traditional uses of the herb, and will perhaps suggest new uses. In the meantime, as the World Health Organization suggests, ashwagandha should be considered as a treatment for a variety of conditions, and we should commit further research to the use of this medicine.

Information on Ashwagandha

Names in various languages: *Andhra Pradesh-pulivendrum, panneru Bangali-ashwagandha, Gujarati-asandha, ghada aahana, Hindi-punir, asgandh; Kannada-hiremaddu, Kerala-amukkiram; Malayalum-amukkuram Marathi-asandha, doragunja, Sanskrti-ashwagandha, turangigandha; Tamil-aamakulang, Telugu-piniru, aragi,* English-winter cherry

Energetics

Taste: sweet, bitter

Energy released in gut: warm

Quality: heavy, moist

Systemic effect: heavy

Constituents

Steroidal alkaloids, steroidal lactones (withanolides), withaferin A-Y, sitoindosides I-X, glycowithanolides

Actions

Adaptogen, alterative, anti-inflammatory, anodyne, antiseptic, antitussive, aphrodisiac, astringent, bitter, deobstruent, diuretic, immunomodulator, nervine, sedative, spasmolytic, and tonic. Reduces *vata* and *kapha* (two ayurvedic "types" of constitutions). Leaves and roots are considered narcotic.

Traditional Uses

Root: arthritis, asthma, bronchitis, cancer, consumption, cough, debility, diuretic, dropsy, dyspepsia, epilepsy, female disorders, hiccups, hypertension, insanity, lumbago, narcotic, psoriasis, rheumatism, ringworm, scabies, scorpion sting, senility, sexual weakness, swelling of the hands and feet, syphilis, tumor, witchcraft, and wound healing

Leaf: febrifuge, locally on lesions, painful swellings, sore eyes

Seed: chest complaints

Topical: boils, scabies, ulcers, inflammation

Indications

Arthritis: osteoarthritis, rheumatoid arthritis

Deficiency due to: chronic pain, environmental stress, illess, mental stress, physical stress, overwork, overtraining (athletics), weight loss

Immunosuppression: amelioration of symptoms from chemo/radiotherapy, CFIDS/FM/AIDS, deficiency due to all stressors, environmental illness

Nervous system disorders: anxiety, bipolar mood disorder, inflammatory/degradative disorders (Alzheimer's, MS, Parkinson's), insomnia, low back pain and sciatica, wind disorders

Longevity tonic: All tissues, rasayana

Reproductive issues: Enhanced performance, female/male hormonal disruption, male infertility, miscarriage

Respiratory disorders: Asthma, cough

Sleep Disorders: Hypersomnia, insomnia

Dose

Powder: 3–6 grams (⅒–⅕ ounce) daily.

Tincture: 6–12 milliliters (1–2 teaspoons) daily; for pain 15 milliliters (2½ teaspoons) every 2–3 hours and as needed.

Decoction: 20–30 grams (⅔—1 ounce) cooked in cow's milk.

Medicated ghee: 5 milliliters (1 teaspoon) two times daily.

Safety Profile/Toxicology

Side effects: At recommended dosage, ashwagandha is well tolerated. Excessive doses are potentially irritating to mucous and serous membranes. This may result in gastro-intestinal upset. In parameters such as blood glucose, creatinine, urea and lactic acid, ashwagandha demonstrates safety in long-term administration. There are no adverse effects on liver, alkaline phosphatase, lipid peroxidation, and hemoglobin. An acute toxicity study in mice showed a good margin of safety.

International Status

In the United States: Regulated as a dietary supplement.

In India: An official herb in the ayurvedic pharmacopoeia of India.

References

Bone, K. *Clinical Applications of Ayurvedic and Chinese Herbs.* Queensland, Australia: Phytotherapy Press, 1996.

Jain, S. K. *Dictionary of Indian Folk Medicine and Ethnobotany.* New Delhi, India: Deep Publications, 1991.

Jain, S. K., and R. A. DePhillips. *Medicinal Plants of India.* Algonac, Michigan: Reference Publications, 1991.

Kapoor, L. D. *CRC Handbook of Ayurvedic Medicinal Plants.* Boca Raton, Florida: CRC Press Inc., 1990.

Nadkarni, K. M. *Indian Materia Medica Plants.* Bombay, India: Popular Prakashan Private Ltd., 1908.

Spelman, Kevin. "Clinical Use of *Withania somnifera* (Ashwagandha)." *The Herbalist.* 1995, Spring/May (17):12-13.

Svoboda, R.E. *Ayurveda Life, Health and Longevity*. London, England: Arkana, 1992.

Wagner, H., and H. Winterhoff. "Plant Adaptogens." *Phytomedicine*. 1994. 1(1):69–70.

Good Health the Chinese Way

≫ by Xingwu Liu ≪

A friend of mine who is also an anthropologist once said that whoever can explain the principles of traditional Chinese medicine, and how this practice works, in a simple way, will be doing a great service to the world. Even I, after more than ten years of deep involvement in promoting Chinese medical formulas and medicinal teas in American society, have some trouble in how to begin writing about the subject. It is very clear that except for acupuncture and the practice of *qigong*, two component parts of traditional Chinese medicine that have become known in this country, the core of the Chinese health regimen—from herbal remedies to life preservation *(yangsheng)*—is virtually unknown in the Western world.

While it is true that many people in today's rational world still believe Chinese medicine is quackery, there are also many people who really do appreciate what traditional Chinese medicine can do for a person. In a sense, it is both poetry and science, and such a combination is all too rare in the world. As an anthropologist, my focus is a bit more scientific than most herbalists, and I tend to take an objective view that I hope may help readers understand this medical system a bit more than they otherwise might. After all, cross-cultural understanding has been the hallmark of cultural anthropology since the science was invented.

Two Divisions

In China, there are two major divisions of medicine. What is called "conventional medicine" in the West is called "Western medicine" in China. This contrasts with what is simply called "Chinese medicine." Both practices are considered comprehensive systems for health and fitness in China, unlike in the West where medical system other than conventional (Western) medicine is treated with some amount of disdain.

Chinese Medicine

There are four major component parts in traditional Chinese medicine:

1. Basic theories

2. Clinical treatment

3. Prevention and preservation of life (yangsheng)

4. Materia medica (herbology)

The basic theories of Chinese medicine represent the theoretical summarization of all the life activities of the human body and of the laws governing diseases and pathological changes. They are the guiding principles of the clinical maintenance of good health and life preservation, and include the theories of yin and yang, the theories of the five elements, theories of visceral activities, and theories on the causes of diseases, pathogenesis, diagnostic methods, categorical identification, treatment principles, and treatment methods. Materia medica, meanwhile, covers the classification, properties, and uses of various herbs, minerals, and animal parts for use in treating and maintaining good health.

Natural and Low-Cost Medication

Traditional Chinese medicines that are use for both prevention and treatment come mainly from natural sources. There are 12,807 recorded medicinal materials, out of which 11,146 are herbals, 1,581 are from animal sources, and 80 are minerals. Formulated using ancient and traditional formulas, these medicines comprise more than one million patent formulas that can be adjusted to suit particular needs with the addition or reduction of certain ingredients. These medicines represent a rich treasure house for health care and fitness.

History and tradition, as well as modern research, have shown that these natural medicines have little-to-no toxicity or side effects, making them on the whole very safe and easy to use. Many of these medicinal materials have bidirectional effects, supplementing in case of deficiency, and discharging in case of excess. For instance, many heat-clearing and toxin-resolving herbs are also antibacterial, and many of them have regulating effects on the immune systems. Another important feather of traditional Chinese medicine is that many herbs and herbal products show a strong selectivity in their attacks against toxins and pathogens. This is unlike modern chemical drugs, which can, in many instances, kill the good cells along with the bad ones.

With the development of modern science and technology, and the current fast pace of life and attendant changes in diet and lifestyle, and with the destruction of the environment, many health problems have developed with which Western (conventional) medicine is helpless. Chemical drugs bring about life-threatening side effects and toxicity. Diseases and viruses have through time developed a high resistance to drugs, and in fact many diseases have originated from the new drugs themselves.

Since traditional Chinese medicine formulas have little or no toxicity or side effects, and are effective on many diseases, they are the best alternative to chemical drugs. It was reported a few years ago that the annual cost for health care per person in China was only ¥150 ($18 USD), while the cost in the U.S. was $1,500—eighty times more expensive. Yet the life span of the Chinese population is almost the same as in the United States.

A Focus on Nutrition

In the Chinese concept of health, the relationship between food and medicine is not thought of as a dichotomy. Instead, the primary model is that health is best promoted by a food-medicine continuum. That is, in traditional Chinese medicine, foods and medicine are considered of the same origin. While some foods are definitely foods (rice, cabbage, and apples), and some medicines are obviously medicines (mahuang, schizandra, and trichosanthe), many substances are both good for food and medicine (coix, dandelion, and wolfberry).

This idea has led to the extensive use of natural plants in promoting good health, and has focused traditional Chinese medicine on nutrition. On the whole, the safe use of certain herbals provide health-conscious people with an abundant supply of medicinal food. And some traditional Chinese recipes are so well prepared that they represent the best combination of flavor and treatment. Medicinal foods such as *yaoshan* are in fact very popular in parts of China, especially southern China.

In traditional Chinese concept, food, especially balanced food, is the best medicine. Generally speaking, a strong medicine is intended to attack the evils (pathogens) in the body. The idea, according to *The Yellow Emperor's Cannon of Medicine*, is to eat five grains for nourishment, five fruits to assist, five animals (meats) for tonification, and five vegetables for supplementation.

Prevention as the Primary Concern

Although an emphasis on the internal factors contributing to diseases and the close interpersonal relations prevent Chinese medical practice from developing definite procedures to isolate sick patients in order to prevent an infection of others around him, Chinese medicine did develop alternative ways to prevent infectious diseases—such as using the herb smoke of attractylodes root, and so on. As a matter of fact, few other medical systems put as much emphasis on prevention as traditional Chinese medicine does.

The Chinese emphasis on prevention has contributed greatly to good health. According to traditional Chinese medical theory, mere pathological factors are not enough to cause diseases. It is only when the equilibrium and balance of various parts of the body break down that disease occurs. Pathological factors are thought to be present all the time, but this affects you only when there is an opening in your defense system.

The most important thing in prevention is to constantly reinforce the immunity of the body and to eliminate any potential pathogenic factors in a patient's life. One of the famous principles in traditional Chinese medicine is to "treat the not-yet-sick." The main approach is to prevent before diseases strike.

The best prevention is, of course, to lead a normal life, to have a nutritionally balanced diet, and to maintain a moderate level of exercise, both mental and physical. This is called yang-sheng, meaning "life preservation." The idea is to maintain the biological balance in a patient through nutrition and the control of emotions. This means the avoidance of any indulgence—we shall talk about this later.

The emphasis in this concept is embodied in the doctor's regular concern for his or her patient's nutrition. Invariably, the traditional Chinese doctor strives to guide the patient along the path of nutrition, both during treatment and in daily life.

Another important aspect of prevention in Chinese medicine is striving to eliminate the possibility of any complications a treatment of one disease may cause to other parts of the body. This is one of the reasons why Chinese medicine is entirely holistic in both diagnosis and treatment considerations.

Balance as the Ideal State of Health

When the relative equilibrium within an organism, or between it and the environment breaks down, problems set in and the organism is thrown into an unbalanced state. This opens up a gap in the system of defense, which otherwise should be closed to avoid any invasion of pathological factors in the environment. Man is not a static system, but a dynamic one in which changes of all kinds are constantly taking place. So a breach in the defense of the body's carefully balanced system is complicated. The role of a doctor in diagnosing treatment in these cases involves identifying the principal and secondary causes of this imbalance. Treatment then involves addressing the principal and secondary causes in a manner similar to how an army general dispatches forces—groups of soldiers, both large and small each with their individual tasks—to fight the enemy. A patient uses a multitude of herbs, each of which has its own role to play in tackling current and future health problems.

On the whole, therefore, we can understand the Chinese way of treatment as rebuilding balance in the patient. The idea of balance as the ideal state of good health leads to another idea—that is, we should always avoid any imbalance created as the result of a treatment. In most cases, the treatment in Chinese medicine is expected to be a slow process, and noninvasive. Of course, while all sick patients would be greatly pleased if they were assured that their disease would immediately be cured, in reality, it is often not possible to restore equilibrium quickly when there is a state of imbalance. And in fact, speed is not desirable in Chinese medicine. Diseases develop slowly. Often, we are not aware of what is happening in our bodies until we suddenly we feel sick at the later stages of a disease. When we feel it, our body is already very much out of balance. To regain this balance takes time. If the treatment is too strong, the patient may be thrown into another opposite imbalance, and the result may be even worse, and possibly too much for the body to take. That is why Chinese medicines normally have little or no side effects. Rather, in Chinese medicine, slow and steady is the way.

Holistic in Diagnosis

In the Chinese concept of reality, the universe and everything in it is a complete, or holistic, system. In reality, everything is connected to every else in a relationship of cooperation and coordination. All are maintained in a relative equilibrium and balanced state. It is a universe of relationships—one element with another, human with nature, one human with others. If there is anything wrong in nature, it is because some relationship has gone out of balance. And if there is anything wrong in society, it is from an inbalance in the relationship between people. Consequently, according to this belief, if there is anything wrong in a human it is in the balance of relationships between the individual and the environment, or between one part of the individual with other parts. This is what Chinese traditional medicine seeks to address.

The occurrence, development, and growth of diseases are subjected to all kinds of factors. In the prevention, diagnosis, and treatment of diseases, everything has to be considered. This includes the season and local conditions, physical and psychological environment, the patient's age, gender, and general physical conditions, family history, and so on. Because Western medicine is so different in terms of this diagnosis, a patient from Western cultures may feel uncomfortable with a Chinese doctor's personal questions.

The holistic approach of traditional Chinese medicine has also led to the classification of the human body into functional systems based not on anatomical order, but more on relationships. The heart system, for instance, includes not only the heart, as one might expect, but also includes the whole cardiovascular and higher nervous systems.

As a result of traditional Chinese medicine's holistic approach, compound formulas of herbs are used, rather then single herbs, in treating complex diseases. This becomes very obvious when one steps into a health-food store and compares Chinese-made dietary supplements with local products. This, together with the abundance of methods and medicinal materials, makes a traditional Chinese medicine doctor a resourceful practitioner. The doctor scarcely knows limits to his or her ability to heal. It is no exaggeration to say that traditional Chinese medicine is an art of healing.

Individualized Treatment

The human being is also viewed as a wholistic system composed of various parts functioning in cooperation and coordination. The human body is a whole organism with the various parts closely related to each other. Each person is an organic unit that adapts to the environment. Good health is the harmonious coordination among the various parts of the body in relation to the physical environment.

Since everyone is a complete organism subject to different physical and psychological environments, and since every organism is changing all the time, every patient is necessarily considered unique in Chinese medicine. Therefore, everyone must necessarily be treated differently. No two patients are alike, and due to differences in constitution, in physical environment, in food and physical behavior, many factors need to be considered by doctors. Every patient need to be examined individually, and individualized diagnoses must be made. Each person's treatment in illness will be unique. For instance, two persons are both diagnosed by modern medical doctors as suffering from essential hypertension. Yet observation shows that the first patient is robust overall, but suffering from red eyes, constipation, irritability, a thick yellow coat on a red tongue, and a wiry, full pulse. A traditional Chinese medicine doctor would provide a treatment to calm down the patient's liver fire, in order to cleanse the organ. At the same time, the second patient has a pale and frail appearance, loose stools, low energy, a pale, flabby tongue, and a weak pulse. The same doctor would formulate a treatment plan, according to Chinese medicine, to invigorate the patient's kidney yang in order to tonify the kidney.

Special Classification System

Those who are not familiar with traditional Chinese medicine are often daunted by its strange classification systems for both diseases and the properties of medicinal materials. Yet the systems really are rather simple once you learn them. Chinese medicine classifies pathogenic factors into six basic categories: wind, cold, dampness, dryness, heat, and fire. Herbs, meanwhile, are identified according to their properties and which parts of the human body they work on. The four natures are: cold, hot, warm, and cool; and the five properties are: sour, bitter, sweet, pungent, and salty. This seemingly folkish way of classification works in Chinese medicine as a practical tool. According to these systems, the same herb can be used to treat all diseases with a common pathogen. For instance, "wind-dispelling" herbs such as *Herba schizonepetae*, *Radix ledebouriellae* and *Herba ephedrae* (mahuang) are all used for cold, or wind-catching, symptoms, in such diseases as urticaria (wind-rash), rheumatic arthritis with migraine pain (wind arthritis), and acute nephritis with edema of the eyelids (wind-edema). At the same time, peptic ulcer and chronic gastritis, pathogenically different from such wind diseases, are diagnosed as a deficiency of the spleen and stomach yang and therefore treated by the same warming-up therapy. And despite the simplicity, these treatments do work.

Practical Prescription Formulation Principles

Since Chinese medicine is nutrition oriented, it treats various health problems in terms of excess syndromes, deficiency syndromes, and deficiency with excess syndromes. Certain common deficiencies include deficiency in *qi* (life force), in blood, and in yin and yang; common excesses include excess in wind, in cold, heat, dampness, dryness, fire, phlegm, and qi. Methods of treatment for excesses include the diaphoretic method (inducing sweat), febrifugal method (dispelling heat), purgation method, mediation method (harmonizing), tonification method (for deficiency), elimination method (for stagnation of food and blood), and emetic method (inducing vomit).

In case of low immunity and debility on the part of the patient, the first consideration is to strengthen the immune system. When outside factors dominate, the doctor will try to dispel the affecting pathogenic factor in order to strengthen the immune system of the patient. The doctor may also try to strengthen the immune system and eliminate the pathogenic factors at the same time if situation warrants. Between symptoms and the cause, the principle is to treat the cause when it is not acute, and treat the symptoms when they are acute. An experienced doctor may make a choice between a straight treatment or paradoxical treatment. A straight treatment is to treat cold with heat, heat with cold, deficiency with tonification, and excess with discharge. But a paradoxical treatment is a hallmark of a good doctor. When he or she determines that the symptoms are simply superficial ones, and not signs of a greater disorder, the doctor may treat cold with heat, treat heat with heat, treat stasis with tonification rather then discharge, treat excess flow with discharge, and treat diarrhea caused by indigestion with purgation! In such cases, the doctor is actually treating the patient rather than the disease.

A compound prescription normally includes four different component parts. They are called Monarch (principal), Minister (adjuvant), Assistant (auxiliary), and Guide (conductor), respectively. (It is not unusual in Chinese to make use of a hierarchical order as an organizing principle. Principal ingredient provides the main curative action, while adjuvant treatments helps strengthen the principal action; an auxiliary treatment is a corrector ingredient to relieve secondary symptoms or to temper the action of the principal when it is too potent, and a conductor treatment directs the healing action to the affected area or site or acts as a minor ingredient.)

In a compound prescription, drug interactions must be considered. According to Chinese medicine, herbs may be either mutually reinforcing (anemarrrhena/phallodendron), mutually assisting, mutually restraining (to weaken or neutralize each other's action), mutually counteracting (to reduce the potency or toxicity of one), mutually neutralizing, or mutually incompatible.

Resourceful in Treating Many Diseases

Recent developments have shown that more and more people in the world are accepting traditional Chinese medicine treatments. The World Health Organization has listed forty-three diseases that can be treated by acupuncture. There have been numerous reports describing how traditional Chinese medicine treatments have done what Western medicine felt helpless to treat—diseases such as eczema and hemiplegia, and so on.

We all know that thrombus is a tough issue, and few people who are half paralyzed after stroke can hope to stand up again, let alone lead normal lives. A few years ago a product called a plasmin capsule made its appearance in China. It was used for treating strokes and hemiplegia and other blood clotting problems, and so far half a million people have been successfully treated for these symptoms (see article on page 165 for more information on this topic).

Safety Issues in Chinese Medicine

It is true that traditional Chinese medicine lacks modern scientific theory and is weak in quantification in manufacturing. The efficacy of much of Chinese medicine still depends much on the experience of the doctors, as many of its concepts are based on folk categories and are difficult for people outside the Chinese culture to understand. In many respects traditional Chinese medicine needs improvement if it is ever to be fully accepted in Western, or at least non-Chinese, societies.

That said, in approaching using Chinese medicine, a person should carefully consider the following:

Traditional Chinese medicine has been used in China and surrounding countries such Japan, Korea, and Vietnam for several thousand years. It is ridiculous to think that traditional Chinese medicine is lacking clinical trials, and that we have to try them on mice before using them.

It is common knowledge that traditional Chinese medicine formulas are much less toxic and have little or no side effects, and therefore are safer than Western medicine. Western medicines are much more generally toxic to individual systems, and many drugs cause severe side effects, and even, in some cases, death. Yet, because people are unfamiliar with Chinese medicine and its concepts, if there is even one case of harm it causes an uproar.

Despite it all, modern scientists are researching ancient Chinese treatments, and they are proving more and more the validity of traditional Chinese medicine. A good example is the traditional Chinese medical concept of "channels and collaterals" *(jingluo)* in the human body. Scientists at the Institute of Biological Physics in China found that when tapping on the body, sensitive modern instruments could detect high-pitched sounds. This is in total agreement with theories written by Huangdi in China 2,500 years ago.

Traditional Chinese medicine is increasingly using modern sciences to arm itself. Chinese medicine is no longer conducted in an ill-lit shed as is typically described. The availability of advanced technology means the practice is virtually as modern as its Western counterpart. Modern medical equipment has been adopted to make both diagnosis and treatment more reliable. As with anything, we have to keep an open mind and be ready to learn. We are not doing ourselves a favor by denying the existence of good things coming from outside our experience. A general manager of a company once told me that he contracted a strange disease in China and did not go to a Chinese doctor. He said that he knew nothing about Chinese medicine. (I understood that he was just being polite. What he really meant was that Chinese medicine was backward and he did not believe it was effective.) He came back with it and tried to get an American doctor to cure it but the doctor did not know what the disease was. A Chinese practitioner likely would have recognized the disease right away.

The Current Status of Traditional Chinese Medicine in China

Traditional Chinese medicine is an officially recognized medical system in China. It exists and serves the Chinese population side by side with Western medicine. It is the official policy in China that all medical practitioners have to be trained in both systems while majoring in one. There is no discrimination against either system. Patients have the choice to seek either type of treatment, and doctors help them make the choice by providing the necessary information about which tradition is better for treating a particular complaint.

With the two systems complementing each other, Chinese medical care has had numerous achievements—most notably a marked increase in life expectancy and general levels of health. Today, with the two medical traditions no longer in competition, but in a state of mutual assistance, patients are the ones who win. Much credit is due to the policies of the government in allowing this peaceful and mutually beneficial coexistence, but even more credit is due to the medical profession in China which has taken solid steps to integrate traditional Chinese medicine with Western medicine.

Integration with Western Medicine

Traditional Chinese medicine has not been an exclusive medical system, perhaps even since its origins. Reading through Chinese history one can note a clear Chinese interest in exchanges with foreign countries—including exchanges in medical practices. Indeed, one of the most important aspects of interactions between China and India is in the area of medicine. Furthermore, as early as the nineteenth century—when Western medicine was first introduced into China—efforts were made to utilize the strengths of Western medicine to make up for the weaknesses of traditional Chinese medicine.

In 1955, the first class was organized for doctors of Western medicine to study traditional Chinese medicine. At the beginning, diagnosis was typically made according to Western medical theory, while treatment was done according to traditional Chinese medicine or in a combination. The result was evaluated according to the standards of Western medicine. Initial successes led to extensive integration of the two systems.

In later years, cooperation between the two systems extended to prevention and to more clinical treatments. This led to many outstanding research results. Now, it is almost universal to treat common and frequently occurring diseases and difficult and complicated cases with combined treatments from both medical traditions. The experience has enriched both traditional Chinese medicine and Western medical knowledge.

Today, the integration of Western medicine with traditional Chinese medicine represents an outstanding advance. The national policy of coordinated medical science and medical care has produced enormous health benefits for the Chinese people. The combined practice of medicine in China has achieved tremendous results in terms of medical science and clinical treatment, and this in turn has attracted much world attention in recent years.

It is generally recognized that Western medicine is based upon structural theory, using analytical methods to explore various mechanisms in the body, so as to understand how diseases work and to apply medicine to treat the diseases. Typically, treatments either focus on eliminating pathogenic factors—sore muscles or glands, offending excretions or fluids—suppressing abnormal functions of organs, or supplementing what is lacking. This way of thinking, and the clinical performance and actual result of such treatments, are all unidirectional and antagonistic. The more a particular drug is focused on one thing, the more its limitations as well as its toxicity and side effects are manifested in the body.

On the other hand, traditional Chinese medicine is characterized with bidirectional considerations. Even when the formula is highly focused, the end result is often manyfold. For instance, heat-clearing and toxin-resolving herbs used in Chinese medicine not only have a wide range of antibacterial functions, but they also have excellent regulating effects on the immune system. Because most of the material used in treatment in Chinese medicine comes from either plant or animal source, they still retain biological modulating properties. Even single-herb formulas may actually be bidirectional in their modulating functions in treating specific diseases.

Many traditional Chinese formulas for medicine control or reduce the toxicity and side effects of Western drugs. In the treatment of tumors for instance, chemotherapy and radiation often damage blood cells and cause adverse stomach and intestinal reactions. Using sea buckthorn seed oil or reishi broken spores often can facilitate the treatment by preventing unnecessary damage to otherwise healthy tissue and cells.

It is also true that Western medicine can often make up for the weaknesses of traditional Chinese medicine in many ways, and sometimes incorporating Western medical practices even may turn traditional Chinese medicine into a stronger treatment for certain diseases. The many traditional Chinese medicinal formulas developed for injection in recent years are good examples of this phenomenon. Clinical experiences show that treatment with the integrated methods of Chinese and Western medicine can increase the efficacy of the treatment, can create more ways of treatment, can expand the scope of the possible treatments, and can shorten treatment time. Such combined treatments can be more effective than simple traditional Chinese medicine treatments, or treatments with Western medicine, alone and not in tandem with each other. A recent article in *The Chinese Medical Report* announced an encouraging result achieved by the Second Affiliated Hospital of Guangzhou University of Chinese Medicine. The article describes an integrated treatment for hypertension-induced cerebral hemorrhage that reduced death rate by 12.8 percent after twenty-eight days and 18.4 percent after six months when compared to treatment which utilized only Western medical methods. "One plus one is more than two," concluded the researchers.

The combination of Western and traditional medicine in China over the past fifty years has shown to the world that this combined way of thinking works. This, in turn, has laid a solid foundation for further development in the medical profession. When traditional Chinese medicine and Western medicine are combined the whole of mankind benefits.

Yangsheng, or Life Preservation, the Most Common, Yet Most Neglected, Part of Traditional Chinese Medicine

As mentioned earlier, a very important part of traditional Chinese medicine is the practice of life preservation. Recently, I bought a huge publication called *Precious Writings of Chinese Yangsheng* that I thought might be useful in my work. After leafing through the pages I suddenly realized that most parts of this book are virtually unknown in the West, yet at the same time some passages have been translated many times into the English language. Simply put, yangsheng, or life preservation, is based on the principle of modulating the yin and yang, harmonizing the qi and the blood, and maintaining a generally healthy mindset that includes many aspects of daily life such as adjusting one's emotions, manipulating the breath, food therapy, medicinal foods, enjoyment of sex and avoidance of sexual indulgence (this part always get my patients' attention; if only thinking about prevention were as popular as thinking about sex), exercise, dieting, and so on.

Misconceptions about Chinese Food

To those whose knowledge about Chinese food is limited to Chinese restaurants, where dishes are full of red meats, or vegetables swimming in oil, you should know this is not a true representation of Chinese thinking about food. Most Chinese do not eat this way, tending more toward healthy vegetable dishes and grains such as rice.

Let us take a look at the role of Chinese restaurants. To an individual, a Chinese restaurant is a place for rare occasions. It is for celebrating an important event—a birthday, a family reunion, opening of a business, and so on. Or, alternatively, it is a place for building public relations where friends and business contacts are wined and dined so that later business interactions will be easier. Or finally, perhaps, it is an ideal place and occasion to dispense favors to those whom you may need at a later date for something important. In reality, few Chinese dine out often, except on special occasions. In fact, a person who goes to restaurants often will be the subject of public talk. People will question how this person has come to have so much money for expensive food, and they will wonder why the person indulges so much in food. They will consider such an eater some kind of scam-artist, no matter if it's true or not.

At home, Chinese people do not eat the same sort of dishes one sees in a restaurant. When I was young, our families mainly lived on food grains and vegetables. Tofu was welcome, and we had it once in a while, but red meat was really a treat that you could expect only on special occasions, such as a wedding or a major festival like the Chinese New Year. Having meat once a month was considered the "good life" in my house, and once a week was only for a rich family. Plain tea and simple food is the way of life for most people.

Today it is a little different. With improved living standards people have begun to indulge in meat and fish more often, though general perception is that plain tea and simple food are still healthier.

In fact, for the sake of our health, plain tea and simple food should not be purely an economic consideration. A balanced diet has always been the ideal way of eating. Problems would occur if you become choosy and indulge in food high in fats or sugars. For instanct, *The Yellow Emperor's Cannon of Medicine*, compiled in the third century B.C., instructs Chinese doctors first and foremost to "investigate the food, beverage, and living conditions of the patients" in order to diagnose correctly and cure effectively. There is no doubt: Moderation in food intake is essential. The Pyramid scripture said: "We live off one fourth of what we eat and the doctors live off the rest." This statement not only pinpoints the necessity of fasting and moderation, but also the idea that what we eat is important to the general maintenance of our health.

Shiyang and Shiliao, or Health Preservation Through Proper Diet and Dietary Therapy

Traditional Chinese medicine maintains that proper diet is of the utmost importance for good health. People should eat various kinds of food. For instance, health manuals advise people with liver trouble to eat more sweet foods such as glutinous rice, beef, dates, and kui (a vegetable); people with heart trouble to eat sour foods such as red bean, plum, and Chinese chives; people with lung troubles should eat bitter foods including wheat, mutton, apricot, and xie (a vegetable); people with digestive troubles should eat salty foods including soybean, pork, chestnut, and pulse plant leaves; and people with kidney troubles should take pungent foods including yellow corn, chicken, peach, and scallions. In general, people with health problem should try adjusting the diet first and foremost. If that fails, only then should the patient turn to medicine.

The general goal of dietary therapy is to use different food items targeted to different health conditions or illnesses. This treatment can occur with or without herbs. On the whole, traditional Chinese medicine has always attached great importance to dietary therapy. The tradition maintains that food and herb medicine are of the same origin, and that foods contain medication. In most cases herbs are often bitter and pungent, not as tasty and delicious as food. The long-term use of certain herbs may, unlike foods, affect the stomach. Used properly, dietary therapy may help the patient achieve a therapeutic result while enjoying good food.

In dietary therapy, foods are divided into three categories: warm-hot, cool-cold, and near neutral. As diseases are classified into categories too—yin, yang, cold, hot, deficiency, and excess—the principle in treatment is to use food having the opposite properties of the diseases. For instance, you should eat foods having cold properties to counter diseases caused by heat, and use foods having a warm property to counter diseases caused by cold. You should supplement in case of deficiency, and discharge in case of excess.

For yang and hot diseases, the objective is to dispel heat and eliminate toxins. Therefore, it is appropriate to use foods with cool and cold properties—such as watermelon, bitter melon, mung bean, eggplants, millets, banana, rabbit meat, and duck meat. If the heat has already hurt the lungs, and the patient suffers from a dry cough, treatment should aim at dispelling the heat, moistening and diffusing the lung. Fritillaria-pear rice soup, loquat leaf rice soup, and other such dishes should be consumed. If the heat has affected the blood, and the patient suffers vexation and sleeplessness, treatment should aim at purifying blood formation and cooling the blood. In this case, bamboo leaf rice soup, talc rice soup, and the like may be taken. If the pathogenic heat is internalized and constipation occurs, treatment should aim at dispelling heat and moistening the intestines; senna leaf rice soup, dried or fresh rehmannia root rice soup, banana cooked in rock sugar, and so on may be administered. If damp heat accumulates, hurting the intestines and related channels, and the patient is suffering from diarrhea with abdominal urgency and pressure in the rectum, treatment should aim at dispelling heat, eliminating toxins, and dissolving dampness; rice soup with purple amaranthus, areca tea with purslane, or lonicera tea with brown sugar should be consumed by the patient.

For yin and cold diseases, the general principle is to warm the yang and dissipate cold. The doctor should suggest that warm-hot foods, such as ginger, celery, onion, garlic, dates, Chinese chestnut, litchi, mutton, eel, and so on, be consumed. If the stomach and spleen is hurt because of too much cold, and the patient is having stomach pains and loose and watery stool, treatment should aim at warming up the stomach and dissipating cold by taking rice soup with fresh ginger, amomum cake, and cardamom bread. If the pathogenic cold is very strong, and the patient is experiencing congestion and chest and back pains, treatment should aim at freeing the yang and dissipating the cold with warm and acrid items; rice soup with shaved cinnamon bark, coix soup with radish seeds, soup with trichosanthes root, and wine may be used. In case of recovery after long illness or post-labor vacuity, and if the patient is feeling cold and experiencing pain in the stomach with watery stool, or cold in the womb with uterine bleeding, treatment should aim at warming the interior, dispelling cold and supplementing vacuity. Veal stewed with dong quai, rehmannia, chicken cubes cooked with Chinese pepper, and so on will be effective in these cases.

For diseases of vacuity, supplementation should be the general approach, but distinctions have to be made to identify which of the following categories it belongs to: yang deficiency, yin deficiency, qi deficiency, blood deficiency. Choose the appropriate treatments according to which condition a qualified practitioner of traditional Chinese medicine diagnoses.

Dietary therapy not only helps chronic complaints, but also can be employed for acute diseases as a complimentary treatment. In this respect, tea has long played an extraordinary role in health and fitness. *Ben cao shi yi*, an addendum to the *Materia Medica* written in the year A.D. 739, claimed: "Medicines are for particular diseases respectively, but tea is medicine for all diseases." The difference between shiyang and shiliao is that in the case of the former the person is enjoying general good health and has no particular health problems. Manipulating what you eat to maintain good health is prevention in the pure sense of the word. A careful reading about the different properties of food items can give you a good understanding of ancient knowledge useful for keeping you healthy in your daily life. Generally speaking, your physical constitution and body shape, the local weather and seasons, and other local conditions have to be taken into consideration in deciding your menu. See a qualified Chinese medical practitioner if you want more information.

Create a Healthy Lifestyle of Your Own

Traditional Chinese medicine is a complicated medical system, but it is not beyond comprehension. As a matter of fact, many people who have no training in traditional Chinese medicine use its traditions to maintain good health every day. Tremendous information, quality health products, and well-trained professionals are available today for health-conscious men and women to use.

There are a variety of products based on traditional Chinese medicine that we can make use of. Beside patent formulas, there are also herb teas, herb pillows, herb cushions, herb baths, and even music compositions that can be used to treat different ailments. You can include herbs of different properties in your own cooking. Many herbs can be used together with conventional food items to make delicious and enjoyable dishes.

It is not easy to switch to something that works slowly in a culture that emphasizes immediate gratification. But nature will reward those who have the courage to try and the patience to learn. Let us take traditional Chinese medicine seriously and leave our cultural biases aside, learning something useful for our good health in the process. After reading and understanding the basics, you will have more control over your own health by doing something about it.

Treating Cardiovascular Disease with Traditional Chinese Medicine

≈ by Xingwu Liu ≈

The Lament of a Chinese Doctor

This story begins on June 29, 2001. A doctor who practices traditional Chinese medicine called me on that day. He said that if what had been in the news was correct and no major facts were missing, Vice President Dick Cheney might not have to get surgery to have a defibrillator implanted in his chest in order to restore regular rhythm of his heartbeat. In fact, he thought it was a pity the vice president of the world's most powerful country had no access to a popular Chinese medical formula called Plasmin, which had been used successfully for years in China to treat half a million people for just the conditions that Cheney suffered from.

I told the doctor that if what he said was true, this was very enlightening. The fact that traditional Chinese

medicine, a medical system that has existed for many thousand years, is still regarded as unscientific and lacking in clinical standards by many in advanced industrial countries is a sad and strange thing.

Prompted by this call, the present writer in time tried to contact the American Association of Cardiovascular and Pulmonary Rehabilitation (AACVPR) to participate in the association's upcoming annual meeting and exhibition as a way of promoting an understanding of this medicine, Plasmin. To my surprise, after reviewing the description of the formula that I sent to the event's organizer, I was politely told that it was not appropriate for me to attend their event, and they wished me good luck elsewhere. When asked to explain, he finally said that the exhibition is only for equipment manufacturers, leaving me wondering why they asked to see the description of the formula in the first place.

The Magnitude of the Problem

According to statistics, 15 million people in the world die of cerebral and cardiovascular diseases each year. In the United States alone, every year about 700,000 Americans are struck down by a stroke, and about 170,000 of these people eventually die. The rest who live often do so with different degrees of disabilities including paralysis (hemiplegia and dysphagia), cognitive deficits (apraxia and agnosia), speech problems (aphasia and dysarthria), emotional difficulties, daily living problems, and pain (not only for the patients, but also their families).

What Can Conventional (Western)
Medicine Do about Strokes?

The degree of success that conventional medicine has in treating stroke victims depends upon the stage of disease. Three stages of treatments are suggested for such patients: prevention, therapy immediately after stroke, and post-stroke rehabilitation. Prevention is important to those who are subject to such risk factors as hypertension, arterial fibrillation, and complications from diabetes. It is also important to everyone because although people forty-five years of age and up are at a greater risk, formation of blood clots that cause ischemic stroke can happen to just about anybody.

Currently there are three kinds of drugs conventional medicine uses to prevent or treat stroke—antithrombotics (anti-platelet agents and anticoagulants), thrombolytics, and neuroprotective agents. Antithrombotics are meant to prevent the formation of blood clots that, if lodged in a cerebral artery, cause strokes. This is achieved through antiplatelet agents, which decrease the activity of platelets that are partially responsible for the blood clotting. Aspirin is the most well-known antiplatelet agent; clopidogrel and ticlopidine are two other common medicines. Anticoagulants are used to reduce stroke risk by reducing the clotting property of the blood itself. The best known are warfarin, heparin, streptokinase, and urokinase. Most of these have to be administered under the supervision of a very experienced doctor.

Thrombolytic agents are used for treating an ongoing, acute, ischemic stroke. The most frequently used is recombinant tissue Plasminogen activator (rt-PA). This has to be used intravenously within three hours of stroke symptom onset to be effective.

Neuroprotectants, meanwhile, are drugs that are used to protect the brain from secondary injury by stroke. These medicines include calcium antazgonists, glutamate antagonists, opiate antagonists, antioxidants, apoptosis inhibitors, and so on.

Surgery can be performed to prevent strokes, to treat acute stroke, or to repair vascular damage of malformations in and around the brain. The most frequently used methods are carotid endarterectomy and extracranial/intracranial bypass. While the former is a procedure to remove fatty deposits from the inside of carotid arteries, the latter is a procedure to restore blood flow to a blood-deprived area of brain tissue by rerouting a healthy artery.

In spite of these treatments, as mentioned earlier, out of the 700,000 Americans who are hit by a stroke every year, 170,000 still will die, and the rest do suffer various degrees of disability as a result of their strokes.

What is called rehabilitation therapy is a complicated post-stroke effort intended to restore function in parts of the body disabled as a result of the stroke. It also is used to help the disabled to fight post-stroke depression. This exhausting and often frustrating enterprise may involved a large team, including a rehabilitation doctor, a nurse, dietitian, physical therapist, occupational therapist, recreational therapist, speech therapist, social worker (in lieu of, or together with relatives), psychologist or psychiatrist, and even a chaplain. With all these people at hand, the patient still can not be sure that he or she may be cured of any of the disabilities.

Yes, conventional doctors and professionals work very hard and have developed many ways to deal with stroke and other cardiovascular diseases. But there is a long way to go for conventional medicine to provide an effective prevention and real cures. Just twenty-four hours after a thrombus is formed, it is enclosed tightly by a shell of collagen. To remove a thrombus, this tough shell has to be opened and removed. That is why people in medical circles have long known that whoever creates an effective collagenase would hold the key to curing thrombus.

Stroke Treatment by Alternative Medical Systems

There are many medical systems in the world and conventional medicine is merely the offshoot of modern chemical industry. For centuries, human cultures had their own medical systems that employed herbs and minerals to cure diseases. Most developed countries have long given up their original medical systems and adopted the new medical science. In this way, other practices have been relegated to a primitive and backward status. In the dilemma of industrial life, a major alternative to conventional medicine, namely traditional Chinese medicine, stands out.

Traditional Chinese Medicine

In recent years, efforts have been made in the West to rediscover traditional Chinese medicine. However, it is still far too early to say that many people understand that system; the system has too great a history to be understood fully in so short a time. To a few in the West, traditional Chinese medicine is a combination of poetry and science. But to the great majority in this part of the world it is still a mystery.

Traditional Chinese medicine is characterized by its emphasis on prevention, wholistic diagnosis, and natural individualized treatment. In today's world of pollution, modern industrial overload, and abuse of pathogenic chemicals, the benefit of these characteristics in treatment by traditional Chinese medicine is not to be ignored. Traditional Chinese medicine has contributed greatly to the welfare and prosperity of the Chinese nation and other neighboring countries. Today, when science and technology have developed to a new height, traditional Chinese medicine still remains an independent medical system with vitality and great potential.

Traditional Chinese medicine has made tremendous progress in the People's Republic of China in the last fifty-odd years since its founding. Mao Zedong might have not really believed in traditional Chinese medicine, as evidenced by his personal physician, but either China was too poor to afford medical care using Western medicine or Mao did not think it was right to dismiss outright something that has been going on for so many thousand years. In time, he made a serious effort in promoting the integration of traditional Chinese medicine with Western medicine. According to this policy, all Chinese doctors have to be trained in both traditional Chinese medicine and Western medicine, though they major in one or the other, and all Chinese hospitals have to provide both traditional Chinese medical and Western medical diagnosis and treatment whatever their principal functions are. A few years ago, the annual cost for health care per person in China was only $18 USD, and the people there enjoyed almost the same lifespan as people in the United States. At present there are more than 2,400 traditional Chinese medical hospitals, with 210,000 beds and more than 540,000 traditional Chinese medicine health workers, 31 traditional Chinese medicine universities, 50 professional schools, and 170 research institutions in mainland China. Altogether, there are more than a millions employees in traditional Chinese medicine, and related fields. With the help of modern science and technology, traditional Chinese medicine has made some outstanding achievements. Its successful maintenance of good health in the Orient, especially in China, is a strong indication that it is a dynamic and viable health system that deserves our respect and warrants our humble learning.

The Story of Plasmin

One of the recent major developments in traditional Chinese medicine is the amazing story of Plasmin, an enteric capsule made of lumbricus (earthworm) extract.

Chinese have been using earthworms in medicine for thousands of years. The famous compendium of herbal traditions and lore, the *Materia Medica*, describes this medicine as: "salty in taste, cold in property, and efficacious in clearing the heart, invigorating blood circulation, dissolving stasis, opening up channels, curing stroke, hemiplegia, and infantile convulsion." The text also pointed out that earthworms have self-dissolving ingredients.

Generally speaking, the Chinese have been quite successful in the treatment of disabilities as a result of stroke. Famous formulas for these ailment include *bu yang huan wu tang* (Decoction for Invigorating Yang), which consists of astragalus, dong quai *(radix angelica sinensis)*, red peony root *(Radix paeoniae rubra)*, lumbricus, ligusticum *(Rhizoma ligustici Chuangxiong)*, peach kernel *(Persicae semen)*, and carthamus flower. The designed action of this medicine is to tonify vital energy, promote blood circulation, and dredge the meridian passage. It is mainly used for stroke aftereffects such as hemiplegia, facial deviation, aphasia, slobbering, lower limbs paralysis, and incontinence to urinate. Sometimes this formula does effectively get people who have been paralyzed to stand again, but it is only sporadically reliable, at best.

With one death of cerebral cardiovascular diseases every minute in Beijing alone, and 1.85 million to 2.19 million first-time strokes taking place every year in China—resulting in a total of 4.29 to 6.20 million patients in the country—efforts were needed to develop something that worked better. During the 1970s, Professor Shan Hongren, a well-known Chinese biochemist, was participating in a research project trying to find effective nonsurgical method to treat eccyesis (a pregnacy disorder) when he and his colleagues discovered that an extract from earthworms had distinct effect on enzymatic functions. For this discovery, he was honored with the United Nations Science Conference Award in 1978. Since then, twenty years of hard work paid off. Working together with Everpride Pharmaceuticals, he successfully extracted the effective ingredients from earthworms and designed a product called Plasmin in 1994.

The response was simply overwhelming. More than twenty hospitals in different parts of the country conducted clinical trials, and their clinical results confirmed the effectiveness of Plasmin on a wide range of complications related to stroke. The rate of efficacy in such cases is generally more than 90 percent, and its convenience of use, nontoxicity, and lack of any side effect are acclaimed by all. Doctors are sure that if taken long term the result will be even better, as Plasmin has proven effective not only during the acute period and the restoration period in strokes, but also good for the aftereffects period.

In the past three years, there have been numerous stories of the success of Plasmin. Thousands of patients with disabilities as results of strokes were cured, and many of those who had been paralyzed for ten or twenty years stood up and began to take care of themselves.

Plasmin has been very well received by the Chinese medical profession. Dr. Dong Ziqiang, associate professor and coctor at the Chinese Medicine Hospital of Pingdingshan in Henan Province, called Plasmin "a breakthrough in the medicine category, an ideal medicine for preventing and treating cerebral infarction and for promoting the rehabilitation of such patients." Professor Wu Songgang, Dean of the School of Biological Science in Fujian Normal University, described Plasmin as "a blessing from nature." Dr. Wu Shijiu, a professor at the Diabetes Division of the South Hospital affiliated to the First Military Medical University of Guangshou (Canton), pointed out that Plasmin "not only has the effect to reduce the high sugar and fat levels for diabetics, but also the ability to treat the complications such as peripheral neuron-pathological changes, limb numbness and limb pain... Plasmin has opened a new page for the treatment of diabetes and its complications, and the drug should be more widely used."

In 1996, Plasmin was approved by the Chinese government for use as a new medicine to treat the effects of heart disease and heart attack. In 1997, Plasmin was first endorsed by the China Gerontology Foundation and then endorsed a year later by the China Gerontology Association Rehabilitation Committee. In 1999, it was listed as a key promotional product by the China Medical Society, a prestigious organization of health professionals that serves as the main advisory organization to the Chinese government. In the same year, Plasmin was listed by the China Administration and Supervision Bureau as a class-two nationally protected traditional Chinese medicinal formula, and in 2000 it is officially listed in the Chinese pharmacopoeia.

As a medicine for the average person, Plasmin comes in a capsule form. The medical matter is made of an extract of a particular strain of earthworms endemic to China. The medicine itself is thrombolytic and fibrinolytic and includes three important enzymes: fibrinolysin, profibrinlolysin activator, and, as was long ago predicted, collagenase.

How Plasmin Works

A capsule of this medicine carries Plasmin into the intestines, and Plasmin is absorbed into the blood circulation system in the human body. As Plasmin has a strong affinity to a thrombus, or blood clot, it attaches to any it finds. The specific collagenase opens up and discomposes the collagen shell around the thrombus, and fibrinolysin enters the thrombus with profibrinolysin activator that activates more fibrinolysin. Fibrinolysin dissolves the fibrin inside the thrombus. As the thrombus disappears, the blood vessel is opened and normal blood circulation restored to the patient.

According to clinical trials, Plasmin is nontoxic and good for long-term use without any side effects. It helps maintain a healthy balance between hemolysis and hemostasis, improves microcirculation, repairs damaged nerves cells, and reduces blood sugar. It also provides many trace elements and vitamins needed by the human body.

Plasmin is recommended for those who have the need to improve their blood circulation, especially those who suffer from ischemic cerebral cardiovascular difficulties, both acute and chronic—such as cerebral thrombus, cerebral embolism, pulmonary embolism, angitis, myocardial infarction, arteriosclerosis, hyperplasminemia, platelet hypercoagulability, the tendency to develop thrombus, high cholesterol, high blood fat, and high blood sugar. It is also good for those with diabetic complications such as nervous pathological changes and microcirculation disturbances

Plasmin is easy to use. But as a caution, it is not recommended for those who have a bleeding tendency, those who suffer from mitral insufficiency and bradycardia, those who are on warfarin, and women during menstruation. When it is used in China, Chinese doctors do not preclude woman in pregnancy.

It is reported that a few patients who are sensitive to high concentrations of protein may experience allergic reactions to Plasmin, causing rashes to break out. In such cases, the patients may reduce the dosage for a while and then increase to normal intake gradually. Such allergies are rare.

Up to the time this article was written, half a million people have found Plasmin to assuage a variety of ills, particularly those who are paralyzed as a result of stroke or suffering from other disabilities such as apraxia, agnosia, aphasia, and dysarthria. The policy of integrating Western medicine with traditional Chinese medicine has made this "unconventional treatment" virtually available to anybody.

Here in the West, we have to work harder to overcome the adverse influence of the vested interests of pharmacological companies in order to eliminate ethnic and professional bias. After all, this is such an important issue that concerns all of us.

Herbs
for
Beauty

Herbal Aphrodisiacs

⇝ by Feather Jones ⇜

T he word "aphrodisiac" is derived from Aphrodite, the Greek goddess of love. According to mythology, she was born of the foam of the sea and was married to Hephaestus, a very ugly god. Her lustiness and passions strayed to gods like Zeus, Hermes, Ares, and Bacchus, the god of wine and drunken orgies. She consequently got pregnant and had a son, Cupid, whose Greek name is Eros, from where we get the word "erotic."

Many early Pagan beliefs concerning love and sexuality are intact even today. For instance, mistletoe, of which Aphrodite ordained that everyone who passed under it should receive a kiss, became an emblem of love. Red roses came to be the symbol of pleasure when Roman brides and bridegrooms were crowned with roses. They are still the desired bouquets for Valentine's Day. Pansies were used for their

potency in love charms, hence they are nicknamed "heartsease." It is this flower that plays such an important part as a love-charm in Shakespeare's *A Midsummer Night's Dream.*

What Is an Aphrodisiac?

An aphrodisiac is a substance or condition that excites sexual desire, or enhances performance and endurance. From a larger point of view, sexual attraction begins from the time two people start thinking about each other in an intimate way. The memory of intimacy and a romantic encounter can linger in one's consciousness for a long time. One can think of an aphrodisiac as an aid that pulls and attracts you into a desired physical relationship.

Spiritual Vitality

Sexual vitality correlates to physical and spiritual vitality. It motivates us to be better persons. Sexual energy carries our life force. We shouldn't suppress it or treat it in other than a positive way. Sexuality is one of the most intimate aspects of life, yet many people perform the act without intimacy. It's a grand distortion to think sex is only for procreation. Sex can be a doorway to higher consciousness. The life force that is used to create a child can also be used to journey into other realms of existence. Looking deeply into one another's eyes can be transformative. Forgetting one's separateness during the experience is one of the most powerful forces on the planet. We are always seeking balance that comes through partnering. We carry both male and female attributes within each of us. When we seek those balances within ourselves, we draw to ourselves a partner who is balanced in the same way. Allowing the heart and mind to express love is a key ingredient in building the essence of spiritual vitality.

Sex is the ultimate event for us to plan and celebrate. At the same time, sex also should be spontaneous, as spontaneity has its ritualistic uses. In general, each of us should stay open, evaluate present beliefs about sexuality, and explore the boundaries. Sexuality is our birthright and our heritage as humans.

Elements of Sexuality

The Orgasm

An orgasm is more than a measured physiological response. It's an emotional coupling, where the vital force of kundalini is activated during the peak of orgasm. Kundalini is the name given to the serpent-like energy coiled at the base of the spine. It is an untapped energy source that resides within the body, which carries a life force that is the expression of the energy of creation. This force travels the chakra system along the spinal cord and is awakened during heightened meditation or during revelationary moments—when we feel energy released at the cellular level. We can make room for this vital force within the body to experience healing and transformation. The *Kama Sutra*, the Hindu book that describes the sacred art of lovemaking, describes spiritual ecstasy attained by allowing kundalini to travel up through the body and around the head. This links one to the natural Goddess source inside oneself. Sex can provide the energy through which one can emerge into higher consciousness.

How to Set the Mood

You can use the following elements to help set the mood for a more spiritual lovemaking session with your partner.

Music: Make it uplifting without being invasive; maybe soft and sultry jazz or blues, nothing too loud or distracting.

Essential oils: Scent is a communication system, and we can send messages through scents. Wear selected essential oils as perfumes. Rose is known for sparking sexual desire and opening the heart; ylang-ylang, whose name means the "flower of flowers," or jasmine, exotic and heady, can unlock our sexual appeal. Other scents include honeysuckle, amber, and sandalwood—these help center your focus and warm your body. Essential oils can be distributed various ways. A few drops on a lit candle will fill the air with aroma but also burns quickly. Use the oils in a spray by putting five to ten drops essential oil into one-half cup of warm water in a spray bottle.

Lighting: Scented candles such as cinnamon, lilac, or spice have a stimulating yet relaxing effect. A fireplace on a cool evening can also be very romantic.

Hot bath for two: For serenity and focus, soak in a hot bath with aromatic bath salts of essential oils of lavender. You may also try lemon, for an uplift, or rose geranium for regulating the body's natural hormonal rhythms.

Flowers: Place fresh-cut flowers or a rose petal potpourri by the bed.

Food: A light, nutritious, and easy-to-digest dessert can provide some extra energy needed for a night of passion.

Massage: Touch is an intimate conversation without words. Massage your partner from head to toes. Do not overlubricate; use just enough oil to create a smooth touch. Be sure to include the erogenous zones on the back of the knees and inner thighs. Essential oils can be used here—for example, ten drops of rose oil per one ounce of sweet almond oil will deeply relax muscles and act as a mental and emotional tonic. Rose is also a gentle antidepressant.

Phone: You may want to take the phone off the hook and turn off your cell phone so you won't be disturbed.

Intention

Making intimacy a ritual with intent can make all the difference to the experience. It doesn't have to be elaborate to be a lasting, loving event—simply set your intent together at the ceremonial beginning of lovemaking. Create a ritual where you acknowledge what you are doing. You can say words like: "I intend to heal all parts of myself and the Earth. I intend to merge fully with my partner in universal love. I intend to remember who I am as a universal spirit. I intend to fly with freedom of thought." Perhaps light a candle, drink ceremonial tea, and smudge with sage, sweetgrass, or cedar. Always remember that your thoughts create your reality. Be playful, have fun, and love one another.

General Contributions to Reproductive Health

Here are some tips to help you generally improve your reproductive health.

Exercise generally in a mild to moderate way.

Avoid excesses in alcohol, tobacco (as it decreases blood flow), antidepressants (which lower libido), high-fat foods, and anabolic steroids.

Use yoga to make you limber.

Generally rest well.

Drink plenty of water.

Viagra Information

Viagra is a prescription drug used for erectile impotence in men. It costs about $10 a pill, assists sustaining blood flow to the penis, and is an enzyme inhibitor that works by enhancing nitric oxide in the body and causing vasodilation. Side effects include headaches, permanent vision problems, heart attack, anxiety, heart stress (and perhaps, in some cases, persistent "viagravation" to women—meaning men won't leave them alone).

A healthy sexual response cycle is needed to maintain physical health. The cycle includes a time for foreplay, a plateau achievement, an orgasm, and then relaxation. Viagra is actually an intervention in this process.

Impotence

There are many reasons for impotence. The absence of arousal can be from emotional distraction. It may be the relationship that's expressing impotence. If it's a long-term symptom, check blood sugar levels too, as they may be low. Also look for sluggish adrenal function, or a lifestyle without creativity. If one does not stimulate the creative life force regularly, one can experience diminished circulation, low immune strength, and a low procreative force. As the body's central organ of sexual response is the mind, an individual needs to find joy and creative stimulation within him- or herself first. Look to lifestyle, particularly a sedentary domestic life or degrading occupation, in these cases.

Sometimes impotence is due to diseases such as diabetes, which causes poor circulation, or tobacco smoking, which constricts blood vessels. Alcohol dulls the central nervous system, including those nerves that stimulate the penis. Other recreational drugs, and some prescription drugs for high blood pressure and for ulcers, can cause similar problems. In traditional Chinese medicine, impotence and premature ejaculation can be the consequences of overindulgence, losing qi, and fatigue. Practice moderation in all things.

Herbal Alternatives to Viagra

Certain botanicals can strengthen the sex organs and stimulate sexual arousal. Some work as a tonic, and some increase blood supply as circulatory stimulants; some bring a greater awareness to local areas via tissue irritation, and some open the heart to receive greater love. (Always check with your doctor or herbalist.)

Ashwagandha *(Withania somnifera)* sometimes called "Indian ginseng": Though literal translation of ashwagandha is "that which has the smell of a horse," this comes from its reputation as a male tonic. Treats male impotence and female infertility as well as spermatorrhea (involuntary emission of semen without orgasm). A reproductive and nervous system restorative for wasting diseases, nervous exhaustion, and loss of muscular energy. Also strengthens the mind and enhances memory.

Bee pollen: Contains gonadotropic hormone, which stimulates the sex glands and supports testosterone production.

High in aspartic acid, it helps rejuvenate the sex glands, improving energy and endurance. Due to its high nutrient content, it helps with prostate problems. Use whatever is collected bioregionally and free of lead.

Cocoa: Contains caffeine, theobromine, and phenylethylamine, a natural antidepressant and stimulant. Chocolate has its own reputation for inspiring romance.

Damiana *(Turnera aphrodisiaca):* This small aromatic, resiny shrub grows wild in Mexico, Texas, and South America, and was an aphrodisiac for the Maya people. A stimulating nerve tonic, it is also a remedy for mild depression. It lifts the spirits and calms the nerves, regulates hormonal activity, and rejuvenates kidney energy. It treats nervous exhaustion, anxiety, impotence, and premature ejaculation, and it increases sex drive. It can be used for anxiety about sexual matters in both men and women, upping sexual interest and triggering erotic dreams. It piques erotic urges and enhances clitorine sensitivity.

Ginger *(Zingiber officianlis):* Stimulating, spicy, and warming, ginger increases circulation to the abdominal region.

Ginkgo *(Ginkgo biloba):* Ginkgo boosts blood flow in the penis without increasing blood pressure. It enhances reflex excitability of the sacral region of the spinal cord and can be used to treat arterial erectile dysfunction, though it may take six to eight weeks to see benefits.

Ginseng, both Chinese *(Panax ginseng)* **and Siberian** *(Eleuthrococcus senticosus):* These both help restore sexual function, and are traditionally used for impotence, increasing sperm production and motility, and prolonging coitus and building sexual stamina. They appears to boost libido through direct action on the higher brain centers, treating some cases of impotence. Siberian ginseng has a slower reviving action than the cured Chinese ginsengs in cases of general exhaustion, weakness, and stress.

Ginseng is clinically shown to be beneficial in treating erectile dysfunction.

Gotu kola *(Centella asiatica)*: Not really an aphrodisiac, but more of a tonic and nervous system rejuvenator. Gotu kola is an adaptogen to the endocrine glands, and helps to bring the body to balance. It also softens the skin and enhances the sensory nerves that innervate the skin, making one more sensitive to touch.

Hawthorne *(Crataegus* spp.): As a cardiovascular strengthener and tonic, hawthorne keeps the heart and blood vessels free of congesting fats and impurities. It has an uplifting influence on the emotions as well.

Kava *(Piper mesthysticum)*: A mood moderator, kava can open the heart when one is feeling closed down. It relaxes the muscles if the body feels tight.

Licorice *(Glycyrrhiza* spp.): Contains saponins that revitalize the adrenal glands for deeper energy reserves and for normalizing ovulation.

Muira puama *(Ptochopetalum olacoides)*: Also called potency wood, this Brazilian shrub is a central nervous system stimulant and tonic. It enhances libido and treats frigidity according to a French study. It also enhances erectile engorgement in both men and women.

Oat seed *(Avena* spp.): Thought to be a sexual appetite booster, oat seed has a positive effect on blood flow, keeping the arteries to the pelvic area open and providing a better erection and vaginal lubrication. It nourishes the nerves and increases sensitivity to touch, and it keeps your energy intact when the action heats up.

Passion flower *(Passiflora* spp.): This vining plant is a good mood elevator. It decreases arteriole constriction, dissolves stress, and melts tension.

Sarsaparilla *(Smilax* spp., or *Aralia nudicalis):* A tonic with phytosterols that resemble steroidal anabolic hormones, sarsaparilla helps the male reproductive organs to function more normally.

Saw palmetto *(Serenoa serrulata):* The berries of this Florida palm exude a distinctive musky odor and support male testosterone production in cases of enlarged or inflamed prostate gland. This herb can be used safely when a boost to male sex hormone levels is needed. It relieves congestion and tones the testicles, ovaries, and uterus, thus increasing sperm count and motility.

Seaweed, all varieties: Seaweed gets your juices flowing by nourishing the glandular and nervous systems, using the minerals to regulate metabolism, blood pressure, and sexuality. Minerals fortify electrical activity so nerves can fire smoothly.

Suma *(Pfaffia paniculata):* A Brazilian ginseng, it has actions similar to other varieties. It restores strength and increases resistance to stress and fatigue.

Virginia snake root, or Indian root *(Aristolochia* spp.): This herb is used to prevent emotional distraction during love making, as well as for impotence and frigidity caused by poor circulation and sluggish digestive function.

Yohimbe *(Corynanthe yohimbe):* Sometimes called West African brown bark, this plant helps restore erectile function by increasing arterial blood flow to tissue of the penis and decreasing blood flow from the penis. It increases sexual appetite and may influence functional impotence. It should be used for short-term acute need, to be used just before lovemaking and with caution. It is considered an antidiuretic with major cardiac and nervous system side effects such as high blood pressure. It also increases heart rate, anxiety, headaches, irritability, pelvic hyperemia, water retention, and liver and kidney disease. It carries similar red flags to Viagra and is not to be used with tranquilizers, narcotics, antihistamines, or large amounts of alcohol. Yohimbine is one of the active constituents found in this plant that has been pharmaceutically manufactured for men with physical or psychological problems in achieving and maintaining erections. Before Viagra, yohimbine was the only FDA-approved medication for treating impotence. One advantage of using the herb over the drug is that it contains a variety of buffering compounds that lessen the side effects. Yohimbe also mildly inhibits serotonin that has shown to lead to loss of interest in sex. Anything that inhibits serotonin has apparent aphrodisiacal influence.

Flower Essences

Flower essences are subtle yet powerful remedies that address any emotional issues that may need attention.

Basil: Integrates sexuality and spirituality.

Hibiscus: Endows the ability to respond sexually with heart warmth and physical passion.

Larch: Helps men who feel inadequate.

Pink monkeyflower: Endows ability to express love and intimacy without fear; also it is used for shame that may be connected to past abuse or rejection.

The Kitchen Pharmacy—Recipes for Love
Lover's Oil

5   drops rosewood oil

5   drops rosemary oil

3   drops tangerine oil

3   drops lemon oil

Lover's Oil enhances any relationship. Just consecrate a candle with Lover's Oil, and light it half an hour before meeting your lover. You'll see sparks all night.

Cupid's Tea

1	tablespoon ginger, grated
5–10	cloves
2–3	sticks cinnamon
4–5	peppercorns
7–10	cardamom pods
¼	teaspoon vanilla extract (optional)
	Soymilk and honey to taste (optional)

Simmer all spices in 3 cups of water for 20 minutes. Strain and add optional vanilla, soymilk, and honey. A warm and stimulating cup of tea.

Love Pills

When making your own pills you can tailor them for certain purposes. The general recipe would include an ounce of any powdered herb to one-quarter ounce gum arabic. Your powdered herb can be a combination of any of the herbs mentioned above—a total of four to five different herbs make a good formula.

Mix to the consistency of dough by adding water a tablespoon at a time. Mix thoroughly and roll out with your fingers to a small pill size. You can shape them as little hearts or other creative icons. At this point, you can cover them with chocolate, licorice, or cinnamon by putting them in a plastic bag with the desired powdered herb dust. Lay your pills atop a piece of wax paper to dry for one to two days. When totally dry, place in a pill jar for storage. Two to three pills each, one-half hour before lovemaking, is a middle of the road dosage. It just depends on how fast you like to drive.

Red to Orange Chakra Express

This herbal wine is easy to make in your kitchen. It has a warming and wild energy and a zesty flavor. Be mindful, guarana contains caffeine. The recipe is still great without it.

½ ounce allspice

½ ounce fennel seed

⅛ ounce cloves

1 ounce astragulus

½ ounce nutmeg

1 ounce ginger

½ ounce cinnamon

½ ounce star anise

½ ounce bay leaf

⅛ ounce guarana

1 bottle Beaujolais or burgundy wine

Use seeds, roots, barks and leaves that are as whole as possible. This recipe makes about one quart. Start with a one-half gallon canning jar and cover herbs liberally with a good Beaujolais or burgundy wine. Allow it to sit for 2 weeks before straining. You can warm the wine before sipping or serve at room temperature.

For Further Study

Chia, Mantak & Maneewan. *Cultivating Female Sexual Energy.* Austin, Texas: Healing Tao Books, 1989.

Green, James. *The Male Herbal: Health Care for Boys and Men.* Freedom, Calif.: Crossing Press, 1991.

Weed, Susun. *The Wise Woman Herbal.* Woodstock, New York: Ash Tree Publications, 1989.

The Songhai Way to Beauty

⤳ by Stephanie Rose Bird ⤳

T he idea of blending elements of cultivated village society with ingredients of a completely natural origin is an ancient concept that can be traced back to the Songhai Empire of Africa. The Songhai see the landscape populated by numerous spirits that live in all aspects of the natural world, and they believe these diverse entities can come together for the good of humankind. As such, the Songhai believe that certain illnesses and disorders can be cured by combining wildcrafted and harvested flowers, herbs, roots, and stems with products associated with domesticated production—milk and cheese, grains, and eggs. The advantage of each type of energy enhances those of the other.

In the following recipes you will find the Songhai philosophy activated through the combination of cultivated dairy products with wildcrafted and harvested natural ingredients. Dairy

products are nutritious, reinforcing, emollient, and softening, and especially have these properties when paired with fruits, vegetables, herbs, and nut oils in beauty recipes.

Recipes for Beauty
Songhai Smoothie

This multipurpose smoothie is fragrant, soothing, moisturizing, rich, and tasty. Designed for parched skin, it is also the embodiment of the Songhai philosophy regarding blending the elements of nature. The Songhai Smoothie contains vitamin-rich strawberries and alpha-hydroxy-imbued buttermilk that nurture sensitive skin. The emollience of peach flesh, peach kernel oil, and creamy coconut milk, balanced with soothing chamomile and oat straw, makes this the perfect skin concoction. The only problem with this treat is deciding between drinking it or applying it to the body. (I suggest a bit of both.)

- ⅓   cup strawberries
- 1   small, ripe peach
- ½   cup coconut milk
- 1½   cups buttermilk
- 1   bag chamomile tea
- 1   tablespoon oat straw

Wash, peel, and finely chop strawberries and peach. Crush the peach pit with a mallet or in a mortar and pestle. Add these ingredients to baking dish. Pour milks over fruit, add herbs, and stir. Cover; infuse mixture in an oven set at 170°F for 2 hours. Remove from oven; whisk mixture. Pour through a fine sieve. Remove peach kernel and tea bag, then firmly press remaining mixture using the back of large spoon to extract juices and herbal medicine. Whisk again and repeat the straining and squeezing process. Dab on to face and neck, leave on for five minutes, and rinse well with cool water. There is no need for further treatments. You can also pour this in your bath for a luxurious moisturizing soak, or sip it throughout the day, as it is tasty and nutritious. Makes 16 ounces. Use within 3 days.

Veggie Milk

The combination of ingredients in Veggie Milk helps alleviate many skin disorders. The bleaching action of the buttermilk makes it especially helpful for those with freckles, scars, and skin discolorations. Alpha-hydroxy-rich buttermilk also gently removes dry skin so you won't look ashy in dry and cold weather. Buttermilk encourages cell renewal, which slows the appearance of wrinkles and tightens saggy skin. The lipids in buttermilk are emollient, so they keep your face moist but not greasy. Cucumbers are astringent, helping to alleviate shiny noses and foreheads. Lettuce is excellent for cleansing skin prone to breaking out with acne. Carrots contain healthy doses of vitamins A and E, which help check the onset of wrinkles while bringing a youthful glow to the skin. Both buttermilk and carrots make Veggie Milk safe for oily and combination skin.

2   carrots
1   cup iceberg lettuce
½   cucumber
2   cups buttermilk

Set oven at 170°F. Scrub carrots and cucumber; rinse them and the lettuce. Drain vegetables in a colander. Peel carrots and cucumber. Cut the cucumber in half and scoop out seeds. Shred drained lettuce, carrots, and cucumber in a food processor with shredder attachment or with a hand grater. Put the vegetables in an overproof bowl or small baking pan, and cover with buttermilk. Let steep for 2 hours, stirring occasionally. Drain through sieve placed over a large bowl. Pour veggie milk into a sterilized bottle. To use, pour a small amount of the milk on to a cotton swab and dampen face and neck gently. Leave on for 3–5 minutes. Rinse thoroughly with cool water; pat lightly with towel to dry. Use instead of soap in the morning and before bedtime. Makes approximately 12 ounces. Shelf life: one week if refrigerated.

Nerfertiti's Milk Bath

There is not a lot of information about the mysterious Queen Nefertiti of Egypt, though her legendary beauty has survived the ravages of time because of her famous sculpted portrait. In Northern Africa and the Middle East, queens often took milk baths to moisturize and heal their sun-dried skin. If you want to feel like a queen, lie back and enjoy the sensual, moisturizing treat of the bath of the ancients.

Nerfertiti's Milk Bath contains choice ingredients gathered from around the world. South African aloe vera soothes and encourages new skin growth. Used in moderation aloe vera gel acts as a humectant, keeping skin moist in the harshest conditions. Roses were, and still are, revered for their hypnotic fragrance. Fresh rose petals, rose oil, and rosewater lend an air of romance to Nerfertiti's Milk Bath. Frankincense is mentioned throughout history, and was sought after as a precious preservative. It has a heady scent for incense and perfumes, and it nurtures the skin. Try Nerfertiti's Milk Bath alone or with someone special, for a romantic getaway, right in your own home.

- 2   cups powdered milk
- 1   cup rosewater
- ¼   cup aloe vera gel
- ½   teaspoon rose fragrance oil
- ¼   teaspoon frankincense essential oil
- 1   cup fresh scented organic rose petals or other organic flower petals (optional)

Plug tub. Run warm water. Add milk. Put rosewater in a bowl. Whisk in aloe vera gel, followed by rose and frankincense oils. Pour mixture under tap. Once tub is half full, turn off the water and add the rose petals. Set fragrant candles around the tub and burn incense. Sit back and relax, soaking in the ancient skin nourishment of the queens of Egypt, for as long as you please.

Mango Laasi

In Indian cuisine, mango laasi is a delightful accompaniment to spicy foods and complex flavors. It is a cooling fusion of dairy products and fresh fruit, which calm the palate. The enzymes in fresh mango are also softening. In this recipe meant for your hair, the ingredients are useful for conditioning. The combination of yogurt and fresh mango juice helps smooth, moisturize, and detangle hair. The lemon adds shine. If you decide to use the optional essential oils, they will leave an exotic aroma. Cardamom is earthy, unique, and spicy; peppermint is lively, green, and stimulating to your scalp.

- 1 ripe mango
- ½ lemon
- ½ cup whole-milk yogurt
- ⅛ teaspoon cardamom essential oil (optional)
- ⅛ teaspoon peppermint essential oil (optional)

Peel mango and slice lengthwise to remove flesh from pit. Cut into 1-inch sections and put into blender. Add juice from ½ lemon and ½ cup of yogurt to the blender. Blend on medium-high until smooth, about one minute. Pour into spouted container. Pour through fine cheesecloth or sieve. Add essential oils (if using); mix well. After shampooing pour over hair, covering all strands well. Massage and rinse. Try doubling the recipe using half as a conditioner and other half to add to the bath. Makes approximately 6 ounces. Shelf life: 24 hours.

Makela, Queen of Sheba's Royal Conditioning Frappé

Makela, Queen of Sheba (or Shabu), has been subject of many a fanciful tale in Arabian folklore, involving magical flying carpets and talking birds that were purported to fly around her. Makela began her reign at age fifteen, gaining enormous wealth, respect, and knowledge (for which she had a neverending thirst). She was very beautiful, with a melodic and elegant public speaking voice. This hair frappé was created with her mystique in mind. Included are ingredients that are nurturing and kind to curly hair: frankincense, myrrh, aloe vera, and roses, and a couple of the gifts presented to her by King Solomon when they wed—wine and honey. For our purposes wine is softening, and honey attracts moisture.

3	tablespoons aloe vera gel
⅛	teaspoon frankincense essential oil
⅛	teaspoon myrrh essential oil
⅛	teaspoon patchouli essential oil
⅛	teaspoon rose fragrance oil
1	teaspoon avocado oil
½	cup coconut water
½	cup coconut milk
1	tablespoon raw clover blossom honey
2	tablespoons red wine

Put aloe vera gel, essential oils, avocado oil in blender or food processor; blend 30 seconds on medium. Add coconut water, coconut milk, honey, and wine. Blend 1 minute more. Pour over hair, and massage in. Rinse well with cool water. Makes approximately eight ounces. Use immediately.

Gift of the Herberas

❧ by Stephanie Rose Bird ❧

Fruits high in enzymes couple well with medicinal herbs to make health and beauty aids. Scientific documentation proves that certain enzymes help break down tough tissue and spark cell renewal. Used in small portions and blended with other wholesome ingredients, these fruit enzymes also help soften and hydrate skin and nails, and reduce tangles in hair. Of course, this is no secret to women of the Mexican diaspora. Mexican *curanderas* and *herberas* have created recipes featuring parts of the papaya tree for hundreds of years.

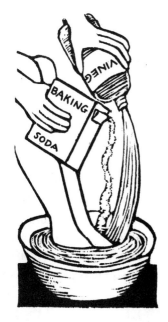

The concept of "live" food is one currently captivating contemporary society, and with good reason. Foods in their natural (live) state contain vitamins and minerals. Such foods have a softening action when used as beauty products, and they strip away chemical buildups of industrial beauty products. Futhermore, these effects are often lost or weakened by industrial processing and the adding of various sorts of preservatives. In general, I encourage you to use fresh juices, and eat natural and fresh foods whenever possible. Sip a glass of fresh juice and eat a handful of raw almonds as you work, instead of a soda pop and a bag of chips. In no time, you will begin to reap the benefits of natural foods. The vitamins and minerals in the recipes are coupled with healthful AHAs (alpha-hydroxy acids), EFAs (essential fatty acids), enzymes, moisturizers, and delightfully sensual essential oil perfumes to help beautify while illuminating your spirit.

Herberas Recipes
Mexican Soapless Shampoo

Rather than relying on commercial suds, this recipe relies on naturally occuring saponins in soapweed (yucca) and papaya leaf, coupled with the brightening and cleansing properties of lemon and the gentle conditioning action of chamomile. This shampoo is wonderful for all hair colors and will encourage shimmering highlights. The most noticeable effect in color will be in blond and gray hair, which appears significantly brighter after washing. Mexican Soapless Shampoo is best used on hair with oily tendencies or oily buildups. Each ingredient has a venerable place in Mexican healing tradition, and once you try the recipe you'll understand why.

  6   ounces distilled water
  ⅓   cup yucca root
  2   tablespoons chopped dried papaya leaf
  1   chamomile tea bag
  1   tablespoon strained fresh lemon juice

Boil water. Peel, thinly slice, then chop yucca root until fine. Add yucca to boiling water and let cook for 30 minutes on medium. Reduce heat to low, and add papaya leaf and chamomile. Infuse 10 minutes. Remove from heat and let cool for 20 minutes. Strain. Add lemon juice; stir to mix well. Shampoo, rinse, and repeat.

Mayan Hair Butter

Numerous extraordinary plants that grow in Mexico have health and beauty benefits utilized by ancient Mayan healers. Sour cream is a very effective moisturizer and emollient that has powerful softening abilities. Banana juice makes a terrific conditioner for curly hair, and avocado is full of beneficial essential fatty acids, vitamins, and minerals. This Mayan Hair Butter is a wholesome delight for dry and easily tangled hair.

¼ cup spring water

¼ cup fresh corn silk or 2 tablespoons dry

¼ cup sour cream

¼ cup strained banana juice

2 tablespoons sunflower oil

Flesh from 1 ripe avocado

Bring water to a boil. Add corn silk, cover, and reduce heat to low. Simmer 30 minutes. Remove from heat; cool. Mix sour cream, banana juice, and sunflower oil together. In a separate medium-sized bowl, mash avocado, and beat with whisk until a smooth paste forms. Strain corn silk by pouring through sieve over avocado paste. Beat corn silk infusion and avocado until smooth and creamy; add to sour cream mixture. Before shampooing, apply Mayan Hair Butter to wet hair. Massage through, covering hair well. Cover hair with cap; leave on 30 to 60 minutes. Rinse well with cool water. Follow with a fragrant herbal shampoo. Makes approximately 10 ounces; use immediately. Excess can be used as a cell-renewing, moisturizing facial.

Peepaw Peel

Papaya has a long history and wide range of curative properties and is highly prized in Mexico and many tropical islands. Called *peepaw* by the Aztecs, papaya contains the enzyme papain, which is responsible for its healing properties. Peepaw Peel utilizes medicines beloved by the Aztecs, combined with healing emollient aloe and revitalizing lime for a pick-me-up facial to liven up tired sallow skin.

¼ cup fresh papaya juice

1 tablespoon aloe vera gel

1 egg white

2 drops lime essential oil

Pour papaya juice into a glass mixing bowl. Stir in the aloe vera gel. Whisk in an egg white, and blend this mixture well. Drop lime essential oil from a clean and sterilized eye dropper. Apply the mixture immediately to face and neck area. Leave on 30 minutes; rinse well, pat dry.

Andean Agua de Rosa

In the pristine Andes mountains of Chile grows an alpine rose that produces the skin- and hair-rejuvenating oil rosa mosqueta. In the spirit of the beauty found in the Andes and its fantastic flora and fauna, Andean Agua de Rosa is a deep-red rinse containing rosa mosqueta oil and two types of red flowers combined with the heady scent of roses.

1½ cups mountain spring water

¼ cup dried rosehips

3 dried hibiscus flowers

1 tablespoon Andean (Chilean) rosa mosqueta oil

½ teaspoon rose fragrance oil

Boil water. Add rosehips and hibiscus flowers. Cover; reduce heat to medium. Simmer 40 minutes. Reduce heat to low; simmer 20 minutes. Remove from heat; let stand 30 minutes. Pour through a fine sieve. Add rosa mosqueta and rose fragrance oil. Apply rinse to shampooed hair. Use once a week until desired shade is achieved. Makes approximately 8 ounces. Shelf life: 30 days, if kept cool.

Homemade Aloe Vera Gel

The magical, spiritual, and medicinal qualities of aloe vera gel have been traditionally utilized by people in such varying locales as

North and South Africa, the Caribbean and South America—wherever the plant can grow. And as the African and Latino diasporas have spread, so has the knowledge and appreciation of aloe vera's magical qualities. It is common knowledge that aloe helps soothe irritated and burned skin. It is also an inexpensive yet highly effective finishing gel for a wide range of hairstyles. A little dab of aloe vera gel makes your locks look great. Aloe vera makes a firm holding gel when creating braids, corn rows, French braids, twists, plaits, roller sets, and scrunching. Aloe can also be used to set and define natural curls. A little dollop serves well to top-dress smooth updos, chignons, and French twists. Just slit open an aloe vera leaf. Scrape the inner gel into a bowl using a sharp knife. When all the gel has been harvested, put the gel and chunks into a food processor. Dilute with water to get to the desired consistency. Blend 60 to 90 seconds until smooth. Pour through a sieve to remove any remaining hard lumps.

The Three-Step Foot Softening System

This is a multicultural recipe, with ingredients gathered from places and cultures around the world. Mexican curanderos (healers) use the sunflower seed meal to soften skin, reduce swelling, and treat sore muscles and even arthritis. Native American medicine men and women often include sunflower seeds in recipes and rites for skin softening and moisturizing. Corn meal has been used historically throughout Mesoamerica for healing, for rituals and ceremonies, and as a food. Buttermilk and sea salt are used in various African countries not only for cooking, but also for skin treatments. East Indian ayurvedic concepts are incorporated by the inclusion of ghee and sesame oil. Both oils are used in India for intensive healing.

Step One: Earthy Foot Scrub

2   tablespoons shelled sunflower seeds

2   tablespoons coarse sea salt

½   cup cornmeal

3   tablespoons buttermilk

1   tablespoon ghee

1   tablespoon sesame oil

Grind sunflower seeds and sea salt until fine, using a food processor, clean coffee grinder, or a mortar and pestle. Add cornmeal; pulsate for 30 seconds, or hand-grind an additional minute or two. Pour into mixing bowl. Add buttermilk, stirring to form a thick paste. Drizzle in ghee and sesame oil. To make ghee, melt 3 tablespoons butter over low heat in skillet, being careful not to burn. As it bubbles, skim solids off the top and discard. After about five minutes of skimming, the remaining liquid will be clear and is called ghee or clarified butter. Ghee can also be bought prepared. Stir the mixture well. Makes approximately 5 ounces. Use immediately.

To do so, clean feet (remove nail polish), and then pat lightly with a towel. Smooth paste onto your feet, making sure all surfaces are covered. Scrub nails, soles, top of feet, and between toes. Pay special attention to your heels, massaging well. For tough jobs and deeper exfoliation use a pumice stone or scrub gloves. Use gentle motions, to prevent scratching your skin. Rinse and pat dry.

Step 2: The Two-Minute Jacuzzi

Now that you have removed the rough dry skin from your feet, it is time to encourage the growth of new skin to replace the old. Apple cider vinegar contains high concentrations of alpha-hydroxy acids, which renew skin cells. Vinegar helps eliminate foot odors, fungi, and athlete's foot. Baking soda softens skin, making it easier to remove callouses, and deodorizes. The chemical reaction set off by the mixture of the two ingredients (acetic acid and sodium bicarbonate) causes bubbles and foam. The result is a calming foot bath that relieves the tensions of the day, while softening, sanitizing, and deodorizing funky feet.

1   cup apple cider vinegar

2   cups warm water

¾   cup baking soda

Pour ingredients into a foot basin or deep pan in order given (double ingredients for a deeper foot soak). Dip feet into the bubbling mixture. Soak 10 minutes. Rinse. Pat dry. Makes approximately 30 ounces. Use immediately.

Step 3: Peppermint Patty Moisture Seal

With your baby-soft, scrubbed feet, it is now time for the finishing touch—a moisture seal. This recipe brings together the art of the *sobradora* (a Mexican healing masseuse), of aromatherapy, and ayurveda. Ghee and sesame oil are used in ayurvedic treatments for warmth and moisturizing during healing massage treatments. Cocoa butter and shea butter are favored by Africans and are coming into vogue worldwide as rich and nongreasy moisturizing oils. Peppermint, green papaya sap, and ginger root are used by many cultures and have been especially useful to Mexican American herbalists for their stimulating and regenerating capacities and softening ability. Ginger and peppermint are widely used in the African American hoodoo healing tradition. Peppermint, papaya, and ginger contain digestive enzymes that help the Peppermint Patty Moisture Seal soften cuticles, callouses, and rough skin. Safflower oil is a light, relatively inexpensive, readily available, neutral oil that contains a high concentration of vitamin E.

3 tablespoons cocoa butter

2 tablespoons shea butter

1 tablespoon ghee

2 tablespoons fresh papaya juice

¼ teaspoon peppermint essential oil

⅛ teaspoon ginger essential oil

1 tablespoon safflower oil

To make ghee, see directions above for the Earthy Foot Scrub. Melt cocoa butter and shea butter in an oven set at 190°F. Add the ghee, followed by the Mexican papaya sap if available. Whisk in the essential oils, and drizzle in the safflower oil. Mix well. Makes approximately four ounces. Use immediately.

If your lover has a foot fetish, ask for help massaging your feet. Not only will this be a sensual treat but you may end up having your toes nibbled, since the oil mixture smells like peppermint patties. Or you may choose to double the recipe and give mutual foot rubs—don't be surprised if sparks are soon flying.

Either way, relax and massage each foot for at least five minutes, while taking deep breaths to drink in the stimulating aroma. Try this treatment twice a month and you will see results!

Herbal Dental Care

✺ by Leeda Alleyn Pacotti ✺

O ne of the most versatile organs of the body is right under your nose: your mouth. Or oral cavity, as it is known medically. With it, you can do wonderful things—flash a winning smile; talk a blue streak about your feelings or ideas; kiss your baby, or even someone more exciting. Purse your lips, grimace, frown; stick out your tongue, or grin and bear it. And, of course, your mouth is necessary for eating.

Considering how useful the mouth is for everything we hold important—communication, nutrition, and nurture—isn't it odd that most of us know so little about this organ?

The Health of Our Mouths

Acording to reports put out by the U. S. Public Health Service, about 98 percent of Americans suffer from some

form of dental disease. Americans have let their fears of the drill and memories of whirring noises cloud their intellects. Shying away from the pain of the dentist has a huge eventual cost. These costs can be measured in more than dollars, although the payment for delaying necessary dental repair can be extreme if not dealt with earlier.

When the mouth is diseased, it is usually indicated by pain, soreness, or tenderness in some area. We find it difficult to chew, which impairs digestion and prevents important nutrients from returning to tissues and structures in the mouth, delaying their repair. Nerves become sensitive from throbbing, which can catapult into inflammation and progress into a painful infection. From irritated nerves, we suffer additional emotional responses, as the other sensory organs of the head become overly sensitized. Noise becomes unbearable; bright lights tear the eyes; and the nose stuffs up into a painful sinus headache.

Physical and emotional reactions aren't the only complications of mouth disease. With prolonged gum or tooth pain, we become less alert, finding our judgment hampered through distraction. Our attention and concentration are drawn to the pain, creating a vicious circle of irritation.

Getting to Know Your Mouth

Fortunately, the majority of the mouth's structures are accessible and visible. We have lips, cheek lining, a variety of teeth, gums, a tongue, taste buds, and the hard and soft palates or roof of the mouth—all culminating with the uvula, the unexplainable thing that hangs in the back of the mouth near the throat. The mouth leads into the pharynx, which closes off the nasal cavity when we swallow, preventing food from going up or out the nose.

Of the visible parts of the mouth, the lips, cheek lining, and palates are most easily injured, resulting in irritating pain in the case of injury. Consider the rawness after you accidently bite your cheek, or the blisters from the oft-experienced pizza burn, or searing twinges when smiling with a split lip.

The gums, which should be a lively red, are overcoats for the roots and neck of the teeth. They are intermeshed with filament nerves, which is why we feel the impact of chewing, and they contain a network of fine blood vessels. The gums are flesh constantly washed by the mouth's saliva. But, unlike skin, the gums don't have several layers of epidermis to protect them. As a result, when the gums bleed they take a longer time to heal.

In considering dentistry and dental problems, we usually think of the teeth only. And teeth are important, performing the vital tasks of tearing and grinding food. They also prop out the facial muscles, preventing sunken cheeks, and help us create specific speech sounds, such as aspirated vowels, some of the hard consonants, and resonating diphthongs. What generally isn't known is that teeth continue to replenish themselves, including regrowing dentin and enamel, as long as their interior pulp receives proper nourishment. It's important to remember that teeth are not bones, although these two structures use many of the same minerals for hardness and durability.

Of the visible mouth, the tongue is the flexible part. This organ is employed primarily in speech, but also is useful in whistling and making other attention-getting sounds. Covered with papillae, the tongue moves food around in the mouth during chewing and assists in swallowing. In Chinese medical and naturopathic health approaches, the tongue offers an important health diagnostic of the prevailing physical condition. On different sections of the tongue, variations in color, texture, size, coating, shape, or spotting reveal the dysfunction or disease of specific internal organs.

Taste buds aren't really visible. They cloister themselves within the papillae, which are the rough, nipple-like elevations covering the tongue. Have you ever noticed that you like to eat certain foods in certain parts of your mouth? This is because not all taste buds are the same. Taste buds toward the back of the tongue near the throat respond to bitterness. Those along the sides of the tongue respond to acidic foods, while the taste buds in the middle of the tongue respond to sweet, sour, and salt flavors.

Obvious from the outside, but directly unobservable, are the jaw bones, which provide an anchor for the teeth, and for the neural network, which reaches along the upper and lower jaw to every tooth, and the salivary glands, which help to cleanse the mouth and provide powerful enzymes to begin the breakdown of food when we chew. These invisible structures play incisive roles in the proper functions of the rest of the mouth.

Making up the jaw are two major bones, the maxilla and mandible. The immobile maxilla houses the upper teeth, while the moveable mandible sockets the lower teeth and shapes the lower part of the face. We naturally protect these bones, like those covering the rest of the face and skull, by avoiding impacts to them. When these bones break, the rest of the mouth is rendered useless. When we suffer calcium deficiency, these bones become brittle and erode, as the teeth are forced to draw vital minerals from them.

From behind the throat, one main nerve splits toward the jointed hinge of the jaw bones. At the joint, it splits again, running forked over and under the teeth on each side of the face. Because all the nerves to the teeth originate from one main nerve, toothache or gum soreness often causes a phenomenon called "referred pain." Have you ever experienced a toothache where it seemed that the tooth directly above or below ached also? Or, if you let the toothache go too long, did you notice a matching tooth on the opposite side of the mouth also ached? What you experienced was referred pain. In the first instance, the neural messaging reversed at the joint, traveling to the tooth matching the bite. In the second instance, the neural messaging reversed behind the throat, sensitizing the aching tooth's complement on the other side of the mouth. This phenomenon can cause us to believe we have more than one toothache.

The salivary glands, the mouth's moisture pumps, exist primarily in three major pairs. Located in front of the ears, under the tongue, and below the base of the tongue, these fleshy organs secrete saliva, which moistens food for swallowing and carries enzymes that start the breakdown of foods, particularly grains. When we are well nourished, watery saliva carries mineral salts that bathe and cleanse teeth and gums.

Commonsense Dental Care

Despite all the complicated chores the mouth performs, attending to its needs isn't difficult. For most people, though, the effort takes a few extra minutes, paying attention to sensations and signals and determining to keep good habits. Caring for the oral cavity is a routine, which pays off in less disease, stronger teeth, better digestion, and fresher breath.

Your Cleaning Frequency

No one set schedule for teeth cleaning works well for everyone. Depending on the strength of your tooth enamel and the number of times you eat or snack during the day, you are the best person to decide how often you should clean your mouth. As a rule of thumb, cleaning should be done at least twice each day—after waking from and before retiring to your longest regular sleep period.

Flossing and Tooth-Picking

Flossing is one of the less glamorous duties in oral hygiene, but is very important to the overall health of your mouth. Floss is available either in waxed or unwaxed thread or as a dental tape, although the tape is used primarily between gapped teeth. Fortunately, flossing needs to be done only once each day to remove accumulated plaque between teeth and under the surrounding gum wall. An up-and-down motion, working the thread as deeply as you can between each tooth and its surrounding gum, is very effective. The first few times the gums will be a little sore afterward, so it's best to floss just before you sleep. Within one week, you'll be able to perform this chore in about one minute.

Toothpicks are helpful to remove food particles or work on plaque if spaces exist between teeth or if you have bridgework. With them, you can get between the bridged teeth near the gum, which is very difficult to do with floss.

Prerinse

A new product and one of the finest discoveries of the twentieth century is the antiplaque prerinse, which is swished in the mouth for about thirty seconds prior to actual brushing. It not only loosens existing plaque, but retards its reformation. With prerinse, you'll be amazed at how smooth the surfaces of your teeth are between professional cleanings.

Toothbrushes

A toothbrush is your primary hygienic device, available in both manual or electric models. While electric brushes have artificial bristles, manual toothbrushes come with either natural or artificial bristles. Bristle strength varies from extra soft, usable by small children or people with extremely sensitive gums and teeth, to hard. For brushes made from artificial materials, soft bristles are the most frequently recommended, while medium bristles are best for natural brushes, which tend to soften with use.

People with bridgework and crowns need to investigate using the proxibrush, a stem holder with a small conical brush at either end. This brush cleans between spaced teeth and can be used to clean gently into the deep pockets of diseased gums.

Changing your toothbrush frequently is very important, because both artificial and natural bristles tend to harbor bacteria. The most recent recommendation is to start each month with a new brush. Consequently, forego the more expensive toothbrushes that wiggle and bend for a simpler style that you don't mind throwing away. When you are not using your toothbrush, keep it soaking in hydrogen peroxide or rubbing alcohol. When the solution becomes cloudy, you'll know it's time to get a new brush.

Toothpastes, Powders, and Salt

Most people are unaware of how much sugar there is in the more well-known commercial toothpastes. Avoid any toothpaste or powder with sugar, sweeteners such saccharin or other artificial sweeteners, and sparkles. The chemicals from these compounds are absorbed directly through the gums into the bloodstream.

Health-food stores carry chalk-based toothpastes and powders, which come in several interesting natural flavors, such as cinnamon, fennel (tastes like licorice), ginger, orange, and strawberry. For sensitive or painful gums or teeth, some of these pastes and powders also contain tea tree oil, which is antifungal and antiseptic, or *neem*, an ayurvedic remedy which is antibacterial and anti-inflammatory. Surprisingly, these toothpastes tend to foam up more than regular commercial toothpastes, which means you need use only half as much.

For people who experience an intermittent bleeding from the gums, brushing with plain baking soda, salt, or a combination of both produces good results. The sodium portion neutralizes acidity in the mouth, preventing further irritation and soreness. The chloride in the salt is a natural cleanser. Brushing with salt can produce a short period of stinging, but, within five to ten minutes, the sensation will be reduced or completely gone. Use baking soda and/or salt before bedtime. With either, don't swallow, but spit and rinse completely.

Brushing

The battle rages over brushing techniques: up-and-down, side-to-side, in a circle, or some combination of these. One way to find a brushing routine that suits you is to use disclosing tablets, made with vegetable coloring, usually red, that sticks to plaque. Most major drugstores carry these tablets. After you brush, chew one; then give yourself a big, bright smile. Most people are shocked to see their choppers are covered with crimson or pink splotches. An extended second brushing removes the tablet residue, which will only come off with brushing, and lets you observe the best motion that actually cleans your teeth. No matter which technique you prefer, spend at least three minutes of thorough brushing, which means getting the bristles gently between teeth and the surrounding gum line, where offending plaque forms. Finally, give your gums, the hard palate, and your tongue a light brushing to clean and stimulate them. You'll never need a tongue scraper.

Postrinse

After brushing, swish your mouth with the coldest water you can stand. You may be a little sensitive to it the first few times, but so are bacteria. Follow this rinse with an antiseptic mouthwash to further arrest bacterial growth. Unfortunately, antiseptic mouthwashes contain alcohol and will dry out gum tissue and the tooth structure, which eventually leads to, you guessed it, cavities. However, alternating an antiseptic mouthwash with a solution of hydrogen peroxide, which whitens teeth, or a homemade mouth rinse produces beneficial results.

Herbal mouth rinses are easy to make. From your health-food store, purchase clove or peppermint oil, goldenseal, or myrrh. Add two tablespoons of oil or one tablespoon of herb to two cups of boiling water, which has been removed from heat. Let the mixture steep until cool, when it is ready to use.

Exercise

Exercising your oral cavity is as important for the mouth as with any other of our body's organ. Without regular movement, the mouth loses precious blood flow and the supplied nutrients that blood brings. The joint of your jaw will weaken, feeling tender when you move it. Teeth feel loose in their sockets, emitting an overall dull ache. Gums become sensitive and tender, losing their bright red color.

What exercise helps you maintain strength, tightness, and firmness in your mouth? In a word, chewing. When your dentist or doctor tells you to chew your food twenty-five times before swallowing, it isn't all for predigestion. Chewing raw and solid foods works and tones the muscles of the jaw and face, which helps you to look younger. As food is chewed, enzymatic saliva washes over the teeth, interfering with bacterial growth. Chewing impacts your teeth, which in turn gently massages them against the gum sockets, stimulating blood flow through tissues. So, when you eat, show your food who's boss. Tear, masticate, and grind your way to great oral health.

Some people have difficulty stimulating blood flow into the gums through chewing. If this is your problem, consider a gum stimulator, which is a kind of wand with a pointed rubber tip. Use the tip to massage around the gum area, especially around the molars.

Oral Remedies and First Aid

Mouth pain is nature's signal for disease. In fact, many dentists now recognize that mouth pain often is a precursor of a change in the body's homeostasis, or health balance. This is particularly true prior to the full onset of a cold or the flu. Withheld emotions frequently register in the mouth as either a tingling sensation, salivation, clinching, or grinding. Bruxism, or grinding teeth during sleep, usually indicates anxiety or repressed feelings.

Besides fleeting or intermittent sensations, there are also stinging sensations caused when cavities in the teeth respond to either hot or cold, and sharp aches, when the tooth is decayed or its roots become necrotic. These pains also occur when a crown or filling is lost, exposing previously protected tooth tissue to the air.

Herbal First Aid

For mouth pain, a highly effective remedy is no further away than your kitchen spice chest. Cloves, in powdered form, placed directly on the gum or packed into a tooth cavity, completely relieve pain and sooth irritated nerves within five minutes. Cloves are antiseptic, antioxidant, and anesthetic. Their active ingredient, eugenol, is the same ingredient used in expensive over-the-counter gum anesthetics. In a pinch, grind down one whole clove. At your health-food store, you can purchase clove oil, which is best applied with a cotton ball molded over the tooth or gum area. Cloves are very helpful when you have broken or cracked a tooth. Their anesthetic properties last from six to twelve hours.

Medicine Chest

Of course, crowns and fillings pop out overnight or on the weekend, when your dentist isn't available. When you lose a filling or a crown, a temporary filling material is available at better drug stores. This material, which sells under such brand names as Temparin, can be used for about ten to twelve applications to fill a hole in the tooth or to recement a crown back into place. This little product, which costs about $4.00, is easily applied and hardens within one hour. It's a life-saver, until you can get to your dentist for an appointment.

Dental Fears and Homeopathy

Dentistry is an exacting and helpful health science, which has no parallel in other health disciplines. Preventative oral care and regular dental assessments go hand-in-hand as part of your health regime. Nonetheless, anyone can experience the need for dental repair, which means a visit to the dentist.

Many people start reacting to the dentist's office long before they get there. Anxiety and arresting panic may cause patients to delay appointments or simply turn around and go home. Homeopathic remedies, which are available at health-food stores, can help dentophobic folks overcome your fear of dental care.

Arnica montana is an all-purpose remedy for any kind of dental work, from cleaning to oral surgery. It not only controls pain, but helps with bleeding and sore gums and assists in preventing infection. Take one dose before and after your appointment, with subsequent doses as often as necessary to maintain your comfort.

If you are nervous before any dental appointment, replace Arnica with one of the following remedies:

Aconitum napellus is taken when you are extremely nervous and fearful. Chamomile quells nervousness and hypersensitivity to pain. This remedy is very helpful for children. Chamomile neutralizes unpleasant reactions to anesthetics, especially if you react with fast heartbeat and weakness in your legs. Use Chamomile if you have pain later from needle puncture. *Gelsemium sempervirens* should be used when you are not only nervous, but shaking and suffering from diarrhea.

Bleeding, soreness, and pain can ensue after dental work. Consider one of the following remedies to help you: *Hypericum perfoliatum* helps the irritation of nerves in the mouth, especially after any drilling. *Ledum palustre* helps the pain from needle punctures, especially if the area in the mouth or the skin of your cheek feels cold. Phosphorus controls excessive, stubborn bleeding. *Ruta graveolens* needs to be taken when you feel deep aching, especially if there is any injury or bruise to the thin layer of periosteum, which covers the jaw bone under the gums. This remedy also helps with pain from a dry socket, when the blood clot covering an extraction becomes dislodged.

Eating for Smiles

As mentioned before, chewing isn't just an adjunct to eating satisfaction, but a great exercise for gum and muscle tone. However, what we chew and eat can make a difference in oral beauty.

Teeth benefit from a wide variety of minerals, not just calcium. You get the most absorbable minerals from raw or steamed fruits and vegetables, which still permit you plenty of healthy chewing exercise and help clean the teeth. As a special note for pregnant women, be sure to obtain an appropriately strengthened multivitamin-and-mineral complex for the term of your pregnancy, to help your developing baby and protect your own teeth, hair, and health.

Avoiding sugary foods prevents an environment conducive for bacterial growth. Sugar residue in the mouth, when mixed with saliva, forms an erosive acid, which pits tooth enamel and creates cavities for invading bacteria. Also, stay away from soft or sticky foods, which remain between the teeth after eating and which produce plaque.

Caring for your teeth doesn't have to be a reluctant chore, but it does take persistence, routine, and habit. Your oral regimen will pay off in good health, higher self-esteem, and lower dental bills. Equipped with such excellent knowledge about your oral cavity, open it up and let your smile shine!

Suggested Reading

Maesimund, B.P., and J. Heimlich. *Homeopathic Medicine at Home.* New York, New York: Jeremy P. Tarcher/Putnam, 1980.

Stay, Flora Parsa. *The Complete Book of Dental Remedies.* Garden City Park, New York: Avery Publishing Group, 1997.

Herb Crafts

Potpourri for All Seasons

by Deborah Harding

The scent of flowers brings a comfortable ambiance to the home, and potpourri helps you bring in those sweet scents with a minimum of fuss. Here are a some tips on how you can enjoy the scent of nature's candy throughout the year.

Flowers Through the Year

In spring, the scent of flowers is fresh and delicate as the snow melts and living plants and trees begin to emerge from the winter sleep. In summer, the scent is strong and sensuous as sunlight draws the oils from herbs and flowers in the garden and creates an orgy for our senses. In the fall, the harvest comes in and the leaves begin their change of color and scent. Smells become musty and pungent as everything readies itself for the approach of darker and colder days. In the winter, we seek the comfort of heat while outside it is clean and clear. Many times the only living thing left is the trusty evergreen with its piney scent. Also in the house are the scents of spices used to enliven our taste buds during this time of confinement.

History of Scents

During the Roman era, laundry was scented with lavender, and mattresses were stuffed with rose petals. During the medieval period, potpourri came in the form of what was called "strewing herbs." During this time, homes were made of stone, mud, and straw. The floors were often made of dirt and sometimes wood. There were no sewage systems, and the stench of human refuse could be dreadful at times. Wastes were either thrown out the window, in a stream or lake, or piled outside. Bathing was something that was not undertaken on a daily basis either. In fact, early physicians prescribed one (!) bath a month, or even a year, as it was said that bathing caused illness. One either became used to these scents wafting through the medieval air, or one tried to mask them.

One way to mask odors was to take pungent herbs and sweet flower petals and throw them about the floor, in the corners, under the tables, and in the beds. Handkerchiefs were soaked in flower- and herb-infused water, dried, and brought to the nose to mask any unpleasant odors that one found. Another method of disguising the stench was to carry about a tussy mussy. These were small bouquets of dried flowers and herbs that one could sniff if the smell of the city became too much.

Potpourri, as we know it today, was created during the Renaissance and Victorian times. Kings and queens stuffed pillows, chair cushions, and other household items with scented, dried material. They also set out beautiful bowls of dried flowers and herbs laced with small pine cones, acorns, nuts, and other pretty items. Whole, dried flower heads were placed in the potpourri, as well as bits of lace and ribbon. In addition, potpourri was also placed in lacey sachets to be situated in drawers or closets.

Essential oils were also used to enhance the scent of the dried material. Essential oils are plant chemicals that are extracted from the plants themselves by breaking down the plant's cellular walls. The oils are extracted, bottled, and sold. Essential oils smell very strongly of the plant from which they were extracted. Today we use then to enhance the scent of the dried material used in potpourri and to make the scent last longer.

What You Will Need

You will need the following items to make potpourri from scratch:

1. Glass bowl

2. Wooden spoons

3. Large-mouth canning jars with lids

4. Dried plant material

5. Essential oils and droppers

6. Miscellaneous ribbon, lace, silk flowers, etc.

7. Scissors

8. A fixative

A fixative is a substance that will help the potpourri retain the scent of the essential oil for more than just a few days. There are many different types of fixatives, but the most economic and easy to use are orris root, a powdered substance from a particular type of iris, and oak moss, a leafy dried moss. Orris root is the more expensive of the two and it does have a scent of its own, which oak moss does not. This scent may or may not enhance your potpourri. Fixatives can be found in most stores that sell soap-making items, in shops that cater to aromatherapists, in any herb store, or on the Internet.

When making your potpourri, be sure that all materials are thoroughly dried. Any moisture at all (with the exception of the essential oil) will cause the potpourri to become moldy and eventually ruin the scent.

Making Potpourri

Most potpourris are made using the same method: Place the fixative in a wide-mouth canning jar and use a dropper to add the required amount of essential oil. Place the lid on the jar and shake vigorously until the fixative and oil have combined—all lumps have disappeared and the mixture looks dry. In a separate glass or enamel bowl combine the dried plant material. (Glass or enamel is used because these materials do not retain scents, as plastic or wood bowls tend to do.) Pour your fixative/oil mixture over the dried plant material mixture in the bowl, or, if your jar is big enough, place the plant material in the jar with the fixative and shake. If you are mixing in the bowl, use wooden spoons to toss and completely mix the fixative into the dried material. (Note: the spoon will also take on the scent of these materials.)

If you are adding any other material such as ribbon, lace, cones, or dried berries to make the potpourri look pretty, you should add these afterward. If you are using silk flowers, add those at the time of presentation. All of the following recipes can be made in the manner above. If there are any special notes, or additional materials you may want to add, they will be given after the list of ingredients in each recipes.

Unused potpourri can be stored in reclosable plastic freezer bags. Even though freezer bags cost more than sandwich bags, they are thicker and hold in the scent. You can also store your finished potpourri in Mason jars out of the Sun. As long as your materials are completely dry, potpourri can store for a very long time. If the scent isn't as strong as you wish, you can always add a little more of the fixative/essential oil mixture after defrosting. Many times I make large amounts of my potpourri recipes because it is convenient to do so; I have kept bags of potpourri in the freezer for more than three years.

The following are recipes for seasonal potpourri. All materials must be dried. Suggestions are given for additives that will brighten up the presentation. You may use your imagination when it comes to additives, or may expound on any of these recipes to make them your own. Experiment with different substances to develop your own scents.

Spring Potpourri

Spring demands a fresh and delicate scent; this is the time of year for lavender or citrus fruits.

Lemon Fresh Potpourri

Bring in the scent of the sun with this potpourri.

- 1   cup lemon balm leaves
- ½   cup lemon verbena leaves
- ½   cup lemongrass, chopped
- 1   cup lemon-scented geranium leaves
- 2   tablespoons dried lemon rind
- ½   cup orris root
- 2–4 drops lemon verbena or lemon balm oil

Add a few dehydrated lemon slices; small pieces of red, orange, and yellow ¼- to ½-inch wide ribbon, or dried calendula flowers.

Citrus Mint Potpourri

This potpourri will scent your kitchen or bathroom with the luscious scent of oranges, lemons, and mint.

- 1   cup lemon balm leaves
- ½   cup bergamot mint
- ½   cup lemon mint or spearmint
- ¼   cup dried lemon peel
- ¼   cup dried orange peel
- ½   cup oak moss
- 6   drops bergamot oil

You may add dehydrated orange or lemon slices, cinnamon sticks, and pieces of bright colored ribbon to this mix if you wish.

Spring Lavender Potpourri

Most of the ingredients for this potpourri can be gathered in spring. Peony petals are dried easily, and you can use either the lavender, pink, or bright reddish-purple petals for this potpourri. This will bring a clean breath of spring into the house

1	cup lavender buds
1	cup lamb's ears
½	cup larkspur flowers
1	cup peony petals
6–8	drops lavender oil
4	tablespoons orris root

Dry whole peony flowers by clipping them with about six inches of stem right before they completely open. Hang them to dry out of the sun. It will take about two to three weeks for them to dry completely. Remove the stems before placing them in your potpourri. The petals only take a few days to dry when removed from the whole flower. Collect petals after the flower has bloomed, and place them in a basket or on screens to dry.

Summer Potpourri

The scents of summer are pungent. Roses are in bloom, as are many other beautiful flowers. There are many colorful dried materials that can be added to your potpourri. The following summer potpourris all contain summer's favorite flower, the rose. Use only flowers that have not been sprayed with insecticide.

Victorian Lace Potpourri

This potpourri not only smells like an old Victorian garden but looks like one too. It includes both roses and lace.

2	cups pink or red rose petals
1	cup red or pink globe amaranth

1 cup pink rose buds

1 cup lavender buds

2 cups rose-scented geranium leaves

2 cups white German statice flowers, separated into small bunches

1 cup oak moss

6 drops rose oil

5 drops lavender oil

You may wish to add the rose buds after everything is mixed in. They are very delicate and tend to break apart if mixed in without care. Cut lace edging into ½- to 1-inch strips, and add to the potpourri along strips of red or pink ribbon. Check your potpourri to see if you actually need the additives. This potpourri has a wonderful lacey-like presentation all by itself.

Old English Garden Potpourri

Old English gardens are a profusion of scents and colors of summer. So is this potpourri.

1 cup red rose petals

1 cup dark-pink rose petals

½ cup chamomile flowers

1 cup broken-up cockscomb in red or pink

1 cup blue or purple larkspur flowers

½ cup hollyhock flowers (deep shades)

½ cup chicory or borage flowers

1 cup baby's-breath

1 cup oak moss

6 drops rose oil

6 drops honeysuckle oil

This potpourri makes a great presentation on its own, though whole rose petals, ribbon, or nonmetallic confetti can be added.

Sunshine Potpourri

This potpourri is golden, like the Sun, and has a scent similar to that of a fragrant garden in the summer.

  1   cup calendula petals (removed from the flower)
  2   cups scented geranium leaves (use a citrus or fruit scent)
  1   cup yellow or red-and-yellow yarrow flowers
  ½   cup chamomile flowers
  ½   cup tansy flowers
  1   cup coins from a money plant
  ½   cup orris root
  6   drops jasmine oil
  3   drops honeysuckle oil

Add the money plant coins right before presentation, as they are very delicate and can break up. You can add yellow, orange, or white silk flowers for presentation. Metallic gold ribbon strips can also be added for some shine, or try some metallic confetti—especially those with suns and stars incorporated in them. Another good additive is bright gold or orange tissue paper that has been cut into small pieces. Tissue paper soaks up any excess oil and tends to retain the scent.

Autumn Potpourri

The scent of autumn is crisp. Most flowers intensify with color now as they begin to dry in preparation for their winter's nap.

Apple Harvest Potpourri

We had an apple orchard when I was young and when the cool temperatures of autumn arrive I can't help but smell the scent of apples in the air.

  1   cup apple- or nutmeg-scented geranium
  1   cup red rose petals

1   cup red or pink straw flowers

½   cup red globe amaranth

¼   cup broken cinnamon sticks

⅛   cup whole cloves

1   cup dried, thin slices of apple

½   cup oak moss

10   drops apple oil

3   drops clove oil

3   drops cinnamon oil

Add dried apple slices after mixing well, as these tend to break up. You can dry apple slices several ways. Cut your apples and place them on a cookie sheet to dry naturally. This does tend to bring in bugs, so watch out for those. Or you can place the cookie sheet in a warm oven, set to the lowest setting. Keep the oven door open and check occasionally to make sure they aren't burning. It will take about three to four hours, and sometimes longer, to dry the apple slices—depending on how thick you slice them. It makes the house smell wonderful so you may want to think about baking an apple pie after the slices are done. Apple slices can also be dried in a dehydrator. This will take several days, so give yourself time; follow directions provided with your dehydrator.

You can add about ½ cup star anise if you like the scent. Other additives can be whole allspice nuts, whole red cockscomb, small dried twigs from an apple tree, or bits of red ribbon or red tissue paper (I have cut pieces of a red-and-white-checked paper tablecloth and used it in this potpourri).

Pumpkin Spice Potpourri

Pumpkins are a part of the autumn experience whether you eat them in pie or use them to make jack-o'-lanterns. Let this potpourri be a part of your autumn experience too.

2   cups dried pumpkin peel

2   cups nutmeg- or spice-scented geranium

2   cups dried orange peel

2   cups rhododendron leaf

1   cup broken cinnamon stick

½   cup whole cloves

½   cup hemlock cones

1   cup yarrow flowers (yellow or red)

1   cup oak moss

6   drops musk oil

2   drops cinnamon oil

2   drops clove oil

Pumpkin peel can be dried by cutting thin pieces from the pumpkin and placing them on a baking sheet. Drying as with apple slices above; the pumpkin peel should be dry within 2 to 6 hours, depending on the thickness. If the peel feels leathery it is not done. Pumpkin peel can also be dried in a dehydrator. This will take a few days. Orange peel can be air dried, just watch out for fruit flies. You may want to cover it with some plastic wrap so flies can't get to it. Orange peel should not be dried in the oven or dehydrator because the scent oils will be lost.

Orange or orange-red ribbon would be welcome in this potpourri. Dried Chinese lanterns (a dried flower) will also work, well as well as acorns, any other kind of nut, whole allspice, or dried seed pods.

Scent of the Woodlands Potpourri

This potpourri goes well in the office or in a man's bathroom or den.

2   cups cedar shavings

2   cups nutmeg- or any spice-scented geranium

1   cup dark-red rose or peony petals

¼   cup evergreen needles (pine, balsam, or cedar)

½   cup broken cinnamon sticks

¼ cup whole cloves

⅛ cup bay leaves

2 tablespoons juniper berries

¾ cup oak moss

8 drops patchouli oil

4 drops balsam oil

Purchase colored tree leaves made of silk or paper from the floral section of a discount store. Cut these up and place them in the potpourri as well.

Winter Potpourri

The scents of winter are fresh, cool, and vibrant. Most winter scents are of evergreen or spices and bring the memories of home to mind. These potpourris are full of warmth and comfort.

Fireside Potpourri

Set this potpourri in a basket near your fireplace. The heat from the fire will activate the scent.

2 cups cedar needles and/or cedar chips

2 cups eucalyptus leaves

1 cup pine needles or leaves of a pine- or balsam-scented geranium

1 cup broken cinnamon sticks

½ cup whole sage leaves

½ cup German statice or baby's-breath

¼ cup rosemary leaves

⅛ cup rose hips

⅛ cup whole cloves

¼ cup oak moss

6 drops balsam oil

3 drops cinnamon oil

Add optional pine cones, acorns, nuts, cone roses, red or green stings of beads, or red and green ribbon.

Holiday Spice Potpourri

Spice and citrus scents are associated with the fragrances of cooking and baking during the holidays.

1   cup lemon-scented geranium leaves
1   cup dried orange peel
1   cup dried lemon peel
¾   cup lemon verbena leaves
½   cup broken cinnamon sticks
¼   cup whole cloves
⅛   cup rosemary leaves
7   bay leaves
¾   cup oak moss
6   drops bergamot oil
3   drops cinnamon oil

Add whole dried lemon or orange slices, acorns, nuts, gold or orange tissue paper, or ribbon sections.

Winterlude Potpourri

This potpourri evokes the scents of deep winter.

2   cups balsam- or pine-scented geranium
1   cup pine needles
1   cup cedar chips or shavings or cedar needles
1   cup white baby's-breath
¾   cup dark red rose petals or rose buds
¼   cup rose hips
¼   cup holly berries

¼ cup juniper berries

¼ cup star anise

Add hemlock or sections of gold-painted pine cones. Add bits of lace or blue ribbon of various shades.

Presentation

To make a pleasant display for your potpourri, pour it into any glass or enamel bowl to display on tables, desks, or shelves in your home. Use crocks, deep dishes, Staffordshire china, wooden boxes, carnival glass, old sugar bowls, or creamers. Be creative with your choices. There are also commercially made potpourri holders that are made of glass and have a metal filigree top that allows the scent of the potpourri to circulate the room. If you are concerned that the potpourri will spill or that domestic animals or children will get into them, place the holders in a jelly jar. Cut a circle of netting that is at least two inches larger than the opening and place it on top. Screw the metal lid on, minus the part that would cover the jar completely. This way animals and children can't get into the potpourri, but you can still see the pretty ingredients and smell the wonderful scents.

Potpourri is a great way to share scents of each season. Decorate your home or office not only with seasonal knick-knacks, but with potpourri as well.

For Further Study

Harding, Deborah C. *The Green Guide to Herb Gardening*. St. Paul. Minnesota: Llewellyn Worldwide, 2000.

Newdick, Jane. *At Home with Herbs*. Pownal, Vermont: Storey Communications, 1994.

Ohrbach, Barbara Milo. *The Scented Room*. New York, New York: Clarkston N. Potter, Inc. 1986.

Shaudys, Phyllis V. *Herbal Treasures.* Pownal, Vermont: Storey Communications, 1994.

―――. *The Pleasure of Herbs.* Pownal, Vermont: Storey Communications, 1986.

Siegler, Madeleine H. *Making Potpourri.* Pownal, Vermont: Storey Communications, 1991.

Making Herbal Papers

P apermaking is an ancient art
that celebrates our interwoven
relationship with plants, written
communication, and culture. The
methods and techniques used to make
paper are essentially the same now as
they were over two thousand years ago.
That is, a diluted slurry of beaten plant
fibers and water are made to flow over
a porous screen. The water drains out
through the screen, leaving a thin mat
of fibers on the screen's surface. This
wet mat is removed from the screen,
the water is pressed out, and the resulting sheet is dried into a strong, flexible
piece of paper.

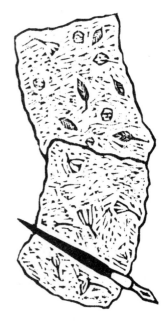

Over the centuries the process of
papermaking has spread throughout
the world. Each succeeding culture has
adapted the basic methods of papermaking to the materials available in the
native environment to suit cultural
needs. Tsai Lun, an emperor's eunuch,

is credited with inventing the first "true" paper in China in A.D. 105. The invention of paper in China in turn allowed Chinese calligraphy to flourish. Meanwhile, oceanic peoples created papers and cloths called tapa, made from the beaten inner bark of the paper mulberry. The Maya, in A.D. 900, had extensive libraries of books made from sacred junn paper and filled with hieroglyphs; these papers were also made of beaten bark.

Handmade papers from plants and recycled fibers are now enjoying a renaissance around the world. Paper recycling is necessary now in industrialized nations facing a shortage of trees for making paper. In some poorer countries, cottage industries have developed to make paper by hand using older methods. The abundance of plants fibers suitable for making paper will ensure the survival of the traditional craft of papermaking.

Almost all plants in fact are suitable for making paper, though some are better sources than others. All plants have a fibrous material called cellulose in their stalk, stems, leaves, and inner barks. Native peoples have in fact been using fibrous plants for ages to make their baskets, rope, cloth, mats, and even shelters. A quick exploration of your backyard and gardens yield several of these plants. In general, you will find that fibers gathered at different seasons will produce different kinds of papers. Quite often, fall- and winter-gathered fibers are very strong and lustrous as they have been "retted," or separated by natural rotting and dissolution of noncellulose plant parts caused by wind, rain, dew, and temperature change. Papermaking from plants is an enjoyable botanical experience that is inexpensive and easily accomplished in the comfort of your own backyard.

How to Start Making Paper

There are several excellent handmade papermaking books circulating now. Twenty years ago, inspired to make my own holiday cards out of recycled paper, I went to the library, did a quick bit of research, and bought a used blender to make paper for solstice Christmas cards. After reading the article, and experimenting a bit, my cards were a great success. With a little self-inspiration and the help of some of the excellent resources available, you can get going as I did with little hassle. You can have, as I did, positive encounters with endless plant spirits. Be creative, experiment, and remember to enjoy the process as you learn about the plants.

For me now, papermaking has become part of the seasonal rhythm of gardening, harvesting, and creating as I work with plants. Almost all the best fibrous plants are also some of the most medicinal and useful herbs.

Typically, I will design my garden and order my seeds in January and February, and I will gather and store any winter-retted fibers I plan to make paper from. I plant pansies for their colorful blooms, which can be pressed and used in paper. I prune and strip roses, mulberries, willows, elms, bamboo, and other woody papermaking plants for the season; I dry the inner barks of these plants and store them for later use.

By March, I plant potatoes and flax, both good papermaking plants, and I plant nourishing cover crops of oats and clover (the oat straw makes excellent paper after its late spring harvest). I make new compost beds and piles of such biodynamic plants as nettle, comfrey, yarrow, chamomile, valerian, dandelion, and oak bark. All of these plants yield beautiful papers from the fiber in their flowers and leaves.

In spring, I fill my plant presses with the blooms from irises, poppies, flax, redbud, willow, dogwood, and morning glories—just to name a few. By May, here in the Shenandoah Valley, it is warm enough to plant canna lily bulbs, whose foliage is very fibrous. The weather is also stable enough to set up my outdoor papermaking lab. The beating stones are cleared and repositioned from winter settling, and I fill the vats with processed inner-bark fibers. The increasing daylight allows for longer fresh-air drying times, and although one can make paper inside, I have found it easier to control the wet mess outside. If you cover your vats and fibers, and add some essential oils to disguise any odors, I have found that fibers will last a good fourteen days.

Sometimes, though, I will use up fibers quickly—creating a large sheet by pouring the fibers onto a large window screen. You will develop your own techniques with experience.

Throughout the rest of the growing season, I keep the plant presses full with different blooms—hollyhock, hibiscus, corn, iris, nettle, blackberry, rose of sharon, and hosta. By fall, dews and winds and temperature change reveal the herbaceous woody and non woody stalks and stems of the plants, thus beginning the retting process. Canna lillies and corn are ready for gathering, and the cooling fall evenings make the fiber preparation and cooking process very comfortable now. Experiment by adding fall leaves directly onto your sheets of paper—sometimes the color holds perfectly. As winter sets in, observe which plants in your gardens leave you clues as to their suitability for papermaking. "Skeletons" of cellulose will be left after, crisp and rattling in the wind, as plants die back for the season.

Basic Papermaking Procedures

Papermaking incorporates all the elements. If you are seeking to make an archive-quality paper, the fibers you collect will have to be cooked in an alkaline solution in order to break down the fiber and dissolve the lignin, pectins, gums, and waxes that hold the fibers together. Be advised however: Naturally field-retted plant fibers do not need to be cooked to remove the non-cellulose material; the fiber in such plants will be visible and easily removed from the stalk, stem, or leaf.

Often, during the summer and fall I throw fresh nettles or iris leaves directly into my blenders. The colors of these plants are fresh and intense, though they do fade in the drying process. Always cut plant material into one-inch pieces before blending, or they could tangle in the blender blade. Add freshly scraped or peeled fiber. Many fibers require cooking in a gentle alkali diluted in water in order to separate for papermaking. Soda ash is inexpensive and least dangerous. Some fibers need to be cooked in a stronger alkali such as lye, though you will have to take great precautions when cooking with it. The amount of alkali used is based on the weight of dry fiber—a standard rule is to use 20 percent of the dry fiber weight. When cooking, use only enamel or stainless-steel cooking pots. The fibers need to be soaked or hydrated before cooking to allow the cell walls of the fibers to swell for better alkali penetration. In the pot, make sure the fibers are completely covered with the water/alkali mixture. Always cook in a well-ventilated area; bring to a quick boil, then allow to simmer. Check your fiber, and stir often to test it for the correct consistency. When the fibers separate easily, they are done. Try not to overcook your fibers or they will become weak. Rinse your fibers completely after cooking, using a fine-mesh strainer to protect against fiber loss during your rinse. In your rinse, avoid water that has been chlorinated, or is tainted with iron, other rust, or sulfur—a neutral pH is best.

Once you have rinsed your fibers and the water is clear, you are ready to beat the fibers. The method you choose will affect your paper's final look. Blenders are an excellent choice for an inexpensive and quick method for home use. They chop the fibers shorter and to quite fine consistency, but the resulting paper is not as strong. Hand-beating is more time consuming, but produces a strong, long-fibered paper. For hand-beating at home, find a large, flat stone or hard, wooden surface on which to set your cooked fibers. Grooved wooden mallets work best for beating the fibers; a wooden baseball bat will do in a pinch too. Mass the fibers together, and then pound the mass into a homogenous pile. After fifteen minutes or so, check the fibers to see if they separate; add more water, and beat again. Continue this process, checking the fibers as you go. You can do a pulp test in a quart jar full of water. The fibers should not clump. With experience, you will learn how much beating makes the desired paper texture. With either method, hand-beating or blending, the results and variations should be recorded to enable you to recreate any papers you like.

During the beating process, the papermaker also decides what type of additives to use to enhance papers. Synthetic internal sizing is available from papermaking suppliers—it comes in a liquid form and is added during beating. Sizing coats the fibers, making them water-repellent and bleed-resistant for use as a base for calligraphy and watercolor paint. Other additives like buffers and brighteners can make your paper smooth and whiter or opaque. Pigments and dyes color papers, though pigments need a retention agent to attach properly to the pulp. These mordants give the pulp a positive charge and so allow the pigment to attach to the fibers (as a rule, if the water in your vat is clear, then the pigment has attached to the fiber). I have used tissue paper to color abaca and flax fibers, as well as poke berries, blackberries, carrot pulp, and other dye plants to influence the hues and textures of my final papers.

The fibers are now added to vats of clean water. The papermaker needs to choose which style of mould he or she will use to make the sheets—there are Western moulds and deckles, Japanese sugetas, Nepalese deckle boxes, and many other creative screen surfaces. The thickness or thinness of your paper sheet is determined by the ratio of prepared fiber to water in your vat. Usually a few cupfuls or handfuls of beaten fibers are added to three or four inches of water in your vat. Deeper vats allow for a smoother pull of your paper making screen; however, you will need to beat more fiber to get a thick sheet. Once again, experience will be your best teacher. You can even make your own large wooden vats, properly lacquered and sealed, when you get really serious about papermaking.

Now that you have your mould or screen ready, mix the fibers by gently stirring the slurry mixture in the vat. Then immediately dip your mould down and under the mixed fibers, and pull upward in a smooth arc. Place the mould on the corner of the vat to drain, and remove the deckle. Be careful not to disturb the surface of the paper in any way—with drops of water or any foreign materials—or flaws will show on your finished paper.

The wet sheet is very fragile. You can, if you choose, add any pressed flowers, strings, feathers, or embossing designs at this time. Most plant material will stick with just a little dab of extra fiber. Heavier items could also be sewn on when the sheet is dried later.

The sheet is now "couched," or laid down, onto damp couching sheets of felt or onto a hard surface. Japanese, Nepalese, and other indigenous papermakers dry their sheets by sponging or brushing the sheets onto walls, boards, large stretched screen frames, or even rocks outside. This quick air-dry process produces a crisp, flat sheet with a surface texture of the drying surface. Weather permitting, drying time can be as brief as two hours. The other, more Western, method of drying involves rolling the wet sheet on to a wet felt and making a continous stack, or "post" of sheets. The wet felts protect the sheets as they are later pressed under some sort of hydraulic jack. The stack of posts may be left to press for a few hours, then brushed on to boards for futher drying or set onto screens or racks. Once you remove the felts they should be cleaned and dried for reuse later. You can also dry your paper on a clothes line outside, once again you will discover which drying method works best for you.

Once you have created your own handmade herbal papers, you will find yourself enjoying just looking at the beautiful variations of each sheet. I like to record my methods for a certain type of paper directly on a sample sheet of the paper. This helps me remember some of the specifics about my procedures. One year I created large journals out of several different plant papers and used photos, recipes, herbal formulas, flower essence journeys, and sketchbook notes to compile a full record of my relationship with each particular plant.

You will find several excellent books at the end of this article that give detailed instructions on how to create your own cards, journals, and artistic books with your plant papers. Papermaking is a simple craft that will rekindle your awareness of the amazing abundance of the plant kingdom. Have fun.

Basic Papermaking Equipment

Recycled paper or plant fibers

Plenty of stainless-steel or plastic buckets for fiber hydration and cooking

Cat litter trays or storage tubs for slurry vats

Blender (look at thrift stores or garage sales)

Screens, a mould and deckle (professional or homemade)

Sticks for stirring, mallets for beating

Pigments and retention agents from papermaking supply companies

Couching felts or boards

A Few of the Fiber Plants

Woody Bast Fibers

Family and Species		Common Name	Best Gathering Time
Moraceae,	*Morus alba*	White mulberry	Fall (steam and strip branches)
	Morus nigra	Black mullberry	Fall
Malvaceae,	*Hibiscus syriacus*	Rose of Sharon	Fall (press flowers, gather inner bark)
Salicaceae,	*Salix nigra*	Black willow	Spring
	Salix discolor	Pussy willow	Fall (gather inner bark)
	Salax babylonica	Weeping willow	Fall (gather inner bark)
Ulmacea,	*Ulmus americana*	American elm	Spring (gather inner bark)
	Ulmus rubra	Slippery elm	Spring (gather inner bark)

Herbaceous Bast Fibers

Family and Species		Common Name	Best Gathering Time
Acocynaceae,	*Apocynolm cannabinum*	Indian hemp	Fall

Family and Species		Common Name	Best Gathering Time
Asclepiadaceae,	Asclepias syrica	Milkweed	Fall
Iridaceae,	Iris siberica	Iris	All year
Linaceae,	Linumus itatissimum	Flax	Fall
Malvaceae,	Alcea rosa	Hollyhock	Fall
Urticaceae,	Urtica dioica	Nettles	Fall

Leaf Fibers

Family and Species		Common Name	Best Gathering Time
Agave,	Yucca filamentosa	Yucca	Fall
Cannaceae,	Canna indica	Canna lily	Fall
Ginkgoaceae,	Ginkgo biloba	Ginkgo	Fall
Iridaceae,	Gladiolus spp.	Gladiolus	Fall
Liliaceae,	Allium cepa	Onion (skins)	Year round
Typha,	Typha latifolia	Cattail	Fall

Rushes, Sedges, and Grasses

Family and Species		Common Name	Best Gathering Time
Gramineae,	Hordeum vulgare	Barley straw	After seeding develops
	Phyllostachys aurea	Bamboo	Year round
	Zea mays	Corn	After harvest
	Avena sativa	Oatstraw	After harvest of green flowers

For Further Study

Bell, Lilian A. *Plant Fibers for Papermaking*. McMinnville, Oregon: Liliaceae Press, 1981.

Hiebert, Helen. *Papermaking with Plants*. Pownal, Vermont: Storey Books, 1998.

Hunter, Dard. *Papermaking: The History and Technique of an Ancient Craft. 2nd ed.* New York, New York: Dover Publ., 1978.

La Plantz, Shereen. *Cover to Cover: Creative Techniques for Making Beautiful Books, Journals & Albums*. Asheville, North Carolina: Lark Books, 1995.

Papermaking Suppliers

Carriage House Paper
   79 Guernsey Street
   Brooklyn, NY 11222   Phone: 800-669-8181
   (papermaking supplies and custom papers)

Dieu Donneí Papermill, Inc.
   433 Broome Street
   New York, NY 10013   Phone: 877-337-2737
   (papermaking supplies and classes)

Lee Scott McDonald Inc.
   P.O. Box 24
   Charlestown, MA 02129   Phone: 888-627-2737
   (papermaking supplies and equipment)

Twin Rocker
   P.O. Box 413
   Brookston, IN 47923   Phone: 800-757-8946
   (papermaking supplies)

Rituals with Natural Essential Oils

❧ by Mindy Green ❧

P lants in many different forms have long been incorporated into human rituals. Before essential oils were isolated, whole plants were employed as healing agents for the physical and spiritual body. Plants have long been thought to connect us to nature, to remind us we are part of something greater than ourselves, and to serve as a catalyst for the transformation of our bodies and souls. Even the most mundane physical exchange we have with plants, that of oxygen and carbon dioxide transference, is essentially magical.

A balance of give-and-take is crucial to all life on earth, and the symbiotic relationship between plants and humans is essential. But the juncture of the spiritual interchange between humans and plants actually occurs through our own sense of smell. This is where we bring the essence of plants into our bodies and therefore effect a change in consciousness, and provide a catalyst for potential spiritual and physical transformation. Whether you think of this as physical chemistry, or as vibrational energetics, it is clear that something magical occurs here. Plants are a manifestation of cosmic energy, transforming and transmuting light into chemical constituents. Most of us partake of this energy by eating the plants. Therefore, we usually think of plants as nourishing us physically, but the truth is they can also nourish us vibrationally.

This is nothing new. Our ancestors believed plants had the ability to communicate with a higher spiritual being—whether one might perceive of it as God, Goddess, or Great Spirit— through the use of plants. They also studied plants by the "Doctrine of Signatures," an age-old classification of the use of plants based on an observation of the plants themselves. That is, it was believed there was a correspondence between the appearance of a plant and what it could be used for, and herbalists noted such details as the shape or markings of a plant (as in lungwort, which is roughly shaped like a lung) or the color of a plant (as in hawthorn, which is red and associated with the heart; the dandelion, which is yellow and associated with the liver; or echinacea, which is purple and associated with blood infections).

The growing environment, taste, and smell also indicated how a plant may be utilized in healing. Paracelsus, the ancient alchemist, tells us that "through the signature the interior may be opened" and the "wisdom in the virtue" made known. Through such observations, herbalists knew which plants healed the body, which were good for arousing sexual desire, which provided a calm mind for meditative practices, and which awakened psychic awareness. Though it is not true in every case, there are a surprisingly large number of plants whose ancient uses prove true through scientific study today.

As ancient peoples incorporated these theories and plants into both their daily life and special ceremonies, so can we. I encourage my patients not to think of herbs just as medicinal agents, but rather to incorporate them into a daily diet. Don't just use essential oils as perfume or for ritual use alone, incorporate them into daily activities such as baths, and in beauty care to keep your body young and your skin smooth. Use them in your office to keep yourself alert and attentive to your tasks. Above all, use them to keep your spirit alive, tuned in, and connected.

Aromatherapy

Aromatherapy is a holistic approach to well-being that promotes relaxation and rejuvenation, and tunes the body, mind, and spirit. It becomes a key element in promoting or facilitating change when used with visualization, meditation, prayer, or ritual. In our Western culture, rituals have generally fallen by the wayside. Some people think of rituals as weird, heathenistic, anti-religious, or worse. However, nothing could be farther from the truth. Some rituals—such as marriage ceremonies, graduations, funerals, prayer, baptisms, and bar mitsvahs—have survived in human culture for centuries. A ritual is simply a ceremony performed to bring an idea into physical form, or to acknowledge a special time. It is a way of putting the universe on notice that you have a desire you want to manifest. It can mark a milestone, an accomplishment, or it can acknowledge new beginnings or bring closure. It can be as simple or complicated as you like, as the occasion calls for. It can be a brief verbal or mental acknowledgment, such as a simple prayer, or a ceremony that lasts for days. The tools can be elaborate and intricate, with songs, musical instruments, crystals, feathers, colors, candles, and more; or the tools can remain very simple. The most important part of any ritual is the intent.

The use of plants in ritual has a long history as old as humankind itself. Different plants were chosen for different types of ritual, unique to each particular culture. The same plant in different cultures can mean different things, but all plants carry associated meanings of some sort. The only requirement in such rituals is to come with a conscious intent, and a clear heart meant only for the highest good. The plant fragrances will then act as catalysts to transform energy. Use plants with love, high integrity, and responsibility—the possibilities are endless.

The Metaphysics of Aroma

As a ritual is a conscious act intended to lead to change in one's life, and magic is the ability to change consciousness at will, scent assists in these through its ability to unlock emotional blocks and old patterns of behavior.

The use of essential oils in psychic/psychological healing can be somewhat arbitrary, depending on a number of factors. These include the combined energies of both giver and receiver, astrological influences, emotional factors, belief systems, personal preferences, emotional programming, and the levels of experience of the practitioners. Though all these determinants can influence choice and effect, what allows magic to happen is attending with a pure heart, inhaling the fragrance, and visualizing an outcome with only the highest good intentions in mind. The merging of plant energies and human consciousness, sparked by the visualization of such a high purpose, can be very powerful. Do not underestimate the power of prayer and ceremony to initiate transformation, and know that each and every person is capable of manifesting it. And always give thanks to the plants that manifest cosmic forces well beyond us.

In choosing the oils for your purpose, the transformative energies of essential oils can be discovered three ways:

1. Studying (myth and history)

2. Observing (the Doctrine of Signatures)

3. Experiencing the effect (on mind and body)

Getting Started: The Productive Uses of Scent

Here is a quick exercise that demonstrates the powers of scent. That is, it is possible to program a "happy" scent for positive experiences. To do so, choose an oil that has no negative memory association and that you find pleasant-smelling. Every time you are relaxed, happy, or in a positive frame of mind, smell that oil. After a week or two, this scent will trigger a memory association in the brain—namely, you will feel happy. Now you may use the scent whenever you are in a stressed situation (but do not overuse it or you will begin to associate it with stress instead).

You should know also that scent can improve memory capacity. Scent memory is twice that of visual memory. Using central nervous system stimulants such as basil, peppermint, rosemary, and lemon can help you expand your memory. Smell them while studying, and again when you need to recall, such as during an exam. This has been proven in scientific studies.

Scent can also unblock emotional trauma. Since our sense of smell has the longest access to memory, it stands to reason that it can also access these deeply recessed areas of unconscious emotional trauma. This idea is based on a lock and key theory—memory is the locked door, smell is the key. Depending on the individual or the experience behind the blocked memory, the scent may vary. Subtle dilutions such as in a diffuser or light room mist are recommended.

There is some research to suggest that scent may be a suitable substitute for tranquilizing drugs. Choose relaxing and soothing scents such as the florals or grounding root oils. Lavender has been suggested in the treatment of Alzheimer's, and to diminish the side effects of drug therapies. Brain mapping studies show that this scent also increases alpha waves in the brain, which are associated with states of relaxation. For those who are lethargic or depressed, jasmine increases beta waves, which are associated with stimulation. It is also suggested that different oils will increase neurotransmitters in the brain, but this depends on an individual's chemical makeup.

Creating a Ritual

Ritual is about opening yourself to positive energy; it need not be associated with dark energies. It can serve as a powerful tool for personal transformation. The use of essential oils can allow you to open to integration and equilibrium. Rituals are performed to honor special times such as birth blessings and other welcomings, marriages and other bondings, and funerals and other separations. They are simply tools to raise your vibrations, invoke protection, strengthen personal vibration, or increase energies.

Beginning the Ritual

Here is a suggested step-by-step framework for creating a customized ritual. In time you will make up your own rituals to suit your own needs. This process can take ten minutes, an hour, or all day; just remember, there are no hard rules here. Create a ritual for whatever has meaning and power for you. The use of essential oils can be incorporated into any part of this process. Choose an oil that has meaning to you for the appropriate stage.

In beginning a ritual, one must prepare mentally and physically. Always it is very important to clearly state your intent before you begin. Are you there to transform, to create, or to empower? Choose an oil of clarity such as rosemary. You may wish to bring in special materials, tools, or symbols such as candles, crystals or specials stones, photos, or other items. Purification is an important beginning of any ritual. This could involve a cleansing bath, smudging (burning of a sacred plant such as sage), and diffusing or misting a clarifying fragrance (such as citrus or fir) to clear away negativity. Eliminate vengeful, greedy, or other negative thoughts, and ask for an outcome of the highest good. (Choose an oil of purity such as rose.) Invite in the dieties you hold as powerful. This creates a sacred space imbued with protection.

At this point the process may vary, depending on what you want to accomplish. You may need to spend extra time acknowledging and releasing the energies that hold you back and keep you from making positive changes—such as negative emotions, behaviors, or memories. They may be spoken, acknowledged in song, or (one of my favorites) written down and burned. It may involve the need to cry, grieve, or recognize your pain in order to let go. (Choose an oil of transformation such as petitgrain.) It is useful to realize that change or suffering often involves loss, but the outcome is opportunity and growth. I found this simple passage helpful in reminding me of this:

My barn
having burned to the ground
I can now see the Sun.

The next step in your ritual is one of affirmation. This is a good time to clarify and reaffirm your intent, being certain that what you ask for is truly what you want because you just might get it. This may involve visualizing, writing, or simply affirming verbally your desires. It may be helpful to make a treasure map to bring dreams into physical form. (Anoint it with an oil of definitive power and manifestation such as sage.) Giving thanks is an important part of any ritual. Once your wishes are made known, you may release your invited helpers and acknowledge their contribution to your process. It is also important to recognize that whatever our challenges, we all have many blessings. Acknowledge these and give them credence as you end your ritual.

Anointing and Visualizing

Essential oils may be used at any or every stage of your ritual. You can anoint physically or psychically injured areas of the body, as well as chakras or auras. To bring continuity to your ritual after it is complete, you may continue using the same oils, or any other blend you created with special intent. Daily use of this blend will reaffirm your goals and serve as a reminder of your intent. As you open it, inhale the aroma and visualize your dream, affirming the qualities you want to enhance. You may wish to anoint significant parts of your body—such as the chakras (see below), organs, hands, feet, heart, and so on, as you had in your ritual.

Intentions Related to Chakras and Other Body Parts

Chakras have been known for millennia as energy vortexes in the body. Anointing them enhances the qualities they represent. At the end of every list is a suggested blend that may be added to one ounce of a carrier oil such as almond, apricot, sesame, olive, or other vegetable oil. Chant the associated sounds as you rub oil on each chakra.

1st chakra: Also known as the root chakra. Location: Base of the spine, perineum, or feet. Related to: Security, survival, grounding, and getting to the root of the matter. Element: Earth. Stones: Garnet and hematite. Colors: Brown and red. Sound: "lam." Oils: Resin oils, vetiver, myrrh, patchouli.

2nd chakra: Location: Sacral/sexual organs. Related to: Creativity, balancing (between male and female), and accessing deepest emotions. Element: Water. Stones: Carnelian and coral. Color: Red and orange. Sound: "vam." Oils: Sandalwood, jasmine, rose.

3rd chakra: Location: Solar plexus, liver, pancreas. Related to: Focusing willpower. Element: Fire. Stones: Amber, topaz. Color: Yellow. Sound: "ram." Oils: Juniper, neroli.

4th chakra: Location: Heart, actions that come from love. Related to: Balance, mediation between higher and lower chakras. Element: Air. Stones: Rose quartz, emerald. Color: Green. Sound: "yam." Oils: Rose, bergamot.

5th chakra: Location: Throat. Related to: Speaking truth freely; self-expression. Element: Sound. (Ring a bell, sing a song, recite a poem.) Stone: Turquoise. Color: Blue. Sound: "ham." Oils: German chamomile, myrrh.

6th chakra: Location: Brow/third eye. Related to: Seeing clearly, intuition. Element: Light. Stone: Lapis. Color: Indigo. Sound: "aum." Oils: Rosemary, lavender.

7th chakra: Location: Crown. Related to: Opening where the soul enters and leaves; understanding. Element: Thought. Stone: Amethyst. Color: Violet, white, rainbow. Sound: Higher octave of "aum." Oils: Frankincense, rosewood.

Other Areas to Anoint

Hands: Gives meaning to everything you do or touch.

Feet: For walking the path of your intention.

Knees: For moving forward in life's journey.

Sex organs: For sacred sexuality.

Pulse points: To connect heart and blood and attune personal energies.

Base of skull: For accessing past lives and memories.

Spine: To give you "backbone" and uphold values.

To draw energy inward, massage the area in a counterclockwise (downward) direction. This symbolizes spirit put into manifestation. For example, massage the throat chakra and say, "May this oil help me speak my truth clearly."

In general, use very low dilutions of 1 percent or less (5–6 drops of essential oil in 1 ounce of carrier) for any work involving the psychic uses of essential oils. On very sensitive individuals you can use the oils in the aura only. Create daily affirmations, speak them aloud, and always use a positive statement such as, "I find comfort and strength in myself." Avoid using negating terms such as "not," "never," or "no."

Creating Blends

Here are a few guidelines to creating fragrances that result in scents that are balanced and pleasing. The terms "top," "middle," and "base" notes refer to an oil's evaporation rate. The proper combining of these oils can result in blends with staying power.

Top Oils

The fastest evaporating oils, or top notes, tend to be light, fresh, sharp, and penetrating. Top notes are fast acting, stimulating, and useful for depression. Examples include fruit oils, such as citrus oils, or lemon scents such as lemon eucalyptus, citronella, or lemon grass.

Middle Notes

Middle notes are harmonizing and balancing to the body, mind, and spirit. This category includes chamomile and marjoram, and amphoteric (balancing) oils such as lavender and geranium. Middle notes can include flowers, leaf, and seed oils such as dill, celery, fennel, anise, coriander, nutmeg, and so on.

Base Notes

Base notes are grounding, and provide a long-lasting and deep, sensual, and romantic quality. These fixatives should be used rather sparingly, they often are not very pleasant scents of themselves; though when used in proper proportion they can add great depth and stability to a blend. Sedating base notes are used for anxiety, stress, impatience, insomnia, and relaxation. These include most woods, resins, and roots, and tend to be among the most expensive essential oils. Some of the more pleasing base notes include cedarwood, vanilla, sandalwood, frankincense, and jasmine. Base notes that you should use more sparingly include spikenard, vetiver, valerian, myrrh, cistus, and patchouli.

Safety

Safety is always the first consideration in using oils (especially on the physical body). Be sure to research the oils that you choose for purity (never use synthetic oils), consider any contraindications or possible skin sensitivities, and adjust dilution accordingly for those who are sensitive, convalescing, or elderly. Avoid direct application with pregnant women. When essential oils are inhaled or applied to the subtle body only, there are far fewer safety precautions to take.

Blending

Start by making a list of all the appropriate oils you want to use in your blend, and be ready to eliminate down to no more than five. Keep detailed notes of your blends and rituals. Label your blend with the date, ingredients, dilution, and so on.

If you have a list of ten oils, one way to narrow the options is by smelling the oils. Eliminate the ones that you find unpleasant. Then open the bottles one by one and imagine in your mind how they would blend with each other. You can hold the bottle caps to your nose in differing combinations, or better yet, place a dab of each on strips of blotter paper or tissue and smell.

Get ready to mix. Start small, blending by the drop. Use no more than twelve drops of essential oil per one ounce of carrier; remember that six drops is a lot when treating the subtle body. Sniff as you go and continue to take notes on the blend. Always mix the essential oils together in the bottle first before adding the carrier. Before the carrier oil is added it is a good idea to hold the blend in your hands, shake or roll the bottle, and simply affirm the purpose and intent. This may well be the most important step in your ritual of blending; reaffirming intent adds a powerful human energy that positively charges your blend.

Now you are ready to add the carrier oil. Jojoba oil has the longest shelf life of any fixed oil. If you are making a small amount that will be used up within a couple of months, any good vegetable oil will suffice. If the blend is very high in resinous oils use pure grain alcohol. Water may be used as a carrier if you want to make a light body or room mist mixture. A small amount of alcohol may be added to help disperse the oils, but they still must be shaken before use. Use about five drops of essential oil blend per ounce of water for a mist.

Your blends may be left as concentrates if you prefer. When blended into a carrier oil they should ideally be used up within two to six months. This shelf life depends, in part, on the carrier used, environmental conditions, and whether or not the blend is stored properly away from heat and light.

If you choose to wear your ritual blend as a perfume, follow these precautionary guidelines. If your blend contains a citrus oil, wear it on an area of your body that won't be exposed to sunlight (these oils increase sun sensitization). Some ingredients can also stain clothing. Here are some more tips for using essential oils:

• Never wear too much of any oil.

• A successful blend is achieved if the fragrance is not over-bearing, is appropriate to surroundings, is dermatologically safe, and provides a sense of well-being.

• Your blend can be used as an anointing oil during your ceremony and added to body lotion afterward to trigger your intentions. It can also be used as an after-shower mist or room spray. Your stock bottle may be used in the bath by adding five to eight drops mixed in a teaspoon of carrier oil per full tub.

Recipe Suggestions

The following recipes will provide rough guidelines for you to make any combination you desire.

Cleansing New House

To clear the energy of previous occupants, use any of the following oils: juniper, pine, rosemary, eucalyptus. To generate good, positive energy, use any of the following oils: bergamot, cedar, lavender, orange, neroli, rose, sandalwood, vetiver.

Uplifting Bath Blend

2 parts each lemon, geranium, juniper; 4 parts rosemary, 1 part peppermint

Relaxing Bath Blend

2 parts each clary sage, bergamot; 4 parts lavender, 3 parts marjoram, 1 part chamomile

Antidepressant Bath Blend

1 part ylang ylang, 2 parts clary sage, 3 parts bergamot, 6 parts sandalwood

Spiritual Sexuality

Varying amounts of jasmine, sandalwood, neroli, rose, vetiver ; use to spray the sheets.

Mother and Child Reunion

1 part Roman chamomile, 4 parts lavender, 2 parts each rose, neroli, 3 parts mandarin

Death Ceremony

2 parts each ylang ylang and melissa, 1 part cypress, 7 parts mandarin, 6 parts sandalwood, 4 parts oakmoss, 5 parts rose

Psychic Uses of Individual Oils

Angelica: Tuning in to the higher self.

Benzoin: Increases physical strength while calming and grounding. Dispels anger.

Bergamot: Heals the heart chakra, especially when grief prevents giving and receiving love. If the heart is open, helps radiate love and healing.

Black Pepper: Mental stimulant and physical energizer. Helps move us from "stuck" places.

Chamomile: Calming and soothing. Helps us communicate clearly, without anger.

Carrot seed: Strengthens inner vision in times of confusion. Removes blocks, allowing free flow of energy.

Cedarwood: Used for temple construction in many ancient civilizations; cedar enhances spirituality and connects us to the divine. Used for mental clarity and to develop and maintain a sense of balance and control in our lives.

Clary sage: To enhance and remember our dreams and gain insight through them; strengthens the "inner eye." May be too intense for some.

Cypress: For transitions, moving one's home, making major decisions, letting go of a relationship, bereavement, loss of a loved one. For thousands of years cypress has been planted in cemeteries as a reminder of life everlasting.

Elemi: Balancing essential oil. Harmonizes and focuses group activities.

Eucalyptus: Cleanses negative energies, both verbal and physical.

Fennel: Protection against psychic attack.

Frankincense: Meditative aid for the highest spiritual aspirations. Breaks ties with the past, especially those that hold back personal growth.

Helichrysum: Activates the intuitive, right side of the brain assisting meditation, intuition, visualization, and creative works.

Hyssop: Used as a cleansing herb in the temples of Egypt; can be used to cleanse any room where healing takes place.

Inula: To strengthen the "faint of heart," and those needing to express and experience love; develops skills and allows the inner self to shine.

Jasmine: Long recognized as an aphrodisiac; unites apparent opposites and aids spiritual development. It has both male and female associations and is said to transcend physical love and develop our understanding of spiritual sexuality. Develops creativity and the artistic senses.

Juniper: A cleanser and detoxifier of the physical and subtle. Clears negativity, helps one deal with large groups of people (at work, traveling, or public places) you would not normally choose to be with.

Lavender: Calming, balancing, cleansing, harmonizing. Aids in meditation and integrating spirituality into everyday life.

Mandarin: Delicate and refined, this essential oil bring us in touch with our inner child.

Marjoram: Diminishes the desire for sexual contact; it can be used by those on a spiritual path or those separated from a partner. Eases loneliness and grief, especially following the loss of a lover. Prolonged use can deaden the emotions.

Melissa: Has the ability to bring comfort, especially in the case of sudden death. Dispels fear and regret, brings understanding and acceptance. Aligns our will with the divine will. Helps us recall past lives.

Mugwort: Protects against evil, heightens dreams. May be too intense for some.

Myrrh: Said to enhance and strengthen spirituality. Used in meditation or before a healing, especially for those who feel stuck emotionally or spiritually and want to move forward in their lives.

Neroli: A symbol of purity; used to reconnect to the higher self, enhance creativity, and calm the mind and body. Also used to spiritualize sexual partnerships.

Orange: Used to bring cheer and joy into your life.

Palmarosa: An aid to healing, especially absent healing.

Patchouli: Strengthens and grounds "dreamers"; attunes one to the physical body. Useful for those who overmeditate or those who don't take care of earthly matters.

Peppermint: Acts on the ego, dispelling pride, and assists in overcoming feelings of inferiority. Associated with cleanliness; helps those who want to live an ethical life.

Petitgrain: For mental clarity and for decision making.

Pine: Invigorating, energizing; clears the mind and body.

Rose: Used to spiritualize sexuality; encourages angels to enter your space.

Rosemary: For psychic protection and clarity of thought.

Rosewood: For meditation and spiritual work. Calming and aphrodisiac. Endangered, so use conscientiously.

Sage: Promotes wisdom and protection from physical illness.

Sandalwood: Stills the mind; facilitates spiritual development.

Spikenard: Intensifies feelings of devotion and generosity. Good for those working in charity or those with deep inner pain caused by natural or manmade disasters.

Thyme: Strengthening, grounding, and energizing on all levels. Helpful to those readjusting to their normal routine after a vacation or retreat.

Vetiver: For grounding and centering. Aligns, balances, and harmonizes. Also for those who are a psychic sponge and take on too much of another's energy, especially when doing healing work. Harmonizes group activities.

Ylang ylang: Creates peace, dispels anger. Use sparingly.

For Further Study

Ackerman, Diane. *A Natural History of the Senses.* New York, New York: Vintage Books, 1991.

Cunningham, Scott. *Magical Aromatherapy.* Saint Paul, Minnesota: Lewellyn Publications, 1982.

Green, Mindy. *Natural Perfumes.* Loveland, Colorado: Interweave Press, 2000.

LeGuerer, Annick. *Scent: The Mysterious and Essential Powers of Smell.* New York, New York: Turtle Bay Books, 1992.

Incense from Bulk Herbs

⇜ by Tamara Bowden ⇝

W hen I first "met" Scott Cunningham, I was in a transitional place in my life. I found his book *Wicca: A Guide for the Solitary Practitioner* (Llewellyn, 1988) and bought it on impulse. It only took the one book, and I was hooked; I began buying up all of the books by him that I could find. I had finally found the spiritual teacher I was looking for.

In particular, I enjoyed reading Scott Cunningham's herb books, which were rich with descriptions of teas, tinctures, aromatherapy, and incense. In time, encouraged and tutored by Scott's work, I felt a strong need to work with magical herbalism.

Serendipity

When you take up a spiritual path, it is often the universe that provides. Shortly after I read *The Complete Book of Incense, Oils and Brews* by Scott Cunningham (Llewellyn, 1989), and began to develop some ideas for creating my own incense, I met a new group of friends who were opening up an occult shop and Wiccan school a few blocks from my house. I received my first formal training in Wicca through these friends, and later I was initiated into their coven.

It was a great time; they loved my ideas, and offered to sell my incense in the shop. And so, bursting with ideas, I began to experiment and create my own unique magical blends of incense. I called them "Vital Essences," and they began to sell rapidly from our little corner shop. Soon, I was teaching my techniques in workshops and was receiving requests to create blends for specific purposes. I began to create personal blends for each of my friends, as well.

After a few months, I learned that Scott Cunningham had passed away, and I felt as if I had lost a friend. I had wished to meet him in person someday and thank him for his amazing body of work, but I never had the chance. I decided then that I would create a special blend of my magical incenses and dedicate it to my spiritual mentor, Scott Cunningham. (The recipe, called "Graduation Incense," is included later in this article.)

When I had the blend ready, I held a small memorial service and invited my friends to attend. I arranged Scott's books on my altar, and lit a white candle in remembrance. I talked about how I had been inspired by and had learned so much from this man. I explained that I had created this special blend in honor of Scott Cunningham, and in honor of all the inspiration and education I had received from his work. Even if I never had met him in person, I felt that he would appreciate my dedication, wherever he was. I started to place some of my incense on a lit piece of charcoal, and out of the corner of my eye I saw someone through the window in the backyard—a man, dressed in white, bending over as if he were picking some of the flowers growing in the yard. As he stood up, I turned to look fully, and he was gone. I whispered my thanks to this man. I truly believe to this day that I had been blessed with a very special "You're welcome."

Coming Full Circle

Years and years have passed now since that event, and I still have a passion for creating my own magical incense. I have wandered farther down my same spiritual path and have learned a lot in the intervening years, but I will never forget the gentle and caring introduction I received from Scott Cunningham.

Graduation Incense: In Memory of Scott Cunningham

This incense is useful for any kind of transition or passage, especially for one who has passed over. It honors and eases passage for those who have gone over, and comforts those who remain.

Red roses (for love, compassion, and healing)

Marjoram (for joy, friendship, and meditation)

Cumin seeds (for health, healing, and protection)

Dill seeds (for wisdom, and communication)

Cinnamon sticks (for protection, physical strength, and purification)

Frankincense (for protection, purification, and courage)

Pure vanilla crystals (for relaxation and dreams)

Grind roses into small bits, then set aside. Grind cumin seeds into small bits, then set aside. Grind the dill seeds, and set aside. Break up and grind the cinnamon sticks into very small bits and set aside. Grind frankincense into a powder. Mix all together with marjoram. Toss in only a pinch or two of the pure vanilla crystals. Charge with energies of love and support, ease of transition, safe passage, acceptance, and release. Burn to remember someone, placing items or pictures on your altar that represent the loved one. Light a white candle for purity and burn the incense on the charcoal.

Supplies

When I became inspired to create ritual incense, I bought a variety of herbs, spices, and resins at my local health food store, food co-op, foreign grocery, and New Age stores. Most are sold by the ounce, and you can purchase a variety of herbs and spices for very little money. Most incense can be made very simply with an inexpensive mortar and pestle. I recommend using a mortar and pestle because it brings your personal energy into the herbs as you grind them. But I also use a coffee bean grinder for larger and more solid herbs like cinnamon, frankincense, cloves, or juniper berries to save a lot of time and effort. You can purchase one for around ten to twenty dollars at most grocery or department stores. If you choose to use a coffee bean grinder, however, don't use it for anything else but your incense, as some herbs such as frankincense are inedible.

Creating Magical Blends

I consult a few different books on herbal folklore to get an idea what each herb represents or is associated with (see bibliography). I consider my ritual purpose, then start selecting herbs appropriate to my intention. I smell each herb to decide if it is right for the blend. I grind each herb and blend them all together in a bowl a bit at a time. I know it is done when it smells right.

Before ritual use, I raise the energy and "charge" the blend by directing the energy appropriate to the purpose into the incense. I will also visualize the energy of the universe, entering through the top of my head as I inhale, and flowing out through my hands into the blend as I exhale. I burn the incense blend on charcoal during my ritual, while focusing on my purpose. As the blend is released through the smoke, my energies and wishes are carried out to the universe.

Recipes for Vital Essences by Sister Moon

Many times, as I create a new blend I can feel the ideas and inspirations just popping into my head, and I am always sure to give thanks for each blend that I create. Here are some of my most popular divinely "inspired" ritual incense recipes, with spellwork suggestions for their use. The herbs I use can all be obtained from Frontier Herb Company (www.frontierherb.com) if you can't find them in stores nearby. I have not included any measurements, because you will have to mix the ingredients yourself and let your intuition tell you when it is ready.

Exploring your own unique perceptions is an important part of this process. If you feel a need to do these recipes differently, by all means, follow your instincts. Let your nose guide you. These are the way the recipes work for me, but you may prefer to use them as a guide to creating your own.

If you don't have herbal books to reference, you can learn a lot by smelling an herb or spice and taking notes on how it makes you feel, or what it makes you think of. Does it represent fire or water? Is it a banishing herb? For example, turmeric and black pepper have sharp, almost unpleasant smells and are traditionally used for banishing (burn these outside, for safety). Rose and jasmine are soothing, loving scents, but patchouli and cumin are earthy. You can experiment with different herbs to build your own reference list. Add as many personal associations as possible as you experiment.

Be as creative as you like with ingredients, methods, and spellwork. Always write down what you are doing so you can recreate it again later. I take notes while I am making a blend, then record my finished incense recipes in a blank book when I am done. I am always energized and enthusiastic about my work with herbs. I hope this helps you to come up with some recipes of your own.

True Love Incense

Red rosebuds or petals (for love, luck, and healing)

Orris powder (for love and psychic awareness)

Ground cinnamon (for protection and purification)

Patchouli root or essential oil (for protection, lust, and
   abundance)

Crush the rose buds or petals, then gently add the orris and cinnamon until it looks pleasing. Add the patchouli until it smells
right. Charge the blend with thoughts of love, acceptance, and
attraction. Release the energy of this blend while burning a red
or pink candle and meditating on being lovable and having love
surround you.

Abundance Incense

Pine (for purification, protection, and money)

Cardamom pods (for peace, purification, and clarity)

Licorice root (for happiness, meditation, and pleasure)

Chop pine needles into smaller pieces with a knife or scissors,
then grind to release the scent. Set aside. Break up licorice root
into small pieces, then set aside. Grind cardamom pods, then mix
all three together. Charge with thoughts of security, prosperity,
abundance, and satisfaction. Release the energy of this blend
while burning a green candle and meditating on being content
and satisfied.

Dreamtime Incense

Chamomile flowers (for purification and the psyche)

Lemongrass (for psychic awareness and wisdom)

Fennel seeds (for divination and purification)

Powdered nutmeg (for luck, psychic awareness, and
   magical power)

Rose geranium oil (for courage, love, and protection)

Blessed salt (for stability, grounding, and peace)

Water blessed by a Full Moon reflection (for
   attunement to lunar energies and the unknown)

Grind chamomile flowers lightly, and set aside. Grind lemon-grass lightly to release the scent, and set aside. Grind fennel seed into smaller pieces, then mix the three herbs until they smell right. Add just a bit of nutmeg (enough to smell faintly). Add one drop of rose geranium oil. Charge the finished blend by the light of the Full Moon. Add some blessed salt and a sprinkle of water that has been blessed with the energy and reflection of the Full Moon. Release the energy of this blend when seeking a vision.

Consecration Incense

Frankincense resin (for protection, purification, and courage)

Cinnamon sticks (for spirituality and protection)

Whole cloves (for divination, exorcism, and health)

Myrrh resin (for protection and spirituality)

Break cinnamon sticks into small, woody pieces, and set aside. Grind cloves into small pieces, and set aside. Pour frankincense into a bowl, and slowly add cinnamon and cloves. Add myrrh until mixture looks pleasing. Burn some of the blend to consecrate the rest. Use for consecration of magical tools, while performing divination or purification, or cleansing a home.

Path Illumination Incense

Cinnamon sticks (for spirituality, psychic awareness, and protection)

Whole cloves (for divination, exorcism, and health)

Cardamom pods (for peace, purification, and clarity)

Break cinnamon into small pieces, and set aside. Grind cloves and set aside, then grind cardamom pods. Mix all three together for the smell of warmth. Charge with energies of illumination and guidance. Release the energies of this blend whenever you need guidance along your spiritual path.

Housewarming Incense

Sage (for purification, cleansing, and spirituality)

Myrrh resin (for protection and spirituality)

Frankincense resin (for protection, purification, and courage)

Sandalwood or cedar (for healing and spirituality)

Dill seeds (for protection, riches, and love)

Rose geranium oil (for courage, love, and protection)

Break up sage into small pieces, and set aside. Grind dill seeds, and set aside. Mix all herbal ingredients together until it smells right, then add one drop of rose geranium oil at a time until it smells finished. Charge with energies of home, happiness, prosperity, protection, love, and peace. Release the energies of this blend to cleanse a living space. Walk with the incense clockwise around each room in the home, wafting the smoke into every corner and closet.

Mysterious Ways Incense

Rose petals (for love, luck, and healing)

Chamomile (for love and psychic awareness)

Raspberry leaf (for toning, health, and female concerns)

Jasmine flowers or essential oil (for lunar energy, peace, and happiness)

Grind roses until they are broken apart. Add chamomile flowers, jasmine flowers, and raspberry leaf until well mixed. Charge with female, passive energies of the Moon while drawing circles or spirals in the blend with your fingers. Release the energy of this blend in any ritual honoring the Goddess, especially one of thanks.

Herb History, Myth, and Magic

Pitcher Plant Lore

≈ by S. Y. Zenith ≈

The island of Borneo is an immense land of great biodiversity. There are vast equatorial rainforests and unreachable jungles on the island that contain various strangely proportioned plant species such as the rafflesia—the world's largest flower—the smallest known pinhead orchid, natural bonsai-like trees, giant mosses that grow to heights of one meter, at least four hundred and fifty types of ferns, and numerous species of the mysterious pitcher plant.

The pitcher plant, in the family *Nepenthaceae* and genus *nepenthes*, is a carnivorous plant. The name *nepenthes* was coined in 1737 by the famous Swedish botanist Carl Linne, also known as Linnaeus, in reference to a passage in Homer's *Odyssey* wherein Helen gives the drug nepenthe in glasses of wine to relieve her guests of their cares. Nepenthe in Greek means "without grief."

Carnivorous plants have specialized leaf organs that are able to trap insects and small animals, dissolve their remains, and extract nutrients from them. Pitcher plants have a modified leaf-type, which forms a well that holds liquid such as rainwater. Insects attracted to the plant fall into the well and drown. They are then digested as part of the plant's nutrient intake. The leaves of the pitcher plant have been variously described as jugs, cups, chalices, pots, urns, gourds, goblets, tankards, and mugs. The pitcher-shaped "body" of the plant is actually made up of leaves. The leaves come in different shapes and sizes depending on the species, but in each the pattern of the midrib and veins of the leaves as a rule embrace the curving body of the pitcher and end in a tiny spur behind the lid of the plant.

The nepenthes' pitcher is a complex structure. The pitcher's mouth is surrounded by a fine grooved rim that sometimes contains sharp points inside and colorful stripes outside. In some species, a small hook forms on the tip of the underside to act as a hinge that secures the lid of the plant over the mouth before the plant is fully mature. The lid prevents rain from diluting the digestive fluid in the pitcher before the cup is completely developed. When the plant reaches its full size, the lid opens to trap ants, spiders, beetles, moths, flies, wasps, scorpions, millipedes, centipedes, snails, and frogs.

The pitcher does not contain any moving mechanisms and is therefore regarded as a "passive trap." The trap itself consists of three parts: the attraction zone around the peristome and under the lid; the zone within the upper portion of the pitcher; and the digestive zone at the bottom. The total life span of a pitcher plant is between sixteen to twenty months. The many species of pitcher plants range from pipe to pint-mug sized. The largest pitcher plant of Borneo is the *Nepenthes rajah*; it is so large that one specimen was found to contain two liters of water and a drowned rat. The flowers of the pitcher plant are the least conspicuous parts of the plant, although they contain nectar glands to attract insects for pollination and have taxonomic features.

Pitcher Plant Folk Uses

The use of pitcher plants in folk remedies has a long recorded history. One of the earliest incidents was related by Paul Hermann, who wrote in 1717 of the species *N. distillatoria's* use as a remedy for snakebite in Sri Lanka. Different Asian regions utilize different species of the pitcher plant in various ways. In some parts of Borneo, the durable stems of certain species are used as binding material or for tying fence posts. They were also used as a substitute for rattan cane in securing timber pieces, although they were rarely used in the weaving of baskets.

The natives of Borneo have been known to use the pitcher plant as an emetic in cases of poisoning and in exorcism rituals. The roots of the *N. gracilis* and *N. ampullaria* were boiled to treat stomach upset and dysentery. In Singapore, a decoction of the stem of *N. ampullaria* was used to treat fever. The peptonised fluid of half-grown pitchers were also used to ease indigestion.

One recorded use from Brunei indicates that the digestive juice from unopened pitchers of any species was useful as a hair oil and as treatment for eye inflammation. Another account from Brunei made a decoction from the roots of *N. gracilis*, mixed with shallots and garlic, to help regulate menstruation. Young shoots of this particular plant species were eaten for the same purpose. To ease the labor of childbirth, women drank liquid from unopened pitchers of the *N. gracilis*. Children also drank this liquid to relieve asthma. Other species analyzed by the Department of Agriculture in Brunei were found to possess astringent, diuretic, and stimulating properties.

In Sabah, the Dusun people use the liquid of unopened pitchers of *N. lowii* and *N. edwardsiana* as skin lotions. On jungle treks in southern Sabah, native guides washed out large pitchers of the *N. reinwardtiana* and packed them with rice to cook in a pot all day. They dined on the rice on their return in the evening. Pitcher plants are also used for steaming rice in Thailand.

In Java, water from the pitchers of *N. gymnamphora* was drunk to treat coughs. The leaves of *N. reinwardtiana* were used for treating skin diseases. The people of Luzon in the Philippines used fluid from unopened pitchers of *N. alata* for diarrhea, and Sumatrans use fluid of the *N. tobaica* as a remedy for burns.

Various Names for the Pitcher Plant

All localities have their own folk names for the pitcher plant. Among the names (translated into English) are "monkey's cooking pot," "monkey's water-scooper," "monkey's jug," "Tiger-ant's cooking pot," and "monkey's rice packet." The plant has also been described as the "little jar of the devil," since it grows in wastelands where evil spirits of the woods and mountains live. It has also been called "devil's jug" and "devil's watercask."

Modern times have seen rapid decline of many traditional uses of the pitcher plant, though the traditions are continued in the most remote locations of Borneo. Plastic twines have replaced pitcher stems as tying material, and Western medicine is quickly replacing folk medicine in urban and suburban locations. These days, pitcher plants are cultivated mainly as peculiar ornamentals. Still, they continue to be part of traditional Malay and Chinese pharmacopoeias. In China, a decoction of *N. mirabilis* is prescribed to reduce high blood pressure and urinary infections. Adventurers roaming into remote forests continue to appreciate pitcher plants for their beauty, the supply of water they give, and for use as cooking pots.

Mexican Herb Lore

≫ by Edain McCoy ≪

I n northern Mexico and the American Southwest, copal, rosemary, and red chili peppers are used for all sorts of magic and healing. All three of these plants are ruled by the element of fire and make use of the power of profound transformation to work their magic.

Copal

Go into any botanica, or herbal apothecary, in the region, and you will find the atmosphere heavy with the cloying scent of copal *(Bursea adorata)*. This aromatic tree resin is renowned for its purifying properties and its ability to bring the truth of any matter to the surface.

Some folk beliefs tell us that one who lies in a room filled with copal will give himself away, or else that an offended god will cause some unusual quirk to occur, such as the popping of

a button or the blowing off of a hat, to indicate that a lie is being told. To use copal in its purification aspect you should visualize spiritual cleanliness filling the air around you as you light a copal incense. Dedicate the incense to your cause with words of power.

> *Copal sweet as an angel's face,*
> *Impart to this place your peace and grace;*
> *Copal warm and powerful charm,*
> *All harm now you must disarm.*

The copal resin is usually crushed to a coarse powder with a *molcajete*, a mortar and pestle made of rough volcanic rock that helps break down hard substances. This device breaks the copal into smaller chunks that burn with ease.

Copal is also a popular ingredient in love magic. When scattered about an area it imparts an aura of romance that's hard to resist. Copal resins are sometimes carried in the pocket or held within a locket or pocket watch to make one attractive to the opposite sex.

Another popular use of copal is in poppet magic, especially magic involving love spells. Poppets are small dolls that have been created to represent specific individuals on whom magic will be worked. This magic is not always positive, and this fact has given poppet spells a sinister reputation among many modern magical practitioners. But poppet magic does not have to be manipulative. The choice whether to make a poppet specific to a person or simply a representation of a type of person is always a choice of free will.

Poppets are usually dressed in the manner that best mimics the one whom they are intended to represent. In Mexico, it is common practice to use a small piece of copal to represent that person's heart. The copal in addition also represents the "heart" of the issue over which a spell will be enacted, and it helps the one who works the spell to connect with the issue. Always try to connect with the heart whenever you burn copal incense in order to renew or strengthen a spell-working.

Rosemary

Rosemary (*Rosemarinus officinalis*, which means "dew of the sea" in Latin) is arguably the most versatile of all magical herbs. It is used in spells for love, protection, beauty, spirituality, healing, and passion. The plant is not native to the Western Hemisphere, but was transplanted from the Mediterranean region of Spain. Though the Spanish name for rosemary is *romero*, in and around San Antonio, Texas, Latinos sometimes refer to the plant as *rubia*, or "ruby," which is also a nickname for the Spanish currency known as the peseta. The origin of this nickname is uncertain, but it clearly attests to the high value placed on rosemary in Southwestern folk life.

The folk healers of Mexico and the southwest, known as *curanderos*, will often use diluted rosemary oil in rituals of healing touch, or as a massage oil for sore muscle and an antiseptic for wounds. The antiseptic properties of rosemary are being investigated by scientists who are not sure why the oil seems to kill bacteria, but the research could someday lead to discovery of new antibiotics.

In many homes in south Texas, rosemary bushes are cultivated beneath windows to protect the home from unwanted spirits who might want to enter. Sometimes the needles of the plant are taken from a rosemary branch and placed inside on the window sill to offer further protection. The clean scent of the needles helps to reinforce the idea of purity and protection when the windows are open and the breeze blows inside.

A curandera I once knew in Texas recommended the placing of rosemary needles in window sills, but asked that they first be put into glass jars to further help deflect negative intentions. As you place your rosemary you should use words of power and evoke any deities, saints, or protective spirits you wish to call.

> *(Name of protector), I place this herb,*
> *So bane and harm shall be curbed;*
> *No negative spirit, nor specter, nor spell,*
> *Can enter this home you guard so well.*

Powdered rosemary is often put into magical candles. Candle magic is very popular in the region, and candles for every magical need are found in many stores—including mainstream groceries and drug stores. Rosemary can be found in candles for love and protection, and sometimes in those honoring the Virgin Mary—the Catholic version of the mother Goddess.

Rosemary incense often forms the backdrop of love magic or for magic enacted by students wishing to pass exams. It is also carried along with "holey" stones to enhance fertility, with lodestones to draw attraction, and with bloodstones when a court case needs the favor of magic. To help turn judges and juries in your favor when you know you are in the right, soak a bloodstone overnight in rosemary water. Place it in your left pocket and go to court. Just before the proceedings begin, reach into your pocket and grasp the stone while reciting your words of power.

> *Stone as firm as judgment stands,*
> *Clasped now in my shaking hands;*
> *Impart the truth and let it shine,*
> *Winning the judgment shall be mine.*

The incense of rosemary has been prescribed to prevent nightmares in children and to promote peaceful sleep in adults. It also seems to soothe those who are restless and anxious. Burn rosemary with lemon incense to help bring someone out of a depressed mood.

Red Chili Peppers

The red chili pepper (*pimienta de rojo* or *pimienta de cayena* in Spanish) that flavor much of Mexico's popular cuisine are also used lavishly in Mexican and Southwestern magic. Their protective influence can be found in many American homes today outside the Southwest at Christmas. It is an old tradition to hang the dried peppers in one's kitchen at Christmas to ensure a safe and happy New Year. This explains why the manufacturers of holiday decoration have created red chili pepper lights to hang on hearths, walls, and Christmas trees during the holidays.

Another use of the hanging peppers is to ensure fidelity from one's domestic partner. To do so, hang them near the bedroom or near the hearth while reciting words of power.

Pepper spicy, red like fire,
Quench in (name of partner) outside desire;
To me for love and sex he (or she) does turn,
For me a passion in him (or her) does burn.
Bring him (or her) home to me each night,
Let the fires of lust burn bright;
By this talisman I do will
Him (or her) faithful by this spell.

Placing two crossed strands of the peppers beneath your bed will strengthen this spell.

Red chili peppers not only protect but can turn back negative energy or entities, cast out evil spirits, guard the house from prying magical eyes, and break curses leveled against someone in the household. The idea that the peppers can block prying magical eyes is of particular interest since this usually means that it puts up a shield against those projecting themselves into your home due to a prurient interest in your private life. This practice is a hallmark of the black (negative or manipulative) curandero's magical arts, and not one practiced by them in general.

There was once a Mexican folk belief saying that evil spirits could not get within the length of seven angels with fully spread wings of a red chili pepper. Though no one has accurately determined just how wide a swipe this is, it explains why hanging the peppers will drive evil from your home.

Crush the dried peppers to break a curse. Trail the powder around the outside perimeter of your home to knock out a curse. Chant words of power as you go.

Pepper powder hot as fire,
Turn back the evil one's desire;
Break the curse that haunts my life,
Remove from me all fear and strife.

Red chili peppers are healing, and those who consume lots of them are said to suffer less from colds and flus. The peppers contain capsascian, an ingredient now touted as a fat burner and energy enhancer. The peppers can also heal by being made into poltices that ease congestion directly by being hung near sick beds to impart the energies of magical healing.

As you hang red chili peppers in your home to heal or protect, do so with a clear visualization of what you wish from them. Seal the spell with words of power.

Red hot peppers do protect,
Negativity and harm do deflect;
Burn away all who wish me ill,
By your power I am whole and well.

For Further Study

Cunningham, Scott. *Cunningham's Encyclopedia of Magical Herbs.* Saint Paul, Minnesota: Llewellyn Publications, 1987.

Davis, Kenneth W., ed. *Black Cats, Hoot Owls, and Water Witches: Beliefs, Superstitions, and Sayings from Texas.* Denton, Texas: University of North Texas Press, 1989.

Devine, Mary Virginia. *Magic from Mexico.* Saint Paul, Minnesota: Llewellyn Publications, 1987.

Trotter, Robert T., et al. *Curanderismo: Mexican American Folk Healing.* Athens, Georgia: University of Georgia Press, 1997.

The Magic of the Pansy

≫ by Scott Appell ≪

Yes, in the poor man's garden grow
Far more than herbs and flowers—
Kind thoughts, contentment, peace of mind,
And joy for weary hours.

Mary Botham Howitt (1799–1888)

We all carry memories of pansies with us from our earliest childhood recollections of gardens and gardening. The beaming faces of these flowers create indelible images, though of course, they are not the only plant that lodges in our young minds; we remember our first encounter with gigantic sunflowers too, our first whiff of pungent tomato foliage, and our earliest taste of freshly picked raspberries. But the pansy alone stands out as the only flower to smile back at you, and when you are young (and child-sized) the flowers faces seem as big as your own.

Pansies are available in a disarming array of color combinations. When this attribute is combined with their light and sweet scent, their ease of culture, their passionate and romantic

magical and medicinal history, and their inclination to bloom throughout mild winters, it is easy to see why pansies have become one of the most widely cherished herbaceous garden flowers in America and Europe.

Aspects of Pansies

One of most interesting aspects of the modern garden pansy is that it does not exist in the wild. While most of the familiar garden objects—trees, shrubs, perennials, annuals, and herbs—were derived from the careful selection and propagation of wild plants, the garden pansy was intentionally developed by gardeners who hybridized several European wildflowers to create a genetic base. The pansy therefore did not exist until the 1820s, and it never grew in American soil until just prior to the Civil War. And, truth be known, the parental history of this flower is complex and steeped in mythology, folklore, religion, and magic.

The modern garden pansy belongs to the plant family *Violaceae*, or the violet family. The flowers typically have five petals—four arranged in pairs—with each pair differing (this configuration is known as zygomorphy to botanists). The genus *Viola* encompasses about 500 species, including the garden pansy, viola, violetta, and violet. Etymologically, the name Viola comes from Greek myth. Zeus hid his love for Io, a virgin priestess, from his wife Hera by transforming her into a white heifer. He made sweet violets spring from the ground for her to graze upon, and named the flowers, *ion*, or *vion*, depending on pronunciation, which eventually became viola.

Botanically, the garden pansy is known as *Viola x wittrockiana*. Taxonomically, the little "x" in the scientific name tells us that plant is the hybrid offspring of different species parents—either from natural or human-induced mutation. Interestingly, at the turn of the century, the flower was alternately known as *Viola tricolor maxima* (the "Big" Johnny-jump-up), and *V. t. hortensis* (the "garden-worthy" Johnny-jump-up). The modern garden pansy was bred and selected in Victorian England during the 1820s through 1840s by a horticulturistknown only as Thompson. Mr. Thompson worked on hybridizing *Viola tricolor*, a native of Europe, Asia, and the Baltic region, with *V. lutea* subsp. *sudetica* (the yellow-flowered Hudson Mountain pansy), which is indigenous to western and central Europe. Botanists also speculate whether he incorporated a third species into the mix—*V. altaica* (the Altai Mountain pansy), a native to the Crimea and Altai Mountains. By midcentury, there were over 400 cultivars available of the pansy, divided into two types—fancy pansies and show pansies. Varieties of the latter are furthered subdivided into three classes according to flower color—selfs, white grounds, and yellow grounds. The selfs have black, maroon, primrose, white, or yellow flowers.

The common name "pansy" may have originated from two different derivations. The first is from the French word *pensée*, meaning thought or remembrance. The other may be a corruption of "pain's ease," an allusion to the flower's analgesic properties. Indeed, all parts of the Johnny-jump-up variety are medicinally valuable. The salicylic acid it contains is an active disinfectant, fungicide, and tissue solvent that can be applied as a poultice to soften hard skin, corns, and warts. The mucilaginous quality of the foliage also lends itself to expectorant, demulcent (inflammation soothing), laxative, and diuretic recipes, and it may be taken internally to cleanse the system and stimulate the metabolism. The juice pressed from the fresh foliage is also prescribed for rheumatism and skin diseases such as cradle cap (tinea capitus or ringworm of the scalp), impetigo, and scabies. For cradle cap and impetigo, take a daily dose (2–5 drops for children, 15–100 drops for adults) by mouth for a week or two. For scabies, use it in combination with baths taken with green soap and sulphur powder or ointment until symptoms are alleviated.

Viola tricolor has additional homeopathic uses as well. An overnight infusion of a quart jar filled with fresh leaves and topped with boiling water (and subsequently strained) is good for cancer, fibrocystic breast disease, or mastitis, and it makes a good gargle or mouthwash for gingivitis, ulceration of the mouth, and pain from mouth and herpes sores. Additionally, this infusion is good for the nervous system, eyestrain, too much sunlight, bronchitis, and sinus and ear infections. (Be sure to see a doctor if you suffer any of these symptoms.)

Though this plant was once formally included in the United States pharmacopeia, do double-check with your homeopathic healer or general practioner before using it, as it is always better to be safe than sorry. Some people react dermatologically when they come in contact with the leaves, and too large doses of the roots (which are edible, and high in minerals) can cause stomach upset, nervousness, high blood pressure, and breathing irregularity.

Pansy Lore

The black markings and the petal arrangement are what has given the Johnny-jump-up the reputation of having a face. This human visage has led to scores of common names for the plant—including monkey faces, Kit-run-about, peeping Tom, and "three faces in the hood." *Viola tricolor* has also been called the herb trinity, in reference to the three colors always associated with it. It symbolizes love and truth, or passion and suffering. Its shade of purple common in artistic depictions of Mary Magdalene and the Virgin Mary after the crucifixion. It is always allegorically associated with the Virgin and with the unicorn (the emblem of purity).

V. tricolor also was beloved as an ingredient of love philters or potions. In the Latin era, this pansy was called *Flos Jovis* (Jove's flower), an allusion to its purported aphrodisiacal attributes. The ancient Celts used the dried flowers and leaves in decoctions intended to seduce and inflame. Folklore has it that at one time all pansies were pure white, but were made purple when pierced by Cupid's arrow. After reading accounts of the flower in the Renaissance herbals of John Gerarde in 1587, William Shakespeare became well aware (as was all of Tudor and Jacobean England) of the pansy's magic. He referred to the pansy (both literally and allegorically) in several of his plays, including *King Lear, Troilus and Cressida, Taming of the Shrew*, and *As You Like It*. The pansy, called love-in-idleness, is integral to the plot of *A Midsummer-Night's Dream*). In this play, Oberon, the Faerie King, inquires of Puck about using the pansy on his estranged, sleeping wife, the Faerie Queen, Titania:

> *It fell upon a little western flower,*
> *Before milk-white, now purple with love's wound,*
> *And maidens call it, love-in-idleness.*
> *Fetch me that flower; the herb I showed thee once:*
> *The juice of it, on sleeping eye-lids laid,*
> *Will make a man or woman madly dote*
> *Upon the next live creature that it sees.*

In addition to love-in-idleness, the pansy had many common names during the Middle Ages and the Jacobean era: heart's-ease or heartsease, ladies' delight, cuddle-me, Kitty-come, cull-me-to-you, tickle-my-fancy, kiss-her-in-the-pantry, and meet-her-in-the-entry-kiss-her-in-the-buttery (which must be longest and most intriguing common plant name in English). The Victorian horticulturist and landscapist Gertrude Jekyll referred to it with the epithet welcome-home-husband-be-he-ever-so-drunk.

English Jacobite poet, Robert Herrick (1591–1674), explained the naming of the heartsease, in "How Pansies or Heart's-ease Came First":

> *Frolic virgins, once there were,*
> *Over loving, living here,*
> *Being here their ends denied,*
> *Ran for Sweethearts mad and died.*
> *Love, in pity of their tears,*
> *And their loss in blooming years,*
> *For their restless here spent hours*
> *Gave them Heart's-ease, turn'd to flowers.*

Romantic-period English poet Mary Botham Howitt (1799–1888) also contemplated the heartsease:

> *Heart's-Ease! One could look at for half a day*
> *Upon this flower, and shape in fancy out*
> *Full twenty different tales of love and sorrow,*
> *That gave this gentle name.*

Another poet of the era, Walter Savage Landor (1775–1864), described his fascination with a single pansy flower in "One Pansy."

> *One Pansy, one, she bore beaneath her breast,*
> *A broad white ribbon held the Pansy tight.*
> *She waved about nor looked upon the rest,*
> *Costly and rare; on this she bent her sight.*

And in 1884, the preeminent female Victorian artist Kate Greenaway (1846–1901) published her *Language of Flowers*, a work she wrote and illustrated. This particular work encapsulates the Victorian tradition of employing flowers and plants to express feelings (as opposed to actually speaking them), both positive and negative, in a subtle manner. That is, people of the era, through the giving and receiving of carefully-crafted tussiemussies, nose-gays, and "talking bouquets," expressed notions of love and desire that could not be spoken. Every blossom and piece of greenery would have a specific subliminal connotation or hidden message, such as:

> *Pansies in a bouquet convey the message of thoughts.*

Today, floral tokens conveying every human emotion can be assembled at home from garden-picked or florist-procured flowers. Of course, deciphering the messages in the flowers is a forgotten skill now. Below are some common varieties of flowers, along with their traditional unspoken meanings.

The Meaning of Flowers and Plants

Arborvitae *(Thuja orientalis or T. occidentalis):* Unchanging friendship

Cinquefoil *(Potentilla spp.):* Maternal affection

Cup-and-Saucer vine *(Cobaea scandens):* Gossip

Double China aster *(Callistephus chinensis):* I partake of your sentiments

Helen's flower *(Helenium* spp.): Tears

Lavender *(Lavandula* spp.): Distrust

Lesser celandine *(Ranunculus ficaria):* Joys to come

Michaelmas daisy *(Aster novi-belgii):* Farewell

Oleander *(Nerium oleander):* Beware

Pansy *(Viola x wittrockiana):* Thoughts

Quamaclit *(Ipomea quamoclit):* Busybody

Sage *(Salvia officinalis):* Domestic virtue

Thrift *(Armeria maritima):* Sympathy

Weeping willow *(Salix alba):* Mourning

Yellow rose *(Rosa* spp.): Decrease of love

Recent History of the Pansy

Garden pansies began to wane in popularity between the two world wars, mostly because they were so labor intensive to propagate. Pansies do not breed true from seed and have to be increased manually by cuttings. During this time many of the older cultivars were lost completely. Still, some heirloom varieties are available today. The bronze and yellow Jackanapes variety (named after Jekyll's pet monkey) dates from about 1890, and the pale lavender and primrose Maggie Mott dates to 1902.

Thankfully, garden pansies have recently grown popular once again. Breeders are developing countless new cultivars, and bountiful varieties of the pansy satisfy every taste. The current trend seems to be leaning away from the flowers with the familiar black blotches, and more towards pastel selfs in varieties such as the tangerine jolly joker, the pale-yellow clear sky primrose, and the silver-pink sterling silver. And whereas garden pansies in the past would dwindle and succumb to summer's warmth, new heat-resistant pansy varieties are being offered—including water colors mixed, frosty rose, and velour clear blue.

To grow in areas with mild winters, sow packaged seed (not collected seeds unless the label of the original seed packet claims the variety "breeds true from seed"), or set out plants in early fall for hibernal blooms. Where summers are hot, sow seed indoors during January or February, and set out young plants in early spring. All pansies prefer a rich loamy soil and plenty of moisture. Picking through the season will keep them in flower.

In addition, we cannot overlook the fact that the flowers and foliage of pansies are delightfully edible—and surprisingly high in vitamin C and A. The lightly fragrant blossoms have a faint lettuce-like taste, and can be used in salads, glazed onto frosted cookies, and affixed to ganache-covered cakes. Also, pansies may be encased within shimmering layers of white wine aspic over cold poached chicken breasts, salmon fillets, or pale wheels of brie and camembert. They may also be frozen in ice to decoratively chill party beverages, and they may be candied.

In 1901, Alice Morse Earle, one of America's first female landscape designers, summed up the pansy most eloquently:

> These little [pansies] have infinite variety of expression; some are laughing and roguish, some sharp and shrewd, some surprised, others worried. . . a few are saucy to a degree, [but] all are animated and vivacious.

Cloves

❧ by Robert Place ❧

L ast spring I had a toothache; it
happened like this: Some time
before I had lost a filling in a
lower premolar, and had neglected to
take care of it. In due time, the gums
under the tooth started to swell and
grew tender to the touch. I made an
appointment with the dentist, but I had
to wait a week before she could fit me
in. And that week seemed a long time
to wait. The sensitivity in my swollen
gums was steady, but it seemed that the
pain might get worse at any moment.

On the Saturday before my dentist
appointment, I woke with an intense
pain in my jaw. I jumped out of bed and
made my way to the bathroom mirror
and discovered that the entire right
side of my face was now swollen—I
looked unlike my normal self. The
flesh on my jaw was sticking out about
a half of an inch further than normal.
This time I didn't hesistate to call
the dentist.

Unfortunately, I only succeeded in contacting an answering machine, which informed me that the dentist was out of town until Monday. A call to another dentist informed me that I would still have to wait until Monday to have the tooth worked on, but in the meantime he offered to prescribe an antibiotic and a painkiller. Normally I hate taking drugs, and I told the doctor so. After some discussion, the dentist convinced me at least to take an antibiotic. I still refused the painkiller. He prescribed penicillin, and a short while later, despite the pain in my jaw, I was on my way to pick up my medicine.

Of course things got worse before they got any better. It turned out that I am allergic to penicillin (I had never taken antibiotics before). After taking first dose of the capsules, I developed red, itchy rashes over my groin and side. The dentist, for his part, told me to try an antihistamine for the allergic reaction, and to go to the nearest emergency room if the rash did not subside.

Meanwhile, the pain in my jaw was getting worse. As I left for the pharmacy a second time, my wife suggested that I buy some oil of clove for the pain. I had never used oil of clove before, and had not thought of it until she mentioned it, but I felt good about trying a traditional tried-and-true herbal remedy.

I bought some of the oil at the pharmacy along with the antihistamine and an alternative antibiotic. The antihistamine worked, I didn't have a bad reaction to the second antibiotic, and now I was able to relax and address the pain in my jaw.

Applying Oil of Clove to Treat Pain

Oil of clove ordinarily comes in a little brown bottle. The bottle I bought had blue letters on the white label that read "Clove Leaf Oil." If you want to apply this remedy to help with tooth pain, simply unscrew the cap and tip it over to get a dab of the thin oil on your finger.

The aroma of oil of clove of course is wonderful, and perhaps part of its secret. Massage the oil with your finger into the infected gum area. The slightly bitter flavor of concentrated cloves will permeate your mouth and sinuses, and you will be instantly drawn into an inner world filled with memories of spice cake and Yule celebrations.

The best part will be when your pain simply melts away. Doubtless you will wonder, as I did, why you hadn't done this earlier. I found that the pain relief from the clove oil will last about a half-hour to an hour. Make another application with your finger when you feel you need it. With cloves as my ally, I got through the rest of the weekend pain-free.

An Ancient Herb

Clove is the common name for *Syzygium aromaticum*, also known as *Eugenia aromatica*, a tropical tree of the myrtle family. The flowers of this plant, commonly dried and used as a spice, have also been given the name clove. An essential oil is made from the distilled buds, leaves, or stems—all of which contain the active ingredient of the plant, eugenol. The tree is a small- to medium-sized evergreen native to the Moluccas, an island group in eastern Indonesia also known as the Spice Islands. It is now also cultivated in Zanzibar, Madagascar, Pemba, and Malaya.

The name clove is derived from its medieval name, *clowe*, which in turn, is derived from the French word *clou*, meaning "nail." Its full name in medieval French was *clou de girofle*, which means "nail of the clove tree." Clove trees were called *girofle* in French, which in turn served as the source of the plant's alternative English name "gillyflower." The small dried buds of the clove, which are dark brown with a thick tapering cylindrical stem and a round head with four symmetrical petals, resembled medieval nails. During the Middle Ages, cloves were commonly associated with the nails of Christ's crucifixion; therefore, in popular belief they possessed some of the magical power associated with a holy relic. The name of this plant should not be confused with the word "clove," as in "a clove of garlic." A garlic clove is derived from an Old English word, which meant to cut and was related to the verb "cleave."

The flowers of the clove are green or reddish when harvested by hand, and turn blackish-brown when dried in sunlight or in wood-fired kilns. High-tech methods have been tried, but the traditional drying methods actually give a higher yield. Dried cloves are delightfully aromatic, with a sharp, spicy flavor when added to foods such as cakes and cookies and curries. Cloves also have numerous practical uses. For instance, they are known to have been used as early as 300 B.C. by the Chinese as a breath freshener and to relieve toothache. The ancient Romans obtained them from Arabic traders and put them to similar use, but they were forgotten by the West when the trade routes were interrupted in the early Middle Ages. Cloves were reintroduced to the Europe in the thirteenth century and became a highly treasured spice. They were one reason why Columbus tried to find a new route to India. In the sixteenth century, the Portuguese discovered the source in the Spice Islands, and by cutting out the middlemen, monopolized the trade. In the seventeenth century, their monopoly passed to the Dutch traders.

Today, cloves are still used to relieve pain. Not only tooth pain but pain from arthritis, from the flu, and from sore muscles. In fact, it is one of the ingredients in the famous Southeast Asian pain-relieving ointment, tiger balm. One should take care when using cloves to treat pain, as it can be an irritant to the skin or mucous membranes if it is over used. Later on, after I recovered from my dental problems, I found out that most dentists recommend using the oil of the buds, which is slightly milder than the leaf oil that I used. I also found that it not only relieves the pain of a toothache but also is antiseptic, antiviral, and promotes healing. In fact, cloves are used in modern dental medicines. It is an important ingredient in the cement used for temporary fillings. By sedating the nerves, it causes the calmed nerve to shrink away from the filling and assists the recovery process. Dentists find that it is safer than aspirin for reliving pain in the gums.

In his book *Back to Eden*, Jethro Kloss recommends combining cloves with bayberry, ginger, white pine, and capsicum as a cure for colds, flu, and fever. The exact recipe follows. Combine the powered herbs in the following proportion:

- 4 ounces bayberry
- 2 ounces ginger
- 1 ounce white pine
- 1 dram cloves
- 1 dram capsicum

Note: A dram is .0625 of an ounce. To use this mixture of herbs as a medicine, make a tea from one teaspoon of the mixture in a cup of boiled water.

Oil of clove is used in aromatherapy to promote a sense of calm. When taken in small doses internally—one or two drops in a glass of water—it is stimulating and helps overcome nervousness and fatigue. It can also cure nausea and expel parasites. The oil of the bud is used in perfumes to add a spicy note.

Interestingly, about half of all cloves grown find their way as an ingredient in Indonesian cigarettes. The herb gives these cigarettes a distinctive flavor, and it fills the air with a delicious incense-like smell. Over all, ground cloves or clove oil in used in seasonings, in baked goods, mouthwashes, toothpaste, candy, and gum. It is an ingredient in Chinese five-spice powder, sometimes in Indian curry powder, and in Worcestershire sauce.

A Magic Herb

As I said above, clove reminds me of foods associated with Yule. Yule, of course, is the ancient holiday celebrated at the Winter Solstice when we have reached the point of the least daylight, and the Sun starts to renew its strength. The name "Yule" comes from the Anglo-Saxon word for wheel. To the Anglo-Saxons this holiday marked the time when the wheel of the year came to an end and a new year began. The Celts celebrated the end of the year on Samhain, which falls on November 1 and is connected with the final harvest (sometimes called the apple harvest). Over time, the customs associated with the two holidays merged and became Christianized as part of Christmas and New Year's Eve.

The celebrations associated with Yule are designed to honor the final harvest, to assure that fertility is maintained through the apparent seasonal death, and to rekindle the light of the Sun. Cloves have been available in the British Isles since the late Middle Ages, but it is difficult to determine when they first became part of the Yule feast. Most of our modern Yule customs were developed or reshaped in the Victorian era. Fruits and spices are used in ceremony as symbols of the harvest and of fertility, as are evergreens, which maintain their green life through the winter. Clove as both a spice and an evergreen is doubly suited for use during the Yule season.

Today, therefore, cloves are a common ingredient in Yule spice cakes and breads. Another Yule treat that can be used to summon spirits, as well as lift them, is spiced apple wine. A Yule apple wine can be made from hard apple cider, or from a mixture of dry wine and soft cider combined with honey and a teaspoon or two of ground cloves, allspice, and cinnamon. Bring the ingredients to a boil, simmer for twenty minutes, and strain. Sliced oranges may be added. Hot apple cider with spice makes a delicious nonalcoholic drink as well.

Perhaps clove's most valuable magical aspect is its aroma. Beside bringing sensual pleasure, the perfume of cloves increases one's sense of calm while heightening one's alertness—a perfect combination for ritual work or meditation. One way to make use of the magical aroma of cloves is to create a clove pomander. Pomanders are of medieval origin. The name derives from the medieval French *pomme d' ambre*, which literally means "an apple of amber." Pomanders were, and often still are, a mixture of aromatic herbs held in bags or in perforated metal boxes and suspended in a room or on a person. They were used as an amulet to ward off infection and other evils.

In modern Yule celebrations, a pomander often takes the form of an apple or an orange studded with cloves and hung as a fragrant ornament; this seems to be another Victorian contribution to the holiday. To make one, take a ripe, round orange and tie two strands of ribbon around it so that they form a cross when seen from the top. Use the ribbon on top to tie a loop that can be used to suspend the pomander when it is complete. Next, use an awl or other pointed tool to poke holes in the exposed surface of the orange. As you proceed, place the stem of a dried clove in each hole. Continue until the entire orange is studded with cloves except where covered by ribbon. Hang the pomander and let it dry out naturally. The dried pomander will continue to add fragrance and protect your house throughout the year. Besides serving as an ornament of fruit and spice, the pomander is a symbol of the Sun that is rekindled at Yule.

In traditional systems of magic, all herbs are associated with a particular planetary god and all the qualities the god represents. The use of the herb magically transfers these qualities and allows the magician to direct them. Cloves are connected with Mercury, Jupiter, Apollo, and the Sun, depending on the correspondence chart used. This discrepancy illustrates the fact that we should not take these correspondences too literally and allow for individual associations. Because cloves permeate the atmosphere with their perfume, are sensual and pleasing, are used as a healing herb and promote meditation, and because they were instrumental in developing world commerce, the best guess is that they are connected to Mercury, the god that embodies all of these qualities. Of course, Mercury is the messenger of Jupiter and often the companion of his brother Apollo, so the associations begin to make more sense when you examine them.

Magical incense and candles containing cloves, combined with nutmeg, cinnamon, and lemon balm, are used to attract money and abundance. Cloves, when combined with other herbs in incense, can be used for health, power, or protection. All of these associations are related to its use in the Yule festival. As

Mercury is one of Venus' lovers, cloves can be combined with the herbs of Venus—such as rose, lavender, or patchouli—to make incense or candles for love rituals.

While researching the uses of cloves, I came across old formulas for ink that used cloves as a setting agent. Cloves serve a similar function in henna art; it is an ingredient in the traditional "magic elixir" used to set the temporary tattoos. As such, the use of cloves in henna art might be another example of clove's function in love magic. After all, the women of the Middle and Near East have been adorning their hands with designs painted with henna since ancient times to enhance their beauty and to attract fertility and luck. In the Islamic world, cloves are traditionally connected with the marriage ceremony.

My wife, Rose Ann, taught me the simplest way to make use of the power of cloves. Take a pinch of cloves and add it to an open pot of water. Bring the pot to a boil, then let it simmer on a low flame. Be observant of the level of water in the pot throughout the day. If the water is low, add more or the pot will burn. It is best to do this while you are near the stove and can see the pot. If you go away, turn it off. You can also leave a caldron of water with cloves suspended in a fireplace or on top of a wood stove.

In time, the aroma of the cloves will fill the house, bringing with it a sense of calm well-being. This also makes a good atmosphere for reading the tarot.

Herbal Spells of Love

᥈ by K. D. Spitzer ᥈

I n olden days, having a mate was a pretty serious business. If you didn't die in childbirth, get carried off by strange fevers, or fall off a siege tower, you were expected to stay married pretty much forever. For a woman, there was often no choice in the matter. Where else was she to go?

Furthermore, in arranged marriages a woman might not even see her groom until the wedding day. And as for laws to protect wives: In England, a woman's husband could legally beat her with a stick (as long as it was no larger than the thickness of his thumb), and he was not liable if he managed to kill her. Even the church offered no protection; women were chattel and that was that.

Into this climate, the only empowerment a woman had was magic. The body of lore surrounding love and sex reaches deep into the ages, back to clay tablets and ancient snips of parchment. Even the Victorians built rituals around attracting the best possible mate and keeping his love. Some of these rites had endured from the Middle Ages. Others were even older.

For instance, sewing herbs into the hem of the wedding gown is one that has lasted for many centuries. Herbs like lavender, elecampane, and clover—representing love or tenderness—would be placed in the gown; wheat grains and oak leaves would ensure fertility, and cedar chips would offer protection. Women helping to sew the gown would include strands of their own hair in hopes that their own wedding day would come quickly.

Apples

For women who were kept quite close to home, finding one's true love was a difficult task. There are virtually hundreds of rituals built around the theme of whom you would marry. Many are just variations of a particular technique. Some involve the apple peel because apples are the special province of Venus, goddess of love. Furthermore, the tree itself is very magical.

To find the initial of the person you are going to marry, take a paring knife and recite the alphabet while peeling an apple. When the peel breaks, the letter you have reached is the initial of your true love's name. To put a little more effort into the process, take the peel of a whole apple and hold it in your right hand; stand with your feet together. Concentrate on your wedding day, picturing yourself in your wedding dress. Throw the apple peel over your left shoulder. Then turn to look at the arrangement of the peel on the floor. It should land in the shape of the initial of the name of the prospective groom. This may take some inventive musing.

If this is not satisfactory, then dry the apple peel and store it. On a cold winter evening, make yourself a comforting cup of hot apple tisane, or herbal tea, sweetened with a delicate drop of honey. Use fresh spring water and an herbal wildflower honey. That night, after retiring, you should dream of the man you will marry. Even if the spell does not take, this is a delicious cup of tea you can easily make for yourself as a late afternoon pick-me-up, just as the French still do.

Dreams

Another reliable source of looking into your future married bliss was through dreams. The best dreams come from sleeping on a dream pillow, and the best dream pillows are made of the best linen cloth, fancifully stitched, maybe even with a bit of lace. The trick here is the stuffing; use *Artemisia vulgaris*, another herb of Venus commonly known as mugwort. A couple nights of sleeping on this carefully prepared pillow should produce the vision of your one true love.

As the ancient rhyme put it:

> *Mugwort! Mugwort! Herb of power,*
> *Bring desire at the midnight hour!*

Bay laurel also played a role in the dream lore. If you pinned a leaf in each corner of your pillow, then you would dream of your intended. Sleeping with a bit of wedding cake under your pillow too was also a sure-fire means of divining your beloved.

Pillows are generally helpful to the lovesick, easing the symptoms of insomnia and giddiness. You need to stuff this pillow with lavender and hops to calm your anxieties and promote the serenity needed to sail through prewedding jitters. Even a catnap on this pillow will be helpful, though an entire night's sleep will bring true rest. Drinking a cup of chamomile or fennel seed tea before bedtime will also alleviate the symptoms of love sickness.

Myrtle

Myrtle is another favored herb of Venus and a very powerful love herb. In the north part of the U.S., myrtle is a tender perennial that is easy to care for. It has tiny, shiny leaves that look great as a winter houseplant. Though now little known, in ancient times the Greeks rubbed their bodies with a poultice of crushed myrtle leaves to attract the lady of their dreams. Since this was a bit messy and impractical as a ritual, it didn't last long.

A bouquet of myrtle and roses was not only lovely to look at, but offered in courtship was a clear declaration of intent. This was a double whammy because roses have a significant symbolism in the love biz. Coupled with myrtle, such a bouquet was very powerful.

Other times, myrtle was steeped in white wine, which was then offered as a wedding toast to secure fidelity and fertility for the bridal couple. Most importantly, a sprig of myrtle placed in the shoe of a roving lover was supposed to bring him or her back home. Since the lover would have to know that the myrtle was in the shoe, you have to wonder if this really worked.

Fidelity

Keeping a lover faithful is another large side dish in the vast stew of love charms. Likely, a great number of love spells include the love potions that promote venery in aging or indifferent partners—though I haven't taken a count lately.

Caraway seeds were once used by women not only to ease flatulence from bean and cabbage dishes, but also by a careful bride who sewed them into the seams of her roving husband's clothing. The seeds were thought to bring him home. And as no one would be the wiser, this would seem to be a better charm than the myrtle in the shoe trick.

Knights returning home from the crusades brought back spells from the Middle East. As a rule of thumb, savory herbs speak of a European background, while sweet spices in charms often hint of a more exotic origin. If the spell calls for rosewater, you can probably trace its ancient roots to Persia. Cloves and cinnamon would also be used to construct elaborate spells to bring a lover safely home.

Versatile cinnamon was smiled on by Venus who not only loves love, but loves money. The bark was also incorporated into prosperity charms, and when sewn into sachets or sprinkled into sweets cinnamon it was guaranteed to keep a lover faithful.

Aphrodisiacs

Failing interest is another aspect of love that requires herbs of powerful magic. An aging husband, before the days of Viagra, might have needed a little something to get him started or a little something to keep him going. An enormous body of tradition grew up around this single fact.

Recall mugwort, that herb of Venus. It has a whole slew of cousins named for Artemisia, the queen of love. Southernwood, or *Artemisia abrotanum*, reveals its use by its common name of lad's love and old man. Fronds of the herb were placed under the bed for encouragement in the house of an aging couple. This was actually a great idea, as southernwood dispels mustiness and mildew as well.

The name of *Artemisia absythium* was used to flavor the now-banned cordial absinthe, but its common name—old woman—also suggests its use in encouraging the marriage bed interest of a longtime married woman. Its stems were also placed under the bed, but an infusion was made with this dangerous herb to drink before retiring.

Many aphrodisiacs are the result of wishful thinking, but also of sympathetic magic. Asparagus is a rigid and upright vegetable, and therefore is thought to be useful for sustaining strength in the male. Bananas also fall into this category.

Other herbs have a mild aphrodisiacal effect. The *Perfumed Garden* recommends a bedtime beverage of herbal honey mixed with ground almonds and pine needles. In three nights, interest in the marriage bed should return; or else at the very least your head cold should ease!

Jasmine is the flower of choice for a frustrated lover. The power of its scent has been known to incite and inflame desire across the ages and across continents. The scent of vanilla beans is very attracting and in some will encourage lust. Ginseng also enjoys a great reputation as an aphrodisiac. Chervil will "excite Venus," and garlic will "provoke venery"—according to medieval texts. And don't forget the love apple, a.k.a. the tomato; it contributed to the allure of the Italian lover, because who wouldn't fall in love with the maker of tomato sauce?

The traditional lore is quite extensive. There seems to be a continuing need in human society for men to arouse women, and for women to keep the interest of an older lover. And I haven't even mentioned the occasional opposite need of marriage partners for anaphrodisiacs—something to cool the ardor of the marriage bed. But perhaps that's a subject for another night.

The Folklore of Witch Hazel

≈ by Carly Wall ≈

P lants have always played a part in magical history. Perhaps this is because they can affect us so powerfully in so many ways—through ingestion, through absorption, or through scent.

Of all the magical herbs, there is one plant that stands out so much that I had to plant two specimens in my yard. I'm speaking of amazing witch hazel *(Hemamelis virginiana)*. This plant, as well as the other species of *Hemamelis*, is steeped in folklore, magic, and also has tremendous healing potential. A lot of power is packed into this humble shrub.

Out-of-Kilter Witch Hazel

The most stunning thing about witch hazel is that it has a blooming cycle out of kilter with the rest of the plant world. Native to the Midwestern woodlands of North America, this plant

blooms in late fall and early winter, usually late October through early December (exactly when the powers of Witches are at their height). That is, when all other trees and shrubs have begun their winter sleep cycle, witch hazel is just getting started—what better indication of its magical properties are we likely to have?

Usually, the bright-yellow clusters of blooms, which look beautiful on a cold, gray day, last for about a month or so. Its long, slender, or feathery petals, and its heavenly scent, also are very appealing. And the magic continues, as the winter moth that pollinates the plant is conveniently one of the few species that can survive low temperatures as an adult. The fruit of the witch hazel becomes dormant over the winter after pollination, and it develops over the course of the following growing season, maturing in the fall almost ten to twelve months later. The seeds are dispersed by gravity, and also by birds that eat the seeds and pass them on in their fashion.

The early growth of the witch hazel is slow, a fact I can attest to. My plant, for instance, is about four years old now and just now is becoming an impressive and sturdy shrub. But it can grow as high as twenty to thirty feet if left to its own devices over its regular lifespan of about 100 years. As witch hazel prefers naturalized settings, it is perfect for natural planting or woodland gardens. Its impressive leaves and flowers make it a beautiful specimen along borders or as a background to highlight flowers and foliage in fall flower gardens.

Witch hazel tolerates light shade and is very hardy, resisting most problems or diseases that affect other plants. It can also tolerate poor soil, as long as it gets plenty of moisture. On the whole, witch hazel can pretty much take care of itself. All you need do is to plant it and let it go, unless you want to prune it to a certain height. Our shrubs are pruned low, and it has become bushy and quite attractive with an abundance of dark-green leaves that hold on long after the leaves of other plants have fallen away.

Since there are other members of its family, I have listed here a few that grow in different climes and that might catch your fancy.

Native vernal witch hazel *(Hamamelis vernalis):* Grows naturally in parts of the Midwest and South. Its flowers appear as early as January or February, though they are smaller than that of other varieties, and of stronger fragrance. The colors of the blooms vary from yellow to red.

Chinese witch hazel *(Hamamelis mollis):* A robust, densely branched shrub with green, round leaves that have gray, woolly undersides. This variety has very fragrant flowers that show up late January; it is one of the first of the plants to announce spring. Leaves are vivid in the fall, turning shades of golden yellow and yellow-orange.

Japanese witch hazel *(Hamamelis japonica):* A large shrub with a vase-like shape that grows wide. It needs ample room to grow and will attain heights of 10–15 feet tall and wide. Leaves turn red, yellow, and purple in the fall. Not as fragrant as the other family members, but it is quite pretty with crinkly petals appearing in February and March. Color ranges from yellow to coppery red with deep-purple calyx cups.

Witch Hazel Medicine

Medicinally, witch hazel has been in great demand. Native American tribes, such as the Mohegan, first made a balm from the crushed bark, as well as a tea from the leaves. They believed the Great Spirit created the long, yellow petals to attract their attention and to help them learn what the plant could offer. The Mohegan rubbed the tea or balm on cuts and wounds, and they also drank the tea for a variety of ailments, including menstrual problems and colds. In the eighteenth century, they distilled astringent potions and lotions from the essential oils in the leaves, bark, and twigs, and they used these extracts as astringents and vasoconstrictors, as well as for other uses. The plant, they discovered, was most powerful in full bloom and when the cold weather had driven the sap to the plant's roots.

As for other uses, witch hazel relieves aching muscles and swelling. It prevents wounds from becoming infected and helps speed the healing process. It comes in handy in soothing sunburn and windburn, and in drying up poison ivy blisters. Witch hazel has been useful in chasing away mosquitoes, and through the years it has been used in hair tonics, aftershaves, as a gargle or eye wash, for bruises, and for stings. Finally, witch hazel was used for such specific ailments as bleeding, diarrhea, hemorrhoids, varicose veins, and swelling in feet and ankles.

From these early beginnings, the plant went on to become a staple in most medicine cabinets. But sadly, today's witch hazel has lost much of its astringent qualities because of the way it is manufactured. The Native American witch hazel tea was infinitely more powerful than today's product, as its astringent tannins dissolve easily in water. Rather than utilizing the methods of the ancient remedy, today's commercial witch hazel is made by steam distillation, which removes the tannins; it is also mixed in a 14-percent alcohol base that further degrades the astringent qualities. Even so, more than a million gallons of the extract is sold in the United States each year alone. The alcohol, since it is astringent itself, probably makes up the difference.

For a natural alternative to modern dilutions of witch hazel, you can make your own witch hazel brew. Just add 1 tablespoon of powdered leaves or twigs to 1 quart of water and boil 10 minutes. Strain, cool, and apply directly, or mix into one of your home remedies.

Witch Hazel Magic

The magical uses of witch hazel abound. As its name implies, it does have a strong witchy connection, and it is purported to protect one "from" a Witch. This belief seems to have been spawned from the belief that hazelnuts and wood were believed to offer protection against fairy enchantment, demons, and Witches. In Scotland, double hazelnuts were hurled at Witches, and cattle were often singed with hazel rods at Midsummer and Beltane fires to keep fairies away. However, these beliefs likely come from a misguided folktale. It seems that in medieval English, the word *wych* meant "flexible," and the term probably was applied to the quite flexible branches of the witch hazel bush.

Another early belief was that witch hazel wood contained powerful energies and was able to help one dowse, or "witch," water and other lost items. In fact, Native Americans found the plant useful for finding water during droughts. There are also legends that witch hazel wood, made into wands, helped lead the owner to find gold and other treasures. I've successfully used witch hazel wood to find a well on our own land—water that we were sorely in need of.

To dowse with witch hazel wood, prepare yourself accordingly. Cut forked twigs from the witch hazel bush, and thank it for its help. Hold each fork lightly in both hands; the twigs will bend downward, drawn to the energies of specific spots. The well drilling man shook his head in amazement when we hit three veins of water that happened to cross at that exact point the witch hazel rod indicated. He told me I would never run out of water, and I never have.

However you work with witch hazel, it can enhance your life in many ways—in healing, in magic work, and in working with nature. Use it wisely, use it well, and its power can affect you in wonderful ways.

The
Quarters and
Signs of the
Moon and
Moon
Tables

The Quarters and Signs of the Moon

Everyone has seen the Moon wax and wane through a period of approximately twenty-nine-and-a-half days. This circuit from New Moon to Full Moon and back again is called the lunation cycle. The cycle is divided into parts, called quarters or phases. There are several methods by which this can be done, and the system used in the *Herbal Almanac* may not correspond to those used in other almanacs.

The Quarters

First Quarter

The first quarter begins at the New Moon, when the Sun and Moon are in the same place, or conjunct. (This means that the Sun and Moon are in the same degree of the same sign.) The Moon is not visible at first, since it rises at the same time as the Sun. The New Moon is the time of new beginnings, beginnings of projects that favor growth, externalization of activities, and the growth of ideas. The first quarter is the time of germination, emergence, beginnings, and outwardly directed activity.

Second Quarter

The second quarter begins halfway between the New Moon and the Full Moon, when the Sun and Moon are at right angles, or a 90-degree square to each other. This half Moon rises around noon and sets around midnight, so it can be seen in the western sky during the first half of the night. The second quarter is the time of growth and articulation of things that already exist.

Third Quarter

The third quarter begins at the Full Moon, when the Sun and Moon are opposite one another and the full light of the Sun can shine on the full sphere of the Moon. The round Moon can be seen rising in the east at sunset, and then rising a little later each evening. The Full Moon stands for illumination, fulfillment, culmination, completion, drawing inward, unrest, emotional expressions, and hasty actions leading to failure. The third quarter is a time of maturity, fruition, and the assumption of the full form of expression.

Fourth Quarter

The fourth quarter begins about halfway between the Full Moon and New Moon, when the Sun and Moon are again at 90 degrees, or square. This decreasing Moon rises at midnight, and can be seen in the east during the last half of the night, reaching the overhead position just about as the Sun rises. The fourth quarter is a time of disintegration, drawing back for reorganization and reflection.

The Signs

Moon in Aries

Moon in Aries is good for starting things, but lacking in staying power. Things occur rapidly, but also quickly pass.

Moon in Taurus

With Moon in Taurus, things begun during this sign last the longest and tend to increase in value. Things begun now become habitual and hard to alter.

Moon in Gemini

Moon in Gemini is an inconsistent position for the Moon, characterized by a lot of talk. Things begun now are easily changed by outside influences.

Moon in Cancer

Moon in Cancer stimulates emotional rapport between people. It pinpoints need, and supports growth and nurturance.

Moon in Leo

Moon in Leo accents showmanship, being seen, drama, recreation, and happy pursuits. It may be concerned with praise and subject to flattery.

Moon in Virgo

Moon in Virgo favors accomplishment of details and commands from higher up while discouraging independent thinking.

Moon in Libra

Moon in Libra increases self-awareness. It favors self-examination and interaction with others, but discourages spontaneous initiative.

Moon in Scorpio

Moon in Scorpio increases awareness of psychic power. It precipitates psychic crises and ends connections thoroughly.

Moon in Sagittarius

Moon in Sagittarius encourages expansionary flights of imagination and confidence in the flow of life.

Moon in Capricorn

Moon in Capricorn increases awareness of the need for structure, discipline, and organization. Institutional activities are favored.

Moon in Aquarius

Moon in Aquarius favors activities that are unique and individualistic, concern for humanitarian needs, society as a whole, and improvements that can be made.

Moon in Pisces

During Moon in Pisces, energy withdraws from the surface of life, hibernates within, secretly reorganizing and realigning.

January Moon Table

Date	Sign	Element	Nature	Phase
1 Wed. 6:42 pm	Capricorn	Earth	Semi-fruitful	4th
2 Thu.	Capricorn	Earth	Semi-fruitful	New 3:23 pm
3 Fri. 10:56 pm	Aquarius	Air	Barren	1st
4 Sat.	Aquarius	Air	Barren	1st
5 Sun.	Aquarius	Air	Barren	1st
6 Mon. 5:57 am	Pisces	Water	Fruitful	1st
7 Tue.	Pisces	Water	Fruitful	1st
8 Wed. 4:15 pm	Aries	Fire	Barren	1st
9 Thu.	Aries	Fire	Barren	1st
10 Fri.	Aries	Fire	Barren	2nd 8:15 am
11 Sat. 4:48 am	Taurus	Earth	Semi-fruitful	2nd
12 Sun.	Taurus	Earth	Semi-fruitful	2nd
13 Mon. 5:08 pm	Gemini	Air	Barren	2nd
14 Tue.	Gemini	Air	Barren	2nd
15 Wed.	Gemini	Air	Barren	2nd
16 Thu. 2:56 am	Cancer	Water	Fruitful	2nd
17 Fri.	Cancer	Water	Fruitful	2nd
18 Sat. 9:29 am	Leo	Fire	Barren	Full 5:48 am
19 Sun.	Leo	Fire	Barren	3rd
20 Mon. 1:32 pm	Virgo	Earth	Barren	3rd
21 Tue.	Virgo	Earth	Barren	3rd
22 Wed. 4:23 pm	Libra	Air	Semi-fruitful	3rd
23 Thu.	Libra	Air	Semi-fruitful	3rd
24 Fri. 7:09 pm	Scorpio	Water	Fruitful	3rd
25 Sat.	Scorpio	Water	Fruitful	4th 3:33 am
26 Sun. 10:26 pm	Sagittarius	Fire	Barren	4th
27 Mon.	Sagittarius	Fire	Barren	4th
28 Tue.	Sagittarius	Fire	Barren	4th
29 Wed. 2:30 am	Capricorn	Earth	Semi-fruitful	4th
30 Thu.	Capricorn	Earth	Semi-fruitful	4th
31 Fri. 7:44 am	Aquarius	Air	Barren	4th

February Moon Table

Date	Sign	Element	Nature	Phase
1 Sat.	Aquarius	Air	Barren	New 5:48 am
2 Sun. 2:55 pm	Pisces	Water	Fruitful	1st
3 Mon.	Pisces	Water	Fruitful	1st
4 Tue.	Pisces	Water	Fruitful	1st
5 Wed. 12:44 am	Aries	Fire	Barren	1st
6 Thu.	Aries	Fire	Barren	1st
7 Fri. 12:59 pm	Taurus	Earth	Semi-fruitful	1st
8 Sat.	Taurus	Earth	Semi-fruitful	1st
9 Sun.	Taurus	Earth	Semi-fruitful	2nd 6:11 am
10 Mon. 1:45 am	Gemini	Air	Barren	2nd
11 Tue.	Gemini	Air	Barren	2nd
12 Wed. 12:19 pm	Cancer	Water	Fruitful	2nd
13 Thu.	Cancer	Water	Fruitful	2nd
14 Fri. 7:04 pm	Leo	Fire	Barren	2nd
15 Sat.	Leo	Fire	Barren	2nd
16 Sun. 10:22 pm	Virgo	Earth	Barren	Full 6:51 pm
17 Mon.	Virgo	Earth	Barren	3rd
18 Tue. 11:48 pm	Libra	Air	Semi-fruitful	3rd
19 Wed.	Libra	Air	Semi-fruitful	3rd
20 Thu.	Libra	Air	Semi-fruitful	3rd
21 Fri. 1:09 am	Scorpio	Water	Fruitful	3rd
22 Sat.	Scorpio	Water	Fruitful	3rd
23 Sun. 3:46 am	Sagittarius	Fire	Barren	4th 11:46 am
24 Mon.	Sagittarius	Fire	Barren	4th
25 Tue. 8:11 am	Capricorn	Earth	Semi-fruitful	4th
26 Wed.	Capricorn	Earth	Semi-fruitful	4th
27 Thu. 2:24 pm	Aquarius	Air	Barren	4th
28 Fri.	Aquarius	Air	Barren	4th

March Moon Table

Date	Sign	Element	Nature	Phase
1 Sat. 10:26 pm	Pisces	Water	Fruitful	4th
2 Sun.	Pisces	Water	Fruitful	New 9:35 pm
3 Mon.	Pisces	Water	Fruitful	1st
4 Tue. 8:30 am	Aries	Fire	Barren	1st
5 Wed.	Aries	Fire	Barren	1st
6 Thu. 8:36 pm	Taurus	Earth	Semi-fruitful	1st
7 Fri.	Taurus	Earth	Semi-fruitful	1st
8 Sat.	Taurus	Earth	Semi-fruitful	1st
9 Sun. 9:38 am	Gemini	Air	Barren	1st
10 Mon.	Gemini	Air	Barren	1st
11 Tue. 9:12 pm	Cancer	Water	Fruitful	2nd 2:15 am
12 Wed.	Cancer	Water	Fruitful	2nd
13 Thu.	Cancer	Water	Fruitful	2nd
14 Fri. 5:06 am	Leo	Fire	Barren	2nd
15 Sat.	Leo	Fire	Barren	2nd
16 Sun.8:52 am	Virgo	Earth	Barren	2nd
17 Mon.	Virgo	Earth	Barren	2nd
18 Tue.9:43 am	Libra	Air	Semi-fruitful	Full 5:35 am
19 Wed.	Libra	Air	Semi-fruitful	3rd
20 Thu.9:38 am	Scorpio	Water	Fruitful	3rd
21 Fri.	Scorpio	Water	Fruitful	3rd
22 Sat.10:33 am	Sagittarius	Fire	Barren	3rd
23 Sun.	Sagittarius	Fire	Barren	3rd
24 Mon.1:48 pm	Capricorn	Earth	Semi-fruitful	4th 8:51 pm
25 Tue.	Capricorn	Earth	Semi-fruitful	4th
26 Wed. 7:51pm	Aquarius	Air	Barren	4th
27 Thu.	Aquarius	Air	Barren	4th
28 Fri.	Aquarius	Air	Barren	4th
29 Sat. 4:26 am	Pisces	Water	Fruitful	4th
30 Sun.	Pisces	Water	Fruitful	4th
31 Mon. 3:04pm	Aries	Fire	Barren	4th

April Moon Table

Date	Sign	Element	Nature	Phase
1 Tue.	Aries	Fire	Barren	New 2:19 pm
2 Wed.	Aries	Fire	Barren	1st
3 Thu. 3:20 am	Taurus	Earth	Semi-fruitful	1st
4 Fri.	Taurus	Earth	Semi-fruitful	1st
5 Sat. 4:24 pm	Gemini	Air	Barren	1st
6 Sun.	Gemini	Air	Barren	1st
7 Mon.	Gemini	Air	Barren	1st
8 Tue. 4:36 am	Cancer	Water	Fruitful	1st
9 Wed.	Cancer	Water	Fruitful	2nd 6:40 pm
10 Thu. 1:54 pm	Leo	Fire	Barren	2nd
11 Fri.	Leo	Fire	Barren	2nd
12 Sat. 7:07 pm	Virgo	Earth	Barren	2nd
13 Sun.	Virgo	Earth	Barren	2nd
14 Mon. 8:42 pm	Libra	Air	Semi-fruitful	2nd
15 Tue.	Libra	Air	Semi-fruitful	2nd
16 Wed. 8:16 pm	Scorpio	Water	Fruitful	Full 2:36 pm
17 Thu.	Scorpio	Water	Fruitful	3rd
18 Fri. 7:51 pm	Sagittarius	Fire	Barren	3rd
19 Sat.	Sagittarius	Fire	Barren	3rd
20 Sun. 9:20 pm	Capricorn	Earth	Semi-fruitful	3rd
21 Mon.	Capricorn	Earth	Semi-fruitful	3rd
22 Tue.	Capricorn	Earth	Semi-fruitful	3rd
23 Wed. 1:58 am	Aquarius	Air	Barren	4th 7:18 am
24 Thu.	Aquarius	Air	Barren	4th
25 Fri. 10:02 am	Pisces	Water	Fruitful	4th
26 Sat.	Pisces	Water	Fruitful	4th
27 Sun. 8:54 pm	Aries	Fire	Barren	4th
28 Mon.	Aries	Fire	Barren	4th
29 Tue.	Aries	Fire	Barren	4th
30 Wed. 9:26 am	Taurus	Earth	Semi-fruitful	4th

May Moon Table

Date	Sign	Element	Nature	Phase
1 Thu.	Taurus	Earth	Semi-fruitful	New 7:15 am
2 Fri. 10:27 pm	Gemini	Air	Barren	1st
3 Sat.	Gemini	Air	Barren	1st
4 Sun.	Gemini	Air	Barren	1st
5 Mon. 10:42 am	Cancer	Water	Fruitful	1st
6 Tue.	Cancer	Water	Fruitful	1st
7 Wed. 8:46 pm	Leo	Fire	Barren	1st
8 Thu.	Leo	Fire	Barren	1st
9 Fri.	Leo	Fire	Barren	2nd 6:53 am
10 Sat. 3:31 am	Virgo	Earth	Barren	2nd
11 Sun.	Virgo	Earth	Barren	2nd
12 Mon. 6:42 am	Libra	Air	Semi-fruitful	2nd
13 Tue.	Libra	Air	Semi-fruitful	2nd
14 Wed. 7:14 am	Scorpio	Water	Fruitful	2nd
15 Thu.	Scorpio	Water	Fruitful	Full 10:36 pm
16 Fri. 6:43 am	Sagittarius	Fire	Barren	3rd
17 Sat.	Sagittarius	Fire	Barren	3rd
18 Sun. 7:03 am	Capricorn	Earth	Semi-fruitful	3rd
19 Mon.	Capricorn	Earth	Semi-fruitful	3rd
20 Tue. 10:01 am	Aquarius	Air	Barren	3rd
21 Wed.	Aquarius	Air	Barren	3rd
22 Thu. 4:41 pm	Pisces	Water	Fruitful	4th 7:31 pm
23 Fri.	Pisces	Water	Fruitful	4th
24 Sat.	Pisces	Water	Fruitful	4th
25 Sun. 2:59 am	Aries	Fire	Barren	4th
26 Mon.	Aries	Fire	Barren	4th
27 Tue. 3:32 pm	Taurus	Earth	Semi-fruitful	4th
28 Wed.	Taurus	Earth	Semi-fruitful	4th
29 Thu.	Taurus	Earth	Semi-fruitful	4th
30 Fri. 4:32 am	Gemini	Air	Barren	1st 11:20 pm
31 Sat.	Gemini	Air	Barren	1st

June Moon Table

Date	Sign	Element	Nature	Phase
1 Sun. 4:27 pm	Cancer	Water	Fruitful	1st
2 Mon.	Cancer	Water	Fruitful	1st
3 Tue.	Cancer	Water	Fruitful	1st
4 Wed. 2:25 am	Leo	Fire	Barren	1st
5 Thu.	Leo	Fire	Barren	1st
6 Fri. 9:51 am	Virgo	Earth	Barren	1st
7 Sat.	Virgo	Earth	Barren	2nd 3:28 pm
8 Sun. 2:30 pm	Libra	Air	Semi-fruitful	2nd
9 Mon.	Libra	Air	Semi-fruitful	2nd
10 Tue. 4:39 pm	Scorpio	Water	Fruitful	2nd
11 Wed.	Scorpio	Water	Fruitful	2nd
12 Thu. 5:12 pm	Sagittarius	Fire	Barren	2nd
13 Fri.	Sagittarius	Fire	Barren	2nd
14 Sat. 5:38 pm	Capricorn	Earth	Semi-fruitful	Full 6:16 am
15 Sun.	Capricorn	Earth	Semi-fruitful	3rd
16 Mon. 7:41 pm	Aquarius	Air	Barren	3rd
17 Tue.	Aquarius	Air	Barren	3rd
18 Wed.	Aquarius	Air	Barren	3rd
19 Thu. 12:57 am	Pisces	Water	Fruitful	3rd
20 Fri.	Pisces	Water	Fruitful	3rd
21 Sat. 10:06 am	Aries	Fire	Barren	4th 9:45 am
22 Sun.	Aries	Fire	Barren	4th
23 Mon. 10:15 pm	Taurus	Earth	Semi-fruitful	4th
24 Tue.	Taurus	Earth	Semi-fruitful	4th
25 Wed.	Taurus	Earth	Semi-fruitful	4th
26 Thu. 11:13 am	Gemini	Air	Barren	4th
27 Fri.	Gemini	Air	Barren	4th
28 Sat. 10:52 pm	Cancer	Water	Fruitful	4th
29 Sun.	Cancer	Water	Fruitful	New 1:39 pm
30 Mon.	Cancer	Water	Fruitful	1st

July Moon Table

Date	Sign	Element	Nature	Phase
1 Tue. 8:13 am	Leo	Fire	Barren	1st
2 Wed.	Leo	Fire	Barren	1st
3 Thu. 3:16 pm	Virgo	Earth	Barren	1st
4 Fri.	Virgo	Earth	Barren	1st
5 Sat. 8:20 pm	Libra	Air	Semi-fruitful	1st
6 Sun.	Libra	Air	Semi-fruitful	2nd 9:32 pm
7 Mon. 11:43 pm	Scorpio	Water	Fruitful	2nd
8 Tue.	Scorpio	Water	Fruitful	2nd
9 Wed.	Scorpio	Water	Fruitful	2nd
10 Thu. 1:48 am	Sagittarius	Fire	Barren	2nd
11 Fri.	Sagittarius	Fire	Barren	2nd
12 Sat. 3:21 am	Capricorn	Earth	Semi-fruitful	2nd
13 Sun.	Capricorn	Earth	Semi-fruitful	Full 2:21 pm
14 Mon. 5:38 am	Aquarius	Air	Barren	3rd
15 Tue.	Aquarius	Air	Barren	3rd
16 Wed. 10:14 am	Pisces	Water	Fruitful	3rd
17 Thu.	Pisces	Water	Fruitful	3rd
18 Fri. 6:20 pm	Aries	Fire	Barren	3rd
19 Sat.	Aries	Fire	Barren	3rd
20 Sun.	Aries	Fire	Barren	3rd
21 Mon. 5:48 am	Taurus	Earth	Semi-fruitful	4th 2:01 am
22 Tue.	Taurus	Earth	Semi-fruitful	4th
23 Wed. 6:42 pm	Gemini	Air	Barren	4th
24 Thu.	Gemini	Air	Barren	4th
25 Fri.	Gemini	Air	Barren	4th
26 Sat. 6:23 am	Cancer	Water	Fruitful	4th
27 Sun.	Cancer	Water	Fruitful	4th
28 Mon. 3:17 pm	Leo	Fire	Barren	4th
29 Tue.	Leo	Fire	Barren	New 1:53 am
30 Wed. 9:27 pm	Virgo	Earth	Barren	1st
31 Thu.	Virgo	Earth	Barren	1st

August Moon Table

Date	Sign	Element	Nature	Phase
1 Fri.	Virgo	Earth	Barren	1st
2 Sat. 1:48 am	Libra	Air	Semi-fruitful	1st
3 Sun.	Libra	Air	Semi-fruitful	1st
4 Mon. 5:12 am	Scorpio	Water	Fruitful	1st
5 Tue.	Scorpio	Water	Fruitful	2nd 2:28 am
6 Wed. 8:11 am	Sagittarius	Fire	Barren	2nd
7 Thu.	Sagittarius	Fire	Barren	2nd
8 Fri. 11:02 am	Capricorn	Earth	Semi-fruitful	2nd
9 Sat.	Capricorn	Earth	Semi-fruitful	2nd
10 Sun. 2:23 pm	Aquarius	Air	Barren	2nd
11 Mon.	Aquarius	Air	Barren	Full 11:48 pm
12 Tue. 7:19 pm	Pisces	Water	Fruitful	3rd
13 Wed.	Pisces	Water	Fruitful	3rd
14 Thu.	Pisces	Water	Fruitful	3rd
15 Fri. 3:00 am	Aries	Fire	Barren	3rd
16 Sat.	Aries	Fire	Barren	3rd
17 Sun. 1:52 pm	Taurus	Earth	Semi-fruitful	3rd
18 Mon.	Taurus	Earth	Semi-fruitful	3rd
19 Tue.	Taurus	Earth	Semi-fruitful	4th 7:48 pm
20 Wed. 2:41 am	Gemini	Air	Barren	4th
21 Thu.	Gemini	Air	Barren	4th
22 Fri. 2:44 pm	Cancer	Water	Fruitful	4th
23 Sat.	Cancer	Water	Fruitful	4th
24 Sun. 11:48 pm	Leo	Fire	Barren	4th
25 Mon.	Leo	Fire	Barren	4th
26 Tue.	Leo	Fire	Barren	4th
27 Wed. 5:27 am	Virgo	Earth	Barren	New 12:26 pm
28 Thu.	Virgo	Earth	Barren	1st
29 Fri. 8:41 am	Libra	Air	Semi-fruitful	1st
30 Sat.	Libra	Air	Semi-fruitful	1st
31 Sun. 11:00 am	Scorpio	Water	Fruitful	1st

September Moon Table

Date	Sign	Element	Nature	Phase
1 Mon.	Scorpio	Water	Fruitful	1st
2 Tue. 1:32 pm	Sagittarius	Fire	Barren	1st
3 Wed.	Sagittarius	Fire	Barren	2nd 7:34 am
4 Thu. 4:51 pm	Capricorn	Earth	Semi-fruitful	2nd
5 Fri.	Capricorn	Earth	Semi-fruitful	2nd
6 Sat. 9:15 pm	Aquarius	Air	Barren	2nd
7 Sun.	Aquarius	Air	Barren	2nd
8 Mon.	Aquarius	Air	Barren	2nd
9 Tue. 3:07 am	Pisces	Water	Fruitful	2nd
10 Wed.	Pisces	Water	Fruitful	Full 11:36 am
11 Thu. 11:09 am	Aries	Fire	Barren	3rd
12 Fri.	Aries	Fire	Barren	3rd
13 Sat. 9:50 pm	Taurus	Earth	Semi-fruitful	3rd
14 Sun.	Taurus	Earth	Semi-fruitful	3rd
15 Mon.	Taurus	Earth	Semi-fruitful	3rd
16 Tue. 10:32 am	Gemini	Air	Barren	3rd
17 Wed.	Gemini	Air	Barren	3rd
18 Thu. 11:07 pm	Cancer	Water	Fruitful	4th 2:03 pm
19 Fri.	Cancer	Water	Fruitful	4th
20 Sat.	Cancer	Water	Fruitful	4th
21 Sun. 9:02 am	Leo	Fire	Barren	4th
22 Mon.	Leo	Fire	Barren	4th
23 Tue. 3:04 pm	Virgo	Earth	Barren	4th
24 Wed.	Virgo	Earth	Barren	4th
25 Thu. 5:49 pm	Libra	Air	Semi-fruitful	New 10:09 pm
26 Fri.	Libra	Air	Semi-fruitful	1st
27 Sat. 6:52 pm	Scorpio	Water	Fruitful	1st
28 Sun.	Scorpio	Water	Fruitful	1st
29 Mon. 7:57 pm	Sagittarius	Fire	Barren	1st
30 Tue.	Sagittarius	Fire	Barren	1st

October Moon Table

Date	Sign	Element	Nature	Phase
1 Wed. 10:21 pm	Capricorn	Earth	Semi-fruitful	1st
2 Thu.	Capricorn	Earth	Semi-fruitful	2nd 2:09 pm
3 Fri.	Capricorn	Earth	Semi-fruitful	2nd
4 Sat. 2:45 am	Aquarius	Air	Barren	2nd
5 Sun.	Aquarius	Air	Barren	2nd
6 Mon. 9:20 am	Pisces	Water	Fruitful	2nd
7 Tue.	Pisces	Water	Fruitful	2nd
8 Wed. 6:07 pm	Aries	Fire	Barren	2nd
9 Thu.	Aries	Fire	Barren	2nd
10 Fri.	Aries	Fire	Barren	Full 2:27 am
11 Sat. 5:05 am	Taurus	Earth	Semi-fruitful	3rd
12 Sun.	Taurus	Earth	Semi-fruitful	3rd
13 Mon. 5:45 pm	Gemini	Air	Barren	3rd
14 Tue.	Gemini	Air	Barren	3rd
15 Wed.	Gemini	Air	Barren	3rd
16 Thu. 6:41 am	Cancer	Water	Fruitful	3rd
17 Fri.	Cancer	Water	Fruitful	3rd
18 Sat. 5:41 pm	Leo	Fire	Barren	4th 7:31 am
19 Sun.	Leo	Fire	Barren	4th
20 Mon.	Leo	Fire	Barren	4th
21 Tue. 1:01 am	Virgo	Earth	Barren	4th
22 Wed.	Virgo	Earth	Barren	4th
23 Thu. 4:27 am	Libra	Air	Semi-fruitful	4th
24 Fri.	Libra	Air	Semi-fruitful	4th
25 Sat. 5:08 am	Scorpio	Water	Fruitful	New 7:50 am
26 Sun.	Scorpio	Water	Fruitful	1st
27 Mon. 4:55 am	Sagittarius	Fire	Barren	1st
28 Tue.	Sagittarius	Fire	Barren	1st
29 Wed. 5:37 am	Capricorn	Earth	Semi-fruitful	1st
30 Thu.	Capricorn	Earth	Semi-fruitful	1st
31 Fri. 8:41 am	Aquarius	Air	Barren	2nd 11:25 pm

November Moon Table

Date	Sign	Element	Nature	Phase
1 Sat.	Aquarius	Air	Barren	2nd
2 Sun. 2:52 pm	Pisces	Water	Fruitful	2nd
3 Mon.	Pisces	Water	Fruitful	2nd
4 Tue.	Pisces	Water	Fruitful	2nd
5 Wed. 12:02 am	Aries	Fire	Barren	2nd
6 Thu.	Aries	Fire	Barren	2nd
7 Fri. 11:29 am	Taurus	Earth	Semi-fruitful	2nd
8 Sat.	Taurus	Earth	Semi-fruitful	Full 8:13 pm
9 Sun.	Taurus	Earth	Semi-fruitful	3rd
10 Mon. 12:14 am	Gemini	Air	Barren	3rd
11 Tue.	Gemini	Air	Barren	3rd
12 Wed. 1:10 pm	Cancer	Water	Fruitful	3rd
13 Thu.	Cancer	Water	Fruitful	3rd
14 Fri.	Cancer	Water	Fruitful	3rd
15 Sat. 12:48 am	Leo	Fire	Barren	3rd
16 Sun.	Leo	Fire	Barren	4th 11:15 pm
17 Mon. 9:36 am	Virgo	Earth	Barren	4th
18 Tue.	Virgo	Earth	Barren	4th
19 Wed. 2:42 pm	Libra	Air	Semi-fruitful	4th
20 Thu.	Libra	Air	Semi-fruitful	4th
21 Fri. 4:24 pm	Scorpio	Water	Fruitful	4th
22 Sat.	Scorpio	Water	Fruitful	4th
23 Sun. 4:02 pm	Sagittarius	Fire	Barren	New 5:59 pm
24 Mon.	Sagittarius	Fire	Barren	1st
25 Tue. 3:31 pm	Capricorn	Earth	Semi-fruitful	1st
26 Wed.	Capricorn	Earth	Semi-fruitful	1st
27 Thu. 4:48 pm	Aquarius	Air	Barren	1st
28 Fri.	Aquarius	Air	Barren	1st
29 Sat. 9:25 pm	Pisces	Water	Fruitful	1st
30 Sun.	Pisces	Water	Fruitful	2nd 12:16 pm

December Moon Table

Date	Sign	Element	Nature	Phase
1 Mon.	Pisces	Water	Fruitful	2nd
2 Tue. 5:56 am	Aries	Fire	Barren	2nd
3 Wed.	Aries	Fire	Barren	2nd
4 Thu. 5:30 pm	Taurus	Earth	Semi-fruitful	2nd
5 Fri.	Taurus	Earth	Semi-fruitful	2nd
6 Sat.	Taurus	Earth	Semi-fruitful	2nd
7 Sun. 6:26 am	Gemini	Air	Barren	2nd
8 Mon.	Gemini	Air	Barren	Full 3:37 pm
9 Tue. 7:11 pm	Cancer	Water	Fruitful	3rd
10 Wed.	Cancer	Water	Fruitful	3rd
11 Thu.	Cancer	Water	Fruitful	3rd
12 Fri. 6:40 am	Leo	Fire	Barren	3rd
13 Sat.	Leo	Fire	Barren	3rd
14 Sun. 4:07 pm	Virgo	Earth	Barren	3rd
15 Mon.	Virgo	Earth	Barren	3rd
16 Tue. 10:46 pm	Libra	Air	Semi-fruitful	4th 12:42 pm
17 Wed.	Libra	Air	Semi-fruitful	4th
18 Thu.	Libra	Air	Semi-fruitful	4th
19 Fri. 2:20 am	Scorpio	Water	Fruitful	4th
20 Sat.	Scorpio	Water	Fruitful	4th
21 Sun. 3:16 am	Sagittarius	Fire	Barren	4th
22 Mon.	Sagittarius	Fire	Barren	4th
23 Tue. 2:55 am	Capricorn	Earth	Semi-fruitful	New 4:43 am
24 Wed.	Capricorn	Earth	Semi-fruitful	1st
25 Thu. 3:13 am	Aquarius	Air	Barren	1st
26 Fri.	Aquarius	Air	Barren	1st
27 Sat. 6:10 am	Pisces	Water	Fruitful	1st
28 Sun.	Pisces	Water	Fruitful	1st
29 Mon. 1:08 pm	Aries	Fire	Barren	1st
30 Tue.	Aries	Fire	Barren	2nd 5:03 am
31 Wed.	Aries	Fire	Barren	2nd

About the Authors

SCOTT APPELL has contributed to numerous books on herbs, and has written four books of his own, all published by Friedman/Fairfax Publishers of New York. Scott lives, writes, and teaches horticulture in New York City, and he has a private horticultural consultation company called the Green Man.

CHANDRA MOIRA BEAL is a freelance writer in Austin, Texas. She lives with a magical house rabbit named Maia and has authored hundreds of articles about everything from mermaids to law. Chandra also self-published *Splash Across Texas*, a guide to aquatic recreation in Texas. Chandra is Sanskrit for "Moon."

STEPHANIE ROSE BIRD is an artist, writer, conjurer, root doctor, and educator. She has been on faculty at the School of the Art Institute of Chicago since 1986. She is also the founder of her own herbal haircare line designed for black women, and she has written for such publications as *Herbal Companion Magazine*. Stephanie is a mother of four, and an avid prairie wildflower gardener who shares her home with butterflies, wild birds, a cockatiel, and a black cat.

TAMARA BOWDEN, a.k.a. Sister Moon, is an eclectic practitioner of Pagan ways and may be too creative for her own good. She is the owner of Sister Moon Designs, though by day she wears the more mundane hat of a technical writer. She facilitates a monthly women's spirituality circle, is a member of Chantress, a Pagan woman's chorale, and lives near Raleigh, North Carolina, with her husband and son.

ROBERTA BURNES is an educator, singer, and storyteller from Lexington, Kentucky. She received a degree in environmental education at Ohio State University in 1986, and has practiced herbalism for fifteen years with particular emphasis on wild edible, medicinal, and dye plants. She currently is the herb specialist at the Good Foods Co-op and science coordinator at the Living Arts and Science Center in Lexington. She teaches workshops on herbs, natural dyeing, astronomy, and natural history, and she performs Shaker music at a restored Shaker village.

DALLAS JENNIFER COBB is a writer who deals with subjects close to her heart: mothering, family, gardening, herbs, and alternative cosmetics. She gardens organically, using her own intuition, and makes herbal-based body and health-care products.

ELLEN DUGAN, also known as the "Garden Witch," is a psychic-clairvoyant and has been a practicing Witch for over fifteen years. She and her husband raise their three magical teenagers and tend to their enchanted gardens in Missouri. Ellen received master gardener status in the spring of 2000. She is currently working on a "Garden Witchery" book.

MARGUERITE ELSBETH, also known as Senihele (Sparrowhawk), is a hereditary Sicilian strega, and is also proud of her Lenni Lenape (Delaware) Indian ancestry. She is a professional astrologer, tarot reader, and spiritual healer, specializing in crisis counseling, spiritual troubleshooting, and difficult relationship issues. Marguerite has published numerous articles in Llewellyn's annuals, and is the author or coauthor of a number of books. She currently resides in the Southwest desert. Please visit her website at: www.practicalSPIRITkeeping.com.

LAUREL (NIGHTSPRING) REUFNER has been a solitary Pagan for more than a decade now. She lives in Athens Country, in southeastern Ohio, with her husband and two daughters. Her website can be found at: www.spiritrealm.com/Melinda/paganism/html.

MINDY GREEN is an herbalist with thirty-years experience specializing in aromatherapy. She is an educator, founding member of the American Herbalists Guild, and author of several books on herbs. She is also a faculty member of the Rocky

Mountain Center for Botanical Studie, and director of education at the Herb Research Foundation in Boulder, Colorado.

MAGENTA GRIFFITH has been a Witch for more than twenty-five years, has been an ordained priestess for thirteen years, and is a founding member of the coven Prodea. She leads rituals and workshops across the Midwest, and is the librarian for the New Alexandria Library, a Pagan and Magical Resource Center (http://www.magusbooks.com/newalexandria/).

DEBORAH HARDING lives in northeastern Ohio with her husband of twenty-one years, two homeschooled daughters, and various cats, dwarf rabbits, guinea pigs, and fish. She has been growing and using herbs, flowers, and vegetables for many years, and is author of *The Green Guide to Herb Gardening* published by Llewellyn. She has published numerous articles on gardening, cooking, crafting, and folklore in magazines and newspapers, and she also performs at Renaissance fairs with her family in a Celtic musical and puppet performance group. Visit Deborah's website at: http://www.geocities.com/debbieh13/prymethyme.html.

FEATHER JONES has been a practicing clinical herbalist, teacher, wildcrafter, and medicine maker for more than twenty years. She is executive director for the Rocky Mountain Center for Botanical Studies in Boulder, Colorado, the founder of Turtle Island Herbs, and past president of the American Herbalists Guild. She is a single mother, strong animal-rights activist, and staunch spokesperson for the Earth.

LENNA KEEFER is an ethnobotanical artist with an awareness of the interconnectedness of all life. Trained as a botanical illustrator, she has experience in naturalist observations and field studies. Currently she is mothering and completing her certification as a flower essence practitioner and a doctor of naturopathic healing.

JONATHAN KEYES is an astrologer, herbalist, and plant spirit medicine practitioner. He holds a degree in health studies from Evergreen State College, has studied shamanism with practitioners in Ecuador, Mexico, and the Pacific Northwest, and is a certified herbalist.

XINGWU LIU has a master's degree in cultural anthropology, and has researched and taught extensively both in China and the U.S. He has contributed to many publications, and currently he is an adjunct professor at DePaul University and president of Health King Enterprises.

EDAIN MCCOY has practiced witchcraft for more than twenty years. She has studied many magical traditions including Wiccan, Judaic, Celtic, Appalachian, and Curanderismo. By day she works as a stockbroker, and by night writes (when she's not ballroom dancing). She is the author of sixteen books.

PAUL NIEDHART has a degree in ethnobotany from Ohio University. Currently, he works on plant propagation and conservation, and since 1994 he has specialized in native prairie plants. Paul also works part-time for United Plant Savers as a land steward, and at the National Center for the Preservation of Medicinal Herbs as their farm manager. In his spare time, he maintains an organic small-fruit farm at his seven-acre home.

LEEDA ALLEYN PACOTTI practices as a naturopathic physician, nutritional counselor, and master herbalist. She incorporates into her practice specialized diagnostics of dream language, health astrology, observations from Chinese medicine, and the resurrected science of personology. Of late, she has investigated neural dysfunctions and the emotional signals of physical illness.

CINDY PARKER is a community herbalist who owns and operates Healing Heart Herbals in southeastern Ohio. She lectures throughout the country on the medicinal and fun uses of herbs, and is currently working on her master's degree in family studies and health communications.

ROBERT PLACE is a visionary artist, and the designer, illustrator, and author of three tarot decks. Robert is recognized as an expert on Western mysticism, the history of the tarot, and divination. He has taught and lectured at the New York Open Center, Omega Institute, the New York Tarot School, and the World Tarot Congress. He can be reached through his website: www.crosswinds.net/~alchemicalegg/.

SHADOWCAT is a priestess and Witch in the American Celtic Tradition of Lady Sheba, but she prefers solitary work. A self-taught, self-proclaimed gourmet cook, ShadowCat spends her days acquiring new manuscripts for Llewellyn Publications. She is also on the board of directors for the Minnesota Book Publishers' Roundtable.

SHERI RICHERSON has more than twenty years of experience in newspaper and magazine writing. Her range of writing expertise has included astrology, herbs, aromatheraphy, and tropical and exotic plants. She is also a lifetime member of the International Thespian Society, and her favorite pastimes are riding her motorcycle and horses, and gardening. She grows herbs and tropical plants at her home.

KEVIN SPELMAN is an eclectic herbalist, writer, and medical researcher trained in biomedical sciences, ayurvedic medicine, and Western herbal medicine. He is on faculty at Tai Sophia Institute, and several other schools of health and medicine, and has practiced clinical herbal medicine for a decade. He has continually cultivated the growth of herbalism as a professional craft.

K. D. SPITZER has loved herbs all her life. She is a master weaver, and one corner of her herb garden is devoted to dye herbs. She teaches in New Hampshire, where she also reads tarot.

CARLY WALL is author of a number of books published by A.R.E. Press and Sterling Publishing in New York. A regular article contributor to Llewellyn's annual publications for the last eight years, she holds a certificate in aromatherapy, is a member of the National Association for Holistic Aromatherapy (NAHA), and is also a member of the Cat Writer's Association. She lives in Ohio.

S. Y. ZENITH is three-quarters Chinese with a dash of Irish in her ancestry. She is a solitary Pagan who has lived and travelled extensively throughout Asia, but for the last seventeen years has been based in Australia. Her fascination with folk traditions, both Eastern and Western, has resulted in numerous articles published both in Australia and the United States. She is currently working on a book titled *Malay Folk Magic*.

Editor's Note

The contents of this book are not meant to diagnose, treat, prescribe, or substitute for consultation with a licensed heathcare professional. Herbs, whether used internally or externally, should be introduced in small amounts to allow the body to adjust and to detect possible allergies. Please consult a standard reference source, or an expert herbalist, to learn more about the possible effects of certain herbs. Llewellyn Worldwide does not participate in, endorse, or have any authority or responsibility concerning private business transactions between its authors and the public.

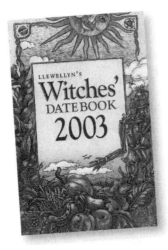

Celebrate Wiccan Days and Pagan Ways

Whether you're planning a ritual, Sabbat feast, or a birthday party, Llewellyn's *Witches' Calendar 2003* has all the information you need to make every day magical: Wiccan holidays; color correspondences; the best days to plant and harvest; the Moon's sign and phase; planetary motion, including retrogrades; and solar and lunar eclipses.

This year's calendar is packed with practical tips, folklore, herb lore, and art by Kathleen Edwards. Articles by popular Pagan authors include:

- **"Prophetic Dreaming" by Migene González-Wippler**
- **"Shamanism" by Richard Webster**
- **"Using Energy in Spell Casting" by Ann Moura**
- **"Pagans and Christians" by Gus diZerega**
- **"Creating a Hoodoo Garden" by Scott Appell**

LLEWELLYN'S *WITCHES' CALENDAR 2003*
36 pp. • 13" X 10"
ISBN 0-7387-0075-4/J073 • $12.95 U.S.
To order call 1-877-NEWWRLD

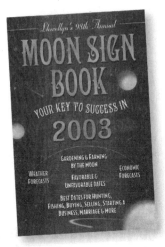